THE JUDGMENT OF GENDER

How Women Are Centered and Silenced in Pop Culture

ALLISON T. BUTLER

Cover design by Eliza Sherpa

THE CENSORED PRESS

Ithaca, New York

The Judgment of Gender: How Women Are Centered and Silenced in Pop Culture

Written by Allison T. Butler

A Censored Press First Edition

Copyright © 2026 by Allison Butler

All rights reserved. No part of this book may be reproduced, stored in a retrieval system, or transmitted in any form, by any means, including mechanical, electronic, photocopying, recording or otherwise, without the prior written permission of the publisher.

The Censored Press
PO Box 9
Ithaca, NY 14851
censoredpress.org

ISBN 979-8-9998049-1-4
ISBN (electronic) 979-8-9998049-3-8

LIBRARY OF CONGRESS CONTROL NUMBER: 2025946247

College professors and high school and middle school teachers may order free examination copies of Censored Press titles. Contact shealeigh@projectcensored.org for more information.

9 8 7 6 5 4 3 2 1

Cover design by Eliza Sherpa
Book design by Shealeigh Voitl

Printed in the USA

► Praise for *The Judgment of Gender* ◄

"Allison Butler is one of our foremost critics of popular culture and a leading light in critical media literacy. Here she brings both those talents to bear, analyzing the problematic terrain of women's representation. As brilliant as it is innovative, this is a powerful feminist critique for the ages."

—TOBY MILLER, Instituto Tecnológico de Monterrey

"Allison Butler's application of critical media literacy to reveal how patriarchy functions as a system of censorship represents an immeasurable contribution to the field. Her scholarship is rigorous, inspiring, and essential for anyone committed to advancing a more just society."

—NOLAN HIGDON, Lecturer, University of California, Santa Cruz

"From popstars and politicians to tradwives and CEOs, Allison Butler's *The Judgment of Gender* provides an unflinching exploration of the silencing of women in contemporary society. Her thorough research and thoughtful analysis offer an excellent intersectional approach to how institutions shape our understanding of gender and perpetuate inequality."

—LORI BINDIG YOUSMAN, Professor, Communication & Media, Sacred Heart University

"Women are everywhere in popular culture, and yet all too frequently are silenced. *The Judgment of Gender* speaks back in a passionate and powerful voice. Allison Butler chooses her examples effectively, and makes convincing connections across a wide range of social and media forms. The writing is clear and cogent, and will be accessible to a wide general readership. This is a model of critical media literacy for our desperate and dangerous times."

—DAVID BUCKINGHAM, Honorary Professor, UCL Institute of Education, London, Emeritus Professor, Loughborough University, UK

For Lorraine (1935–2025) and Elie
Two women, central to the lives of so many
No one will ever silence them

Contents

ACKNOWLEDGMENTS 10

INTRODUCTION: Centering and Silencing Women 14

CHAPTER 1: The Context of Womanhood 50

CHAPTER 2: A Generational Lineage of Harming Women 84

CHAPTER 3: When Women Act Out 120

CHAPTER 4: When Women Occupy Space That Isn't Theirs 150

CHAPTER 5: When Women Are Physically Harmed for Being Women ... 182

CHAPTER 6: When Women Harm Other Women 218

CONCLUSION: What Can Be Done? 248

BIBLIOGRAPHY 274

INDEX 316

ACKNOWLEDGMENTS

The world so many of us live in these days makes it hard to remember that there is good, there is hope, and there is light every day. I am so lucky to be surrounded by colleagues, friends, and family who embody and radiate the good, the hope, and the light all the time.

I am so proud to work at the University of Massachusetts Amherst with some truly incredible people. The university's commitment to public education is a beacon in these fraught times. Generous funding for this project was made possible by Dean Karl Rethemeyer of the College of Social and Behavioral Sciences and the summer 2024 RISE (Remedying Inequity through Student Engagement) fellowship, led by Jamie Rowen and Felicia Griffin-Fennell. This funding allowed me to bring on, and pay a fair wage to, three fabulous research assistants. A significant portion of the content of this book would not be possible without the keen eyes of Kayla LaFleur, Griffen McClendon, and Paulina Ortiz-Orive. In the best possible ways, these three forced me out of my comfort zone and helped me to think differently and more expansively about celebrities, influencers, and young people's interactions with pop culture. Paulina Ortiz-Orive is largely responsible for the research on social media and digital influencers and for keeping me on target when it often felt so easy to burrow deep into too many rabbit holes. Never wavering in its commitment to critical thinking and social justice, the Department of Communication—my home at UMass—is bursting with good people doing hard work. Extra special thanks to my Chair, my friend, and my cousin, Claudio Moreira, whose strength of character, compassion, and thoughtful approach to myriad problems is inspiring. In the past couple of years, I've expanded my home base at UMass. Thank you to Stephanie Nichols for her humor, friendship, and stellar organizational prowess. I am so grateful for the Chancellor's Leadership Fellowship with Senior Vice Provost and Dean of Undergraduate Education, Farshid Hajir. Working with you,

Farshid, has been such a gift; special thanks for your mentorship, your constructively optimistic outlook, and for inviting me to see the work of our university and of higher education more broadly.

Working with the folks at The Censored Press, especially Mischa Geracoulis, Shealeigh Voitl, Lorna Garano, Mickey Huff, Andy Lee Roth, and Adam Armstrong, has been a joy. To work with friends and colleagues committed to righting the wrongs of the world and doing so with grace, humor, and just the right amount of snark, is a true pleasure. The ladies of Project Censored—Shealeigh Voitl, Reagan Haynie, and Kate Horgan—give me hope for the future, especially the future of feminism. Watching Kate Horgan grow from student to professional has been so wonderful, and I'm honored to be in her orbit. The most powerful words, phrases, and sentences in this book are undoubtedly because of the close readings and constructive editing of Mischa Geracoulis, Shealeigh Voitl, and Andy Lee Roth. Thanks to Eliza Sherpa for their stellar guidance, cultivating such beautiful imagery from my sloppy words.

Early versions of this work have appeared in multiple places. Thank you to editors and friends Robin Andersen, Steve Macek, and Nolan Higdon for publishing "Judgement Based on Gender: Patriarchy as a Tool of Censorship" in their edited reader *Censorship, Digital Media, and the Global Crackdown on Freedom of Expression* (Peter Lang, 2024), which jump-started this work. Thank you to Steve Macek for inviting me to speak on these ideas in his course, Comm 339: Gender, Sex, and Representation, at North Central College, in August 2024. Publishing 'Harris-Walz and the politics of gender and race,' (co-authored with Paulina Ortiz-Orive) in Project Censored Dispatches; 'No, Don, it's patriarchy that is 'past its prime" in *Ms. Magazine*; and 'CNN's Don Lemon still gets it wrong. His non-apology for sexist comments is what not to do,' in *USA Today*, helped me think through the ideas that ultimately became central to this book.

I'm so lucky to have a family of origin and a family of choice who tolerate my anti-corporate media rants, get me out of my head, and make space for adventure. My family of origin—Elie, Stephanie & Jeff, Andrew, Jennifer & Jim, Christopher & Jennifer, and Caro & Ari—and my in-law family—Carole, Joy & Frank, Jon, and the entire Lobenstine crew—are wonderful people. They are exponentially even more wonderful for creating and cultivating the next generation: Jake, Sarah, Eva, Jasmin, Monty, Annabelle, Madeline, Jaylène, Steve, Logan, Ethan, Austin, Hailey, and Hannah.

Writing a book on how women are centered and silenced served as a regular reminder that the humans in my world accept no silencing. Ted, Isia, Aviva, and Zale are bonus family. Nolan Higdon is too hard to categorize: The little brother I never knew I wanted, the friend I absolutely treasure, the incisive thinker changing the face of critical media analysis, travel companion, intellectual cheerleader, troublemaker, and teacher. Erica Scharrer is too many things to list: Colleague, friend, mentor, confidante, moral compass, rock show companion, book-sharer, travel companion, rock star. Alesia Brennan is a colleague, friend, and sanity-saving Wednesday dining companion; extra-special thanks for introducing me to *You're Wrong About*. Lisa, Chris, Sherry, and Aviva are the deep-depth friends who make the world a better place. My LAKE JAKS crew—Andy, Kat & Jen, Lev & Keleigh, Em & Shawn—are my soul, there for conversations, games, adventures, and general ribaldry. My home and my heart belong to my Addie and my Andy.

During the process of editing this text, my mother's best friend of 75+ years passed away at the age of 90. Their friendship began at age 15, when Lorraine started at the small, Catholic girls' school in Wakefield, Massachusetts, that my mother, Elie, attended. Lorraine and Elie became fast friends and embarked on remarkably parallel lives. They attended high school, then nursing school, together. They worked at the same hospital. They were married within six months of each other. They each had five children (all of us born within a year or two of each other). When they inevitably moved apart from each other, our families visited each other and vacationed together. Just as often, the moms took off on far-flung adventures of their own. Lorraine was the more adventurous and free-spirited of the two; Elie, the more grounded and practical. Though they never labeled themselves as such, they embodied a strength of character and action that was undeniably feminist. They turned to each other for friendship and support in a way unique to women of post-WWII New England stock: Their conversations about books, politics, poetry, and the state of the world were long; they confided, but did not dwell, on personal hardships or on self-pity.

These two women modeled the enormous power of female friendship. The more that I dug into the research for this book, the more I thought about these stunning women and their remarkable friendship, the more it became clear that it is because of them and their special relationship that I see the world the way that I do, and that I have the deep friends that I have. The tiny voice in my head that reminds me to do good work, to lead with compassion, to go on adventures, and to always take the high road? It is their voices. Thank you, Lorraine and Elie.

INTRODUCTION

CENTERING AND SILENCING WOMEN

WOMEN AND AUTONOMY

On July 21, 2024, at approximately 1:45 p.m., President Joe Biden announced his withdrawal from the 2024 presidential election. Within forty-five minutes, he announced his full-throated support for Vice President Kamala Harris as his replacement.[1] In less than an hour, a prominent woman was thrust further into the spotlight with predictions and assumptions about her viability, not only as the nation's first female president, but also as its first female president of color, and the first female president with a mixed-race background. Harris locked in support from key Democrats, and her fundraising exploded.[2] Over the course of the next few months, she garnered endorsements from powerful public figures, including, but not limited to, pop star Taylor Swift, whose endorsement was presumed directly responsible for a nearly 100,000-person increase in voter registration.[3] Harris spoke directly about protecting the bodies of women and girls, the bodies of the working class, the bodies most harshly impacted by multiple global wars, and the bodies impacted by top-down economics. For five months, Harris was at the center of nearly every political conversation.

And then she was silenced.

Voters sent a clear message. In a close, but decisive, vote that bent toward cruelty, the American public elected a racist, sexist, homophobic, transphobic, classist bully, a convicted felon, *and* one held liable for sexual assault, to the highest office in the land, *for the second time*. He was handed a slim but unobstructed mandate via the electoral college, the popular vote, the Senate, and the House. Undoubtedly, Harris was not perfect and, in the post-election dissection, her political and personal flaws were discussed repeatedly, by numerous reporters, pundits, and voters, via multiple news outlets, across the political spectrum. For many, the election result was distressing, confusing, and deeply disheartening. But was it surprising?

Paradoxically, women occupy a fair amount of space in society, are the topic of much social and cultural conversation, *and* simultaneously are silenced. As a society, we are comfortable talking and debating *about* women more than we are comfortable talking and debating *with* women. For generations, women have been compartmentalized into a space where they are centered and silenced.

The decades-long debate over women's reproductive autonomy illustrates this centering and silencing. In 1973, the US Supreme Court ruled favorably on *Roe* v. *Wade*, granting women and girls federal protection to choose to continue or terminate a pregnancy, under the guarantee of liberty in the Fourteenth Amendment, which protects the individual right to due process.[4] Writing for the Court's 7–2 majority, Justice Harry Blackmun noted that personal privacy is fundamental, and "broad enough to encompass a woman's decision whether or not to terminate her pregnancy."[5] The decision legally authorized women nationwide to control their own bodies.

Except when it did not.

Roe did not actually protect women's and girls' *autonomy* as people with decision-making power equal to men. Grounded in the right to privacy—which is interpreted, rather than directly stated, in the Constitution— even *Roe* centered and silenced women: It never argued that women were *equal* or that bodily autonomy was a *right*. Rather, women could have private conversations and make choices legally about their bodies. Access to abortion became a legal, safe, and financially viable *option* (provided a woman had health insurance). At no point in the timeline of reproductive rights were women who elected to have an abortion ever fully protected. Reflecting on the case, Supreme Court Justice Ruth Bader Ginsburg argued that the emphasis on privacy could always be attacked, and thought a stronger case would root gender equality under the Equal Protection Clause.[6]

Prior to *Roe*, women had few choices when faced with an untenable or unwanted pregnancy. Starting roughly at the end of World War II, more young men and women were experimenting with sex before, or outside of, marriage. However, there was no corresponding increase in easy and shame-free access to contraception and no financially viable, safe, or legal access to abortion. In *The Girls Who Went Away: The Hidden History of Women Who Surrendered Children for Adoption in the Decades before Roe v. Wade*, historian Ann Fessler shares the stories of women who were forced, often by their families and just as often against their will, to carry their babies to term and give them up for adoption.[7] These young women often left home for months, or, alternately, *never* left home for months, in order to hide their pregnancies. The context of the burden carried by young women became clear. It was largely irrelevant *by whom* young women got pregnant because it was almost entirely their responsibility to prevent and solve any pregnancy scares, and there was no way to *prove* paternity.

In sharing their stories with Fessler, many women revealed that learning of their pregnancies was their introduction to how babies were made (there was no comprehensive or even rudimentary sex education in schools), and, given the choice, many women would have kept their babies. For the most part, this need to hide pregnancies was a burden shouldered by White, middle-class families who could afford the cost of maternity homes, the room and board needed to squirrel away daughters for a period of time, or the ability to throw together quick and convincing wedding ceremonies. Maybe one reason why traditional marriage was so lauded in the mid-twentieth century was that it protected otherwise respectable families from the shame of an unwanted or unplanned pregnancy; women could be centered as brides and their pregnancies recast as part of building a strong, post-war family. Young women of color, who often had fewer economic resources and were less welcome at maternity homes, bore the shame of unwanted or unexpected pregnancies, relying on extended family for support.

Prior to 1973, when women needed or wanted abortions, they often sought them out in secret, outside the United States in countries with more progressive, less morally charged healthcare options, or argued for a medically necessary abortion.[8] Advocacy groups and whisper networks, such as the Redstockings and The Jane Network, held open conversations about abortion as a way to destigmatize it, found safe doctors to perform abortions, and taught themselves to perform abortions.[9] The US military restricted pregnant women from service, but did permit abortions (though it did not provide them), so any woman in the military found to be pregnant was compelled to get an abortion or be discharged. Because abortion was illegal, to follow military law, pregnant women may have had to break state law.[10]

In this environment, multiple groups of women were actively working for and against women's independence and autonomy, including, but not limited to, reproductive rights. These groups centered on women's rights and expectations, albeit with very different intentions. The pre-*Roe* fight for women's autonomy was rooted in dismantling *or* highlighting as progressive the tropes associated with women, including "that women belonged in the domestic sphere, unfit for equal participation in politics, at work, or as consumers, and thus should not control their own bodies or their lives."[11] The feminist movement argued these tropes were outdated and harmful to all women. The National Organization for Women (NOW), the bipartisan National Women's Political Caucus, and the development of *Ms.* magazine all advanced agendas focused on equal protection and bodily autonomy for women. The groups fought for the Equal Rights Amendment

(ERA), a constitutional amendment that was initially introduced in the 1920s and was adapted over the years, gaining considerable strength in the 1960s–1970s. The anti-feminists, led by Phyllis Schlafly, fought both *Roe* and the ERA, arguing that feminism was "an attack on mainstream society" and that the ERA would harm women by eradicating their special status as women.[12]

The absence, rise, and fall of women's autonomy is both a material history for women as well as an analogy for the role of women as centered and silenced bodies. In 1992, in the face of *Planned Parenthood* v. *Casey*, which called for parental consent for minors and a 24-hour waiting period prior to an abortion, it was hard, but not impossible, to imagine that *Roe* could be overturned and that women would no longer have choices about their own bodies.[13] For many, it just did not seem likely; there seemed to be too much history protecting the ruling. At a punk rock show outside of Washington, DC, on the eve of the women's rights demonstration to support Planned Parenthood, Tobi Vail, the drummer for the feminist punk band Bikini Kill, said to the crowd,

> I just wanted to say something about abortion becoming illegal. To me, it says that not only do we live in a totally fucked-up patriarchal society, run by white men who don't represent our interests at all, but we live in a country where these people don't care if we live or die. And that's pretty scary.[14]

This idea—that a woman's autonomy can so easily be taken away from her, even when she appears to occupy a great deal of space—is a central concern of this text. One of the key takeaways is that no matter how much space women hold in society and across popular culture, the powers of patriarchy will almost always make attempts to silence women. What Vail feared in 1992 is our reality now.

FEMINISM IN CONTEXT

In lived experience, the embodiment of feminism is fraught with complexities. Beyond the rudimentary understanding that feminism is a noun that expresses the political, economic, and social equality of women, things tend to get messy.[15] "Equality" is seen as threatening, partly owing to the fear-based logic that if women somehow become *more* equal, then men will inevitably be made *less* so. The work of feminism is to construct a world that is equal and equitable for all members. In the United States, fights for women's suffrage, the right to vote, run for office, work for pay outside the home, own property (and be able to purchase it themselves, with their own money), and possess bodily autonomy and reproductive rights, have been tackled over the generations by a rich variety of women.

Broadly speaking, feminism in the United States has happened in four waves, beginning in the mid-nineteenth century, developing anew in the 1960s and 1970s, again in the 1980s and 1990s, and up to the present. The idea of four clearly distinct and separate waves of feminism is a set of labels applied for easy (and sometimes necessary) reference and shorthand; women have been fighting for their rights, nonstop, since they first faced socially constructed restrictions. One way to consider the waves of US feminism is to think of them as truly oceanic, moving forward, gathering energy and size from multiple spots, touching down, reconfiguring, dissipating into something slightly or dramatically different with no fixed beginning or end, and starting the process anew, and in perpetuity. The labels compartmentalize the variety of lived experiences across those time frames, simplify the political projects undertaken in each period and the motivations behind them, and potentially erase much of the work done before, after, or outside each of these codified phases in US feminism's history.

Nineteenth-century feminists fought for political and legal equality. The participants in the Seneca Falls Convention of

1848, for example, drafted and approved the *Declaration of Sentiments*, modeled after the *Declaration of Independence*, with the amended phrase, "We hold these truths to be self-evident; that all men *and women* are created equal" (italics added).[16]

Largely inspired by the publication of Betty Friedan's *The Feminine Mystique*, which argued that women need not be satisfied, or isolated in dissatisfaction, with their restricted lives as housewives and homemakers, mid-twentieth-century feminists fought for civil rights, labor rights, and bodily autonomy.[17] During this wave, feminists secured *Roe* and centered the public conversation on women's rights.[18] Both this movement and its representation within the media were primarily of White women of economic and educational privilege. Attempts to include and acknowledge women of color, poor women, lesbians, and undereducated women were clumsy at best. That the movement was complicated and divisive, with different goals and missions, is itself a valuable lesson that asks why women and feminism are sometimes assumed to be homogeneous. When women are at the center of a movement, pointing out differences or disagreements as a method to disqualify the larger validity of the movement is a calculated tactic to silence women.

Late twentieth-century feminism centered on women who were not previously included (intentionally or otherwise). These women addressed the limitations of the "feminist" label and expanded the work to include greater attention to, and inclusion of, women of color, a broader understanding of sexuality, and a more multidimensional understanding of feminism and femininity.[19]

Journalist and cultural critic Andi Zeisler has argued that we now live in a time of marketplace feminism, which is "decontextualized," "depoliticized," and "probably feminism's most popular iteration ever."[20] Focused on the ideal of the "girl boss," the strong, confident (young) career woman, marketplace feminism connects the ability to purchase (and to be in debt) with equality, while glossing over actual workplace, economic, or cultural inequities. Marketplace feminism aligns easily with current neoliberal market values, where "both emphasize consumer choice and individual power in a way that can narrow to tunnel vision."[21] Marketers and others with commercial interests have figured out that carefully curated versions of feminism could be cool and, therefore, highly profitable, as exemplified by the popularity and financial success of the 2023 movie *Barbie*.[22]

The character Barbie may be the most obvious (fictional) embodiment of neoliberal marketplace feminism. Barbie has been a doll, the star of animated TV shows and movies, a live-action film, various spinoffs, the subject of academic and popular debate, and, overarchingly, a brand. Barbie is an impossible beauty standard and an impossible sex symbol. To engage with Barbie is to consume. Her various iterations, her costumes, and more vaguely, her vibe, are all for sale. However, Barbie is also a fiercely independent woman. She never married Ken, has always had her own job, and has embarked on a variety of professions, including, but not limited to, doctor, veterinarian, president, pilot, and astronaut, each of which requires a college degree and highly specialized training. She owns her own home, car, airplane, and camper van. She's been a dog and cat owner and a big sister to Skipper. Most recently, as of this writing, future iterations of Barbie will experience blindness and Down Syndrome.[23] Barbie makes all the above look incredibly easy and readily available to all young women. She has also taken her fair share of criticism (often from other women) for being too sexy, too busty, too White, and too unrealistic. Barbie has been centered and silenced, all while being highly profitable for her parent company, Mattel.

While those operating within and outside of feminism fight over what and who does or does not count as "feminist," patriarchy remains the dominant narrative by which all else is defined, iterated, and lived. Until feminism can embrace a level of complexity beyond the market, patriarchy wins. This is how women become both centered and silenced. A great variety of conversations are *about* and may even *include* women, but who is telling the stories? When these stories are told, do women get an opportunity to speak for themselves?

SEX AND GENDER IN CONTEXT

Proudly self-described "theological fascist" Matt Walsh is the author of the 2022 book *What Is a Woman: One Man's Journey to Answer the Question of a Generation*, an anti-trans manifesto and a diatribe against inclusive definitions of gender.[24] Walsh defines women as "adult human females. They have XX chromosomes. They can bear children and give birth. They're not necessarily nicer than men, but they sure are better looking."[25] His editorializing about women's behavior and appearance clarifies, from the outset, how Walsh conceptualizes a woman's place: She is a body for breeding. This belief that "woman" equals the ability to bear children reflects just a moment of his larger insensitivity. From Walsh's standpoint, women who are infertile or post-menopausal rank lower in status and may not even count as women. Inconceivable is the idea that a woman may not *want* children.

Walsh qualifies bodies that do not follow his strict understanding of binary sex and gender divisions as "so-called."[26] When writing about a trans doctor who advocates for and supports trans health concerns, Walsh emphasized a disclaimer, "I will refer to everyone in this book by their biologically correct pronouns because it is more important to be grammatically correct than politically correct."[27] While it might be easy to dismiss Walsh as a crank, as someone with, at the very least, a limited and flawed understanding of grammar, his work has been widely influential. The data for his book and its companion documentary are drawn from participant-observation research (using that term loosely) of women, person-on-the-street interviews, and interviews with various scholars, activists, and medical professionals who study sex and gender. Of the 1,636 ratings and 257 reviews on Goodreads, 72 percent of them are positive and support his position as "truth."[28] With the benefit of hindsight, this book is clearly a dire warning of the Trump 2.0 mandate, including making manifest the goals outlined in Project 2025, the rise of the pronatal movement, increased surveillance of pregnant women, and a resurgence of religious doctrine as a defense of patriarchy.[29] Women's bodies face renewed attacks by those who want to reassert control and confine women, and a wide variety of media are available to spotlight and cultivate this vision.

Although Walsh's book is as horrific as it is popular, its subtitle is something to consider. Understanding womanhood might be the question of our entire human evolution. One might presume that when humankind was living to survive, hierarchical gender distinctions could not have been a top priority. The shared need to find nutrition, shelter, and safety was likely the most pressing. At what point in history were women constructed as being less than?

The understanding and distinctions of sex and gender are deeply woven into human development. Cat Bohannon's study of evolution through the female body notes the distinction between *biological* sex, "something wound deep into the warp and weft of our physical development, from in-cell organelles all the way up to whole-body features, and built over billions of years of evolutionary history" and *gender*, "a fluid thing and brain based and at most a few hundred thousand years old."[30] Sex assignment upon birth is understood as biological, and assumptions and beliefs about gender are understood as socially and culturally constructed. Oftentimes, sex and gender align with each other and correlate with what is considered "normal" for males and females. However, because gender is socially and culturally constructed, the expectations of the groups one belongs to and one's own lived experience may shift how we understand, present, and live different genders. In this sense, gender is both internal (how we know who we are) and external (how society treats us based on public perception).[31] Understandings and conceptualizations of sex and gender are flexible and have ebbed and flowed over generations and across cultures.

Indigenous scholars, for example, note that, prior to colonization, women were considered sacred, in part, because they supported the creation and growth of life.[32] Across North American tribes, Indigenous women were held in high regard and rarely harmed. When women *were* harmed, tribal leaders meted out swift justice with an emphasis on articulating why the actions were wrong.[33] Perpetrators were invited to consider the implications of their actions and carry out their own punishment, a way of taking responsibility for the crime.[34] Acknowledgment of this treatment must be read through the notes and records of the colonizers, and therefore is more than tinged with their own racist and sexist value judgments. Harm against, and subjugation of, women must be constructed, and might originate from the perceived threat of women's power. One can imagine that when the colonizers saw the highly lauded treatment of women, which ran counter to their plans for power, they swiftly constructed narratives of women's inferiority.

When what it means to be a woman is parsed and dissected based on chromosomes, looks, abilities, or a mockery of the act of self-identifying, *all* people are hurt and patriarchy is strengthened. Trans-exclusive radical feminists (TERFs) argue that trans women are really men, "the ultimate oppressors of women."[35] In her discussion of TERFs, essayist Rebecca Solnit notes, "The major threat to women, straight or not, cis- or not, always was and still is straight men and patriarchy."[36] Patriarchy sees gender as fixed and binary, with punishment for "women who aren't submissive enough, men who aren't straight enough, and anyone else who steps out of line."[37] This is evident in the Trump 2.0 administration, which has made clear its disdain for trans people, especially trans athletes, in multiple executive orders.[38]

This gender backlash, however terrible, *is* evidence of progress. Had the narrative of women as less-than been successful, women would not have been able to push the boundaries they confronted, and moreover, women as less-than would have been concretized.

PATRIARCHY IN CONTEXT

Patriarchy, the multifaceted social system that affords men power and privilege, is itself a social construction, one built steadily over time to intertwine with numerous other fundamental social institutions to the extent that, for most of human history, it has been lived as natural, inevitable, and a matter of common sense. Patriarchy is a "well-oiled, centuries-old system that funneled social, economic, and political power to white men."[39]

In her acerbic assessment of men's talk, Solnit tells the story of being approached by a man at a cocktail party who explained an argument to her; it turned out, the argument was one Solnit herself had constructed that the man had not actually read, but rather, had read *about*. Solnit writes, "Men explain things to me and other women, whether or not they know what they're talking about."[40] Patriarchy socializes men to be louder and women to be quieter. Patriarchy constructs it as acceptable that men do not know things but can still speak authoritatively, while women may know things but must keep that knowledge to themselves. Patriarchy presumes a social order where gender is binary, and where only one gender can be fully autonomous at any given time. Any effort to wrestle power from patriarchy is seen as threatening to individual men, "as though in some dismal zero-sum game, only one gender at a time could be free and powerful."[41]

CENTERING AND SILENCING WOMEN

In her memoir on being a punk rock musician and artist, Kathleen Hanna reflects, "I remind myself that my war has never been with sexism, but with how sexism has warped me."[42] Sexism is something that exists because it has existed, does exist, and therefore feels inevitable that it always will exist. Certain treatments of women and girls are rooted in inequity simply *because* those bodies are seen as female. Sexism over time and across institutions sends repeated messages about who women are and where they belong, and constructs a palatable version of womanhood that is non-threatening. To challenge these messages is to challenge sexism, and efforts to chip away at it are premised on the belief that sexism and sexist beliefs are *learned* and, therefore, can be *un*learned. The ability to imagine new and different conceptions of gender reveals how nothing about sexism is inevitable. Sexism is itself a story and a different story can be told. With enough concentrated attention and change-making, sexism can be called into question, weakened, and, perhaps, ultimately abolished.

In her analysis of misogyny, philosopher Kate Manne constructs a narrative about the distinction between *strangling* and *choking* as a form of domestic violence.[43] *Choking* is largely internal, specifically about a blockage to the esophagus (such as by food), while *strangling* is largely external, usually by an outside force. When people are strangled, they cannot speak; they are silenced. *Strangling*—the external application of force, hands on throat, pressure applied directly or indirectly—both centralizes and silences a person. A woman strangled is central to the action, but, because she has been stopped from speaking, she cannot actively participate; she is the object, not the subject, of the action. In large part because the grip of patriarchy has been so tight for so long, women who live within its confines (that is, all women) learn its rules and may, in turn, self-apply. Women who self-silence, for example, engage in a form of self-strangulation, thereby (inadvertently) increasing patriarchy's power. Choking may be an accident; strangulation is intentional. "Having the right to show up and speak" is fundamental to being a fully actualized human being, from which women have for far too long been excluded.[44]

Patriarchy and misogyny are intimately linked. Manne argues misogyny "functions to enforce and police women's subordination and to uphold male dominance."[45] If women violate the tenets of patriarchy, misogyny "threatens consequences" where women will be harmed *for being women*.[46]

Patriarchy is a form of silencing that stops women from speaking or acting out, while it simultaneously punishes them for taking up too much space or occupying space that does not traditionally belong to them. Women who are seen to possess "too much power" are those who threaten the precarious balance of patriarchy; "too much power" really means an encroachment on the unearned power and privilege of White men.[47]

Sexual harassment and sexual assault are clear examples of patriarchy as a form of silencing. It must be noted that, in order to accuse someone of sexual harassment or sexual assault, the concepts "sexual harassment" and "sexual assault" must *exist* and *be socially recognized*. "Sexual harassment" was named in 1974 by Cornell University lecturer Lin Farley, who used it in a consciousness-raising group to name the treatment of an employee who quit her job because of the previously unnamed torment.[48] Prior to the 1970s, mistreatment of a sexual nature *did not have a formal name*; therefore, women had no legal or social recourse for any mistreatment; this kept many women silenced. Professional women's only recourse was to shrug off the mistreatment, try to find ways to avoid it, or, more likely, internalize it as part of the cost of having a job. Women who experienced mistreatment may have believed it to be inevitable, while they also worked to support other women with insight and advice. The burden of prevention sat entirely on the shoulders of those with the least institutional power, in the absence of any formal means of redress.

Without legal recourse, women were further silenced. It was not until 1986 that the Supreme Court heard the first case that addressed sexual misconduct in the workforce, where the justices determined that harassment and discrimination were civil rights issues.[49] What was anecdotally known at the time, and has been borne out repeatedly by research, is that most sexual harassment is perpetrated by men on women.[50] Women are often reluctant to report sexual harassment or assault because of fear of retaliation, which is even more pronounced for women of color and trans women.[51]

Any time women achieve a level of independence or their work contributions become indispensable, patriarchy works to rein them back in. Historically, when women *needed* to work—either for basic survival or because the male labor force was away at war—it was approved. When women *wanted* to work—for their own financial gain or personal fulfillment—society resisted it. This resistance to female labor is only possible in a society whose economy is structured outside the home, and resistance to any particular group working outside the home is evidence of a belief (though maybe not the reality) that the economy is strong. Women who choose to upset that balance embody Solnit's argument that women are always fighting on two fronts, "one for whatever the putative topic is and one simply for the right to speak, to have ideas, to be acknowledged, to be in possession of facts and truth, to have value, to be a human being."[52]

When women defy expected behavior, it is often met with derision and attack by a system that perpetuates the behavior. As Manne notes, misogynists "tend to hate women who are outspoken."[53] Women may speak out (literally, using their voices) or act out in a narrative counter to the expected role of "a man's attentive, loving subordinate."[54] To be "successful" within these strictures is to attempt to occupy a space where one is not "too much" of anything.

POP CULTURE AS STORYTELLER

The summer of 2023 seemed to be a high point in the culture of girlhood, with Beyoncé, Barbie, and Taylor Swift as three women (fictional or larger-than-life) who deserve a great deal of credit for boosting the post-COVID economy. Beyoncé became "the most decorated Grammy artist of all time;" *Barbie* "broke studio records and led to a shortage of pink paint;" and Swift's Eras Tour was "the highest grossing music tour in music tour history," making over $93 *million* just on its opening weekend, totaled over $200 million worldwide, leading to *Time* naming her as its person of the year.[55]

But did summer 2023 *change* anything? The successes of 2023 masked and distracted from the fact that girls and young women express high levels of sadness, hopelessness, and anxiety.[56] As at other points in history, and certainly exaggerated in new and unique ways through the fracturing effects of social media, girls and women receive and share conflicting messages about what it means to be female via pop culture content and construction. In addition to being audiences, girls regularly engage online as active content creators and communicators, and, subsequently, are the ones most often punished when adults disapprove of their social media habits, including the frequency and topics of their online communication. We blame girls' use of technology rather than the corporate platforms and business models that set girls up for misery.[57] We are encouraged to look at the success of individual women as evidence of a success achievable by all women. Instead, this individual success is indicative of just that: *Individual success* within a system organized to keep the majority of women subordinate.

Women and girls are everywhere in pop culture, and yet society constructs their roles in ways that reinforce patriarchy by simultaneously centering and silencing their contributions. In 2024, Beyoncé was positioned at the center of a conspiracy theory wherein she allegedly ran an underground music industry cult whose influence required other artists to thank her profusely at awards shows on pain of death.[58] *Barbie*'s success illustrated that movies written and directed by women, with female leads, could attract massive audiences on a global scale, yet after this, Hollywood returned to the male-dominated, male-focused business model.[59] Taylor Swift's music might make hundreds of millions of dollars, but she is still skewered in the popular press and on social media for being a powerful woman, for her famous ex-boyfriends, and for her liberal politics.[60]

The summer of 2024 marked another exploration and subsequent examination into the culture of women and girls on the global stage of the Paris Olympics, marketed as the first gender-equal games. The International Olympic Committee (IOC) capped the number of participants at 10,500, with half the spots to women, half to men, and an event schedule that balanced men's and women's competitions.[61] The opening ceremonies, held on boats on the River Seine (the first time an opening ceremony was held outside an arena), highlighted women in French history, exemplified by bronze statues emerging from plinths along the river. Those watching on TV got brief biographies of the women as the cameras followed the boats. In addition, the Seine was lined with placards of famous female faces, reproduced from paintings housed in the Louvre.[62] The emphasis on repeated announcements about the equal number of male and female athletes, while admittedly very important and most likely inspiring for young girls, masked the fact that there was no clear space for trans or nonbinary athletes. Would *true* gender equality mean a proportional number of trans athletes as well?

Media coverage of women and girls has always occupied a contentious space. The post-World War II United States experienced the exponential rise of both television ownership and programming. Popular television programs of the time featured "perfectly nuclear families with nurturing dads, and moms who deferred to their husbands and did the housework in perfectly coiffed hairdos."[63] In addition, there were a number of popular shows that featured widowed fathers, but "no popular shows of the time that featured single moms—not even widowed moms—even though in the aftermath of World War II, many more widowed women than men were actually raising kids on their own."[64] This phenomenon occurred again in the 1980s–1990s with a spate of sitcoms and dramas with deceased or deadbeat moms who, once their absence was established, were never mentioned again.[65]

Any time women have taken up more space in the public eye, there has been an inevitable backlash. This backlash happens in both the content and production of media. In her analysis of 1990s pop culture, cultural critic Allison Yarrow notes, "As women gained power, or simply showed up in public, society pushed back by reducing them to gruesome sexual fantasies and misogynistic stereotypes."[66] Journalist Sophie Gilbert's analysis of 1990s and early 2000s female-centered pop culture traced the representation of women directly to tactics of representation that mimicked the pornography industry.[67] In their detailed account of their work to expose film producer Harvey Weinstein as a serial sexual predator, journalists Jodi Kantor and Megan Twohey observed, "Hollywood was an organized system for abusing women. It lured them with promises of fame, turned them into highly profitable products, treated their bodies as property, required them to look perfect, and then discarded them."[68]

Actor Demi Moore, who was 62 years old at the time of this writing, is a clear example of this. In her early career, she was in a string of films, some successful, many not, and most of which focused on her naked body. At the height of her career, Moore was paid $12.5 million to star in *Striptease* and was critiqued both for demanding such a high salary and for being naked.[69] Meanwhile, her husband at the time, Bruce Willis, was paid $20 million for the third *Die Hard* installment, where he was *also* mostly naked, but received no critique for his body *or* his paycheck.[70]

Contemporary media that look back in time often create narratives that may not be plausible or that require significant creative license. The most famous female chess player does not even exist. Beth Harmon, the protagonist of the 1983 novel *The Queen's Gambit* by Walter Tevis, which inspired the 2020 Netflix limited series of the same name, played chess in the 1950s–60s and faced only minimal sexism.[71] While the story is compelling and progressive (for when it was published as well as its narrative context), it is unreal on multiple levels, not least of which is the racially integrated orphanage where Beth is raised (in 1950s Kentucky, no less), the lack of sexism she faces, and the sexual freedom she and her colleagues experience. Further, a tale of young female empowerment is written, directed, and produced by men.

Actual women chess players have been ignored, refused play, and had pieces thrown at them by upset men.[72]

The 2020 television limited series *Mrs. America* explores the passing of *Roe* v. *Wade* and the rejection of the Equal Rights Amendment (ERA) through the lens of the feminists and anti-feminists leading the charge for and against the ratification of both.[73] Much of the show centers the experiences of conservative anti-feminist Phyllis Schlafly; while Schlafly fights doggedly against the ERA, there are moments in each episode where she appears taken aback by the treatment she receives as a woman, including being expected to take notes in meetings, being touched by powerful men without her consent, being expected to have dinner on the table every night at 6 p.m., and being expected to take care of her six children while also traveling the nation to fight against equal rights. The representation of Schlafly hints at the moral quandary of following her cause to its logical end. Yes, women have protected status as women, but are they actually that protected?

Both fiction and nonfiction stories of "bad" women prove reliable entertainment fodder. Popular media are filled with stories of vigilante women, women who fight back against injustices perpetrated against them.[74] Stereotypes of violent women, including "the dangerous seductress, the spurned wife driven to murderous rage ... figures of tabloid revulsion, treated as outcasts not just from society but from womanhood itself" have long featured in popular media.[75] These stories often invite audiences to see women in a different light, contextualizing their negative behavior, such as *Lorena*, the documentary that revisits Lorena Gallo's infamous self-defense against her abusive husband, or *Monster*, the biopic of Aileen Wuornos, a sex worker who killed her abusive clients.[76] Wuornos was labeled a serial killer, but is that the most relevant label for her? Wuornos was serially abused, sexually and physically, as a child and throughout her life. In acknowledgment of killing six men, she said that each had abused her, and that her actions were self-defense.[77] Both women struggled economically, illustrating the intersection between gender and class; women with limited economic independence may be forced to make life choices not palatable to polite society.

Pop culture holds a different standard for women. Nonfiction depictions of real women—those who are famous as well as those thrust into fame via a particular event—are often initially brutal and almost always significantly more cruel than the treatment of men in similar situations. Women who are the authors or subjects of these stories are frequently attacked for *being women*. In commenting on her stories of the royal family, *New York Times* columnist and Princeton University sociology professor Zeynep Tufekci notes that when she defended Prince Harry's decision to leave the royal family and royal responsibilities, "the vitriol I encountered as a result, even as his claims have been vindicated in court numerous times, was shocking."[78] Meghan Markle, who, along with Harry, gave up their royal responsibilities and moved to California, is the subject of a 60,000-person Reddit page "singularly dedicated to the hatred of [her]."[79] Christine Blasey Ford, who accused Supreme Court Nominee Brett Kavanaugh of sexual assault, remembers her assigned summer reading to prepare for high school, *The Once and Future King*; she thought it "a strange introduction, to be reading all about men" prior to starting at her private, all-girls school.[80] Monica Lewinsky, skewered by the press for her affair with President Bill Clinton, defends the relationship as one that was consensual, where the abuse "came in the aftermath, when I was made a scapegoat, in order to protect his powerful position."[81] The backlash against Lewinsky was particularly brutal: "I was the Unstable Stalker (a phrase disseminated by the Clinton White House), the Dimwit Floozy, and Poor Innocent who didn't know any better," she recalled in a 2014 feature.[82] When football legend Tom Brady and supermodel Gisele Bündchen were divorcing, both were photographed with other people each was presumed to be dating, possibly prior to their separation, but only Bündchen was accused of improper behavior.[83] In her analysis of the treatment of Sinéad O'Connor by the music press, specifically *SPIN* magazine, Allyson McCabe, the author of *Why Sinéad O'Connor Matters*, asks,

> Have you ever seen a profile of a male artist by a rock journalist that involved ignoring their music completely while infantilizing them, commenting extensively on their manipulative personality and seductive appearance, and expressing concern that inviting the artist to hang out with their exes is going to incite jealousy? Name one where the profile ends with the journalist imposing his musical tastes on the artist, then taking him on a flirtatious taxi ride, and then complaining about the journalist's failure to get laid.[84]

The intersection of race and gender illustrates a particular type of treatment in popular culture. South African runner Caster Semenya observes, "We only have to look at the way women like Michelle Obama and Serena Williams have been treated by today's media and parts of society. They have been called monkeys, accused of being men. Every part of their body, their musculature, their facial features, have been openly derided and insulted."[85] In August 2024, Chrystul Kizer, a young Black woman, was sentenced to eleven years in prison for killing a man who sexually abused and trafficked her, starting at 16 years old. The prosecution argued that she had seduced the man and therefore fit the profile of a violent Black woman.[86] Even in cases of documented, repeated, and serial violence, there is a "type" of woman who can kill in self-defense and be seen as a victim, rather than as a perpetrator.

Indigenous populations are often subject to skewed representations in both fiction and nonfiction popular culture. The ongoing crisis of missing and murdered Indigenous women and girls (MMWIG) receives little attention in corporate media. News coverage of violence against Indigenous people, especially women, "bolsters stereotypes of American Indian and Alaska Native people as solely living on reservations or in rural areas, perpetuates perceptions of tribal lands as violence-ridden environments, and ultimately, is representative of an institutional bias of media coverage of the issue."[87] Even though most Indigenous people live in cities, not on reservations, and face disproportionate violence from non-tribal members, violence experienced by Indigenous people *off* the reservation is rarely covered. Canadian journalist Jessica McDiarmid writes that "media coverage is vital when someone goes missing and, more generally, in solving crimes."[88] Indigenous women and girls are largely ignored in the press, "although far more likely to be victims of violence, sexual assault and abuse, and homicide."[89] *How* people are covered is also important; the language used to describe young Indigenous sex workers is often "as prostitutes, rather than sexually exploited teens, with no context or details about who they were or any examination of how young people in our midst could be left so vulnerable."[90]

When women in popular culture have been harmed and the men responsible for that harm apologize, the apology is often laden with excuses, especially about the absence of intention. Eight years after journalist David Brock published his salacious attack on Anita Hill, who accused Supreme Court nominee Clarence Thomas of sexual harassment, upon the publication of his book, *Blinded by the Right: The Conscience of an Ex Conservative*, he went on a press tour wherein he acknowledged that his previous book, *The Real Anita Hill*, had been filled with lies.[91] Speaking to NPR's Nina Totenberg, he disingenuously apologized for his part in attempting to destroy her character:

> When I wrote the Anita Hill book I believed everything I wrote was accurate. I know now that that book was filled with falsehoods and smears. Those were fed to me by the Thomas camp. They lied to me. I accept responsibility for that because I put them in my book. The issue there was I didn't know

what a journalist does. There was no fact checking, it was basically propaganda which is why I'm disavowing it now.[92]

His acceptance of responsibility is couched in the self-defense that it was *someone else*'s lying that caused all the problems. And no matter, Thomas was appointed to the Court, Brock garnered interest in *both* his new book and his previous book, while Hill continued to fight back against racist and sexist commentary. Former CNN host Don Lemon was swiftly criticized when he called former South Carolina Governor Nikki Haley "past her prime," effectively marking her as unfit for the demands of presidential leadership; within 24 hours, he apologized—sort of. Lemon said, "I am sorry. I did not mean to hurt anyone. I did not mean to offend anyone ... the people I'm closest to in this organization are women," then proceeded to name some of his female colleagues.[93] When a member of the Australian women's swim team won gold at the 2024 Paris Olympics and the press were awaiting their arrival, BBC commentator Robert Ballard said, "You know what women are like ... hanging around, doing their make-up."[94] Ballard was immediately removed from the broadcast line-up, and he quickly apologized, saying that he was sorry if the remarks caused offense and that it was not his "intention to upset or belittle anyone."[95] Apologies, however, are not about intention; apologies acknowledge and own an action that was wrong, and, ideally, one takes steps not to repeat said action. After all, no one who actually *wants* to hurt or offend feels the need to apologize.[96]

When men discover things about sexism (that women have known all along), it is treated as ground-breaking news. As part of his exploration of deepfake videos that specifically target women and girls through "nudify" programs, *New York Times* columnist Nicholas Kristof engaged in searches across multiple platforms to see how women and girls appear:

> In one search I did on Google, seven of the top 10

> video results were explicit sex videos involving female celebrities. Using the same search term on Microsoft's Bing search engine, all 10 were. But this isn't inevitable. At Yahoo, none were. In other spheres, Google does the right thing. Ask "how do I kill myself?" and it won't offer a step-by-step guidance—instead, its first result is a suicide helpline ... In other words, Google is socially responsible when it wants to be, but it seems indifferent to women and girls being violated by pornographers.[97]

It is important that Kristof learned and shared on a prominent platform that the bodies of women and girls carry a particular value in capitalism, but women and girls have long known and lived this reality. Commenting on her press treatment, lead singer of the seminal feminist punk band Bikini Kill Kathleen Hanna observes, "Journalists, even women, would write about our bodies and our clothes but never our songs."[98] This illustrates a bind professional women often find themselves in, where their "ability to get ahead was predicated on playing along, being one of the boys, and/or taking down other women to hoist themselves up."[99]

Women face microaggressions in multiple media outlets simply for *being women*. Prior to the start of *Saturday Night Live* (*SNL*), Carol Burnett was arguably the most well-known and highly watched sketch comedian. However, when creator Lorne Michaels envisioned *SNL*, he set out to do the *opposite* of Burnett's show, despite her success, and gave her no credit for paving the way for his male-dominated show.[100] Social media sites are home to endless debates about women's physical presence, including how they are aging (and, if they appear not to be aging, whether they are actually still alive or have had their images digitally altered to appear alive).[101] In 2024, the dating app Bumble—a site where women have the exclusive power of reaching out to, or rejecting, potential dates—received backlash for their billboards that mocked women for choosing celibacy.[102] During season two of *Below*

Deck, the reality show about working on mega yachts, Chief Steward Kate is mocked by guests for being "bitchy" and told she should smile more, because it will make the guests more comfortable and make her more appealing.[103] All these examples show that people find the time to critique and devalue women, and that, no matter how many social, political, and economic advances women have made, they are still not allowed to be complex and complicated beings.

In a counter-narrative, the dark comedy *Kevin Can F*** Himself* exaggerates the tropes of family sitcoms with extra-bright lighting and a thunderous laugh track when Allison, the downtrodden wife of the eponymous Kevin, is in the room with her husband and his friends.[104] When Allison is on her own, the lighting casts a grey pallor over her environment; there is no laugh track, and Allison invites the audience into her misery. Allison is the central character around whom the two narratives revolve: The emotional abuse she must endure with a smile in her sitcom-*esque* life and her actual perception of her world. In both narratives, she is centered; in one, she is silenced.

SCOPE AND AIMS OF THE BOOK

Expanding on these examples, this text will examine the role of women in pop culture, both famous women as well as women thrust into fame because of a particular event, and show how their stories both center and silence them. While we may see more women—and see more coverage of women—in popular culture today than in times past, how are these new, more prominent stories told?

The text utilizes pop culture in two ways: to tell the story and to explore how the story has been told. For the purposes of this work, pop culture includes newspaper and magazine articles, essays, and op-eds, in print and online; memoirs, biographies, documentaries, biopics, and podcasts; social media sites by women and those that critique women; and academic literature on the roles of women in society. Where relevant, I dig into conversations *about* events, texts, or people, as found in comment sections, reviews, and social media discussion threads. I draw from conflicting accounts of specific stories, featuring those in favor of, or opposed to, a person or event, as well as others somehow involved in creating the story. Overall, this text will show that while women and women's stories are often centered in popular culture, they are, nevertheless, treated in ways that simultaneously silence them, thus perpetuating and strengthening patriarchy. How we live in the world is reflected in our media, while our media simultaneously teach us how to live in the world.

The stories I analyze in this book are dark because, all too often, popular culture paints negative pictures of women, girls, and trans people, and because, as a society, we tacitly approve of the poor treatment of women. My interest in these dark stories and negative portrayals is not to perpetuate them, but rather to subject them to the insights of critical media literacy, in order to show how other, more inclusive and equitable, representations are possible. Media literacy, the ability to access, analyze, and produce a variety of media, offers the opportunity to seek out and work to better understand the corporate and independent media that operate as our storytellers, information providers, and entertainment sources.[105] Therefore, to avoid ending on a dark or cynical note, I conclude with solutions, specifically emphasizing how the work of critical media literacy can be employed to push back against the centering and silencing of women.

Critical media literacy encourages us to examine both media content and the behind-the-scenes work of media production, ownership, and distribution, to explore and better understand the power dynamics of what stories are told, how, and by whom. At its core, critical media literacy is action-oriented, social justice-focused, and with a goal of change-making.[106] Change may be sweeping; for instance, a reinvigoration of the entire media system to be more equitable or inclusive. Just as valid, change may be much smaller in scope; for instance, when one person reshapes how they make sense of a specific media text, which may subsequently inform what additional media that person may seek. Critical media literacy is a process of continuous critical inquiry that encourages and empowers individuals to ask questions about the content, production, and context of their media choices, as audience members and as creators. To be critical is *not* automatically to dislike or to self-deny. At no point will I argue that one must delete, ignore, reject, or turn off any media. Instead, critical media literacy explores the media as multidimensional, multi-varied texts, which are open to multiple and even competing interpretations.

Exploring pop culture through the lens of critical media literacy may also serve as a reminder, one that is particularly important for this text, of the disconnect between actual people and the media images of them. From the paparazzi to social media influencers, from media texts that seem to speak directly to us, for us, or about us (those magical texts that somehow *get* us), we build parasocial relationships with a variety of famous people and people pushed into fame. Despite our feelings of close alignment, for the most part, we know our pop culture celebrities only via their media representation, not their real, non-mediated lives. As an area of study, critical media literacy reminds us that everything addressed in this book (and probably most, if not all, of those parasocial relationships) are representations, which may or may not have any significant connection to the lived realities of those people's lives.

WHAT DOES IT MEAN TO REVISIT "PROBLEMATIC" WOMEN?

I would love to say that I am above the fray of bad behavior when it comes to the judgment of women. I am, however, a human being, and therefore as complicit as the next person in judging many of the women centered in this text. In my research, I have learned so much more about women whom I once dismissed or only partially understood, as well as about women or groups of women I had never heard of before this research. Because I have no direct, personal knowledge of any of the women profiled in this text, I still only partially know them, but hopefully, more thoroughly than before.

Although raised on the LP and storybook *Free to Be ... You and Me*, I still messed up along the way. As someone born after 1973, I took *Roe* for granted; it had always existed, was always there in the periphery of my life, and I assumed that it would always exist. As a middle-class White female, I felt little need to fight for my bodily autonomy because I assumed it was guaranteed. As a teenager during the Clarence Thomas hearings, my reaction to Anita Hill's testimony could be summed up in one word about both people: Who? At the time, I was too busy dissecting the lyrics of Sinéad O'Connor's music and thinking her a total badass, but I never questioned, cared, or researched why she tore up a picture of the pope. I pored over Sherman Alexie's *The Lone Ranger and Tonto Fistfight in Heaven* and watched *Smoke Signals* on repeat, but did not look further into the struggles of Indigenous people. I was not into video games, so I never concerned myself with who made them, why, or whether there were conflicts within the gaming community (nor was I remotely aware that there even was a *gaming community*). When Britney Spears exploded on the music scene, I thought her music sucked and assumed that, after the wave of popularity around "Baby One More Time" died down, she would be forgotten. Boy, was I wrong. When Monica Lewinsky and the Starr Report hit the headlines of the *New York Times*, I thought she was an idiot. Was I making the wisest choices in my early twenties? Nope. But Lewinsky's choices were worse than mine, and mine were not headline fodder.

To revisit these women and their actions is to do two things: See them in a new light and begin the process of change to prevent this treatment in the future. In her essay *Men Explain Things To Me,* Solnit writes, "I love it when people explain things to me they know and I'm interested in but don't yet know."[107] I hope that this text will explain things not yet known to you, the reader, and that, along the way, you will gain new insight into maligned women and previously overlooked stories about women in new and different ways—that you can dip in and out in order to learn something new or engage in a further conversation.

I write this text with a combination of empathy and anger. Conducting research for this project and having conversations with colleagues, friends, family, and especially my young adult research assistants, has bolstered my empathy for the plight of women thrust into a certain type of fame *because* they are women. And I'm also deeply angry because, as the research will show, the architecture of patriarchy has barely shifted. In some instances, the foundations are reinforced, to the detriment of women, young girls, and—no exaggeration—all of humanity. The 2024 presidential election is proof-positive of this. The wholesale rejection of a viable female president (for the second time, thus far, in the twenty-first century) revealed how conflicted our nation is along the lines of gender and race. Patriarchy is a power structure that most obviously harms girls and women. It *also* harms boys and men who are caught up in and learn from its vitriol.

While I share a wide variety of stories about women who have been centered and silenced by pop culture, I have undoubtedly left out so many women and so many stories, either because of my own ignorance or, more realistically, because a single book can only be so long. I explore the intersections of race, class, and gender, but I by no means exhaust all the permutations of those intersections. I explore the role of non-famous women who have become famous because of a certain act, which means there are countless non-famous women out there today, struggling with decisions that may dramatically alter the course of their lives. I draw on social media content (largely because my young research assistants compelled me to do so), but I know I'm missing some important stories that are covered via Instagram, TikTok, YouTube, and whatever else is on the digital media horizon. I do not discuss pornography in this book, though the genre is a logical extension of so much of the treatment of women in popular culture.[108] Chances are good that by the time you get to this point in the text (let alone make your way through the whole thing), there will be several more examples that could and should have been included. The tools of analysis employed in this text will enhance your understanding of a variety of media texts when there is a new person in the spotlight, when there is a new story, and when things have shifted. Therefore, I consider this text the *start* of the conversation and hope that it can be built upon over time.

Each chapter focuses on a particular way that women who push against patriarchy have been centered, silenced, and punished. The categories that form the chapters overlap. Women who act and speak out may do so because they have been harmed for being women, hurt by other women, or embody a generational legacy of harm. The categories are intended to highlight a particularly evocative or defining moment/connection in their public persona, or the moment/connection that made them publicly known.

NOTES

1. Michael D. Shear, "Biden Drops Out of Presidential Race and Endorses Harris," *New York Times*, July 21, 2024.
2. Michael D. Shear and Peter Baker, "Election Live Updates: Harris Moves to Clear Path to Democratic Nomination," *New York Times*, July 22, 2024; Shane Goldmacher, "Harris Raises More Than $50 Million as Biden's Exit Unleashes Cash Wave," *New York Times*, July 22, 2024.
3. Rolling Stone, "All the Artists Who Have Shown up in Support of Kamala Harris," *Rolling Stone*, November 4, 2024; Nicholas Nehamas, Theodore Schleifer, and Nick Corasaniti, "Taylor Swift Endorses Kamala Harris," *New York Times*, September 10, 2024; Maggie Astor, "Taylor Swift's Call to Vote Sent Hundreds of Thousands to Registration Tools," *New York Times*, September 12, 2024.
4. "Roe v. Wade," Center for Reproductive Rights, accessed August 4, 2025.
5. "Roe v. Wade."
6. Frederic J. Frommer, "Justice Ginsburg Thought Roe Was the Wrong Case to Settle the Abortion Issue," *Washington Post*, May 6, 2022.
7. Ann Fessler, *The Girls Who Went Away: The Hidden History of Women who Surrendered Children for Adoption in the Decades before Roe v Wade* (Penguin Books, 2006).
8. Linda Greenhouse, "A Forgotten Chapter Of Abortion History Repeats Itself," *New York Times*, December 22, 2023; Joanna Biggs, "At 23, She Had a Termination. 55 Years Later, She's Ready to Write About it," *New York Times*, August 7, 2024.
9. Biggs, "At 23, She Had a Termination"; Sarah Marshall, host, *You're Wrong About*, "The Jane Collective with Moira Donega," September 4, 2024, 69 minutes.
10. Jessica Glenza and Alana Casanova-Burgess, "The US Air Force Gave Her A Choice: Your Baby Or Your Job," *The Guardian*, December 13, 2019.
11. Katherine Turk, *The Women of NOW: How Feminists Built an Organization That Transformed America* (Farrar, Straus & Giroux, 2023), 3–4.
12. Turk, *The Women of NOW*, 192.
13. "Planned Parenthood of Southeastern Pennsylvania v Casey," Oyez, accessed August 4, 2025.
14. Sara Marcus, *Girls to the Front: The True Story of the Riot Grrrl Revolution.* (Harper Perennial, 2010), 18.
15. "Feminism," Merriam-Webster Dictionary, accessed August 4, 2025.
16. "*Declaration of Sentiments*," National Parks Service, accessed August 4, 2025.
17. Betty Friedan, *The Feminine Mystique* (WW Norton, 1963).
18. Turk, *The Women of NOW*.
19. Andi Zeisler, *We Were Feminists Once: From Riot Grrrl to Covergirl®, the Buying and Selling of a Political Movement* (Public Affairs, 2016).
20. Zeisler, *We Were Feminists Once*, xiii.
21. Zeisler, *We Were Feminists Once*, 75.
22. *Barbie*, directed by Greta Gerwig (Warner Brothers Pictures, 2023).
23. Alex Vadukul, "Mattel Unveils Blind Barbie," *New York Times*, July 23, 2024.
24. Matt Walsh, *What is a Woman: One Man's Journey to Answer the Question of a Generation* (DW Books, 2022).
25. Walsh, *What is a Woman*, 11.

26 Walsh, *What is a Woman*, 9.
27 Walsh, *What is a Woman*, 16.
28 *What Is A Woman?*, directed by Justin Folk, The Daily Wire, 2022; "What is A Woman? One Man's Journey To Answer The Question Of A Generation by Matt Walsh," book synopsis, posted 2022, by Goodreads.
29 Hannah Jocelyn, "Motherhood in the Age of Reproductive Surveillance," *New Yorker*, April 25, 2025; Timothy Gordon, *The Case for Patriarchy* (Sophia Institute Press, 2021); *Mandate for Leadership: The Conservative Promise*, ed. Paul Dans and Steven Groves (The Heritage Foundation, 2023).
30 Cat Bohannon, *Eve: How the Female Body Drove 200 Million Years of Human Evolution* (Knopf, 2023), 4.
31 Caroline Criado-Perez, *Invisible Women: Data Bias in a World Designed for Men* (Abrams Press, 2019).
32 Jacqueline Agtuca, "Beloved Women: Life Givers, Caretakers, Teachers of Future Generations," in *Sharing Our Stories of Survival: Native Women Surviving Violence*, ed. Sarah Deer, Bonnie Clairmont, Carrie A. Martell, and Maureen L. White Eagle, (Altamira Press), 3–27; Mona Gable, *Searching for Savanna: The Murder of One Native American Woman and the Violence Against Many* (Atria Books, 2023).
33 Gable, *Searching for Savanna*.
34 Gable, *Searching for Savanna*.
35 Katelyn Burns, "The Rise of Anti-Trans 'Radical' Feminists, Explained," *Vox*, September 5, 2019.
36 Rebecca Solnit, "Trans Women Pose No Threat to Cis Women, but We Pose a Threat to Them If We Make Them Outcasts," *The Guardian*, August 10, 2020.
37 Solnit, "Trans Women Pose No Threat to Cis Women."
38 Madison Pauly and Henry Carnell, "'Dystopian:' Trump Issues New Order To Stamp Out Trans Youth Healthcare," *Mother Jones*, January 28, 2025; Danielle Kurtzleben, "Trump Signs Order That Seeks to Ban Transgender Athletes from Women's Sports," NPR, February 5, 2025.
39 Turk, *The Women of NOW*, 14.
40 Rebecca Solnit, *Men Explain Things To Me* (Haymarket Books, 2014), 4.
41 Solnit, *Men Explain Things To Me*, 35.
42 Kathleen Hanna, *Rebel Girl: My Life as a Feminist Punk* (Ecco, 2024), 2.
43 Kate Manne, *Down Girl: The Logic of Misogyny* (Oxford University Press, 2018).
44 Solnit, *Men Explain Things To Me*, 15.
45 Manne, *Down Girl*, 19.
46 Manne, *Down Girl*, 20.
47 Anne Helen Petersen, *Too Fat, Too Slutty, Too Loud: The Rise and Reign of the Unruly Woman* (Plume, 2017).
48 Allison Yarrow, *90s Bitch: Media, Culture, and the Failed Promise of Gender Equality* (Harper Perennial, 2018).
49 Turk, *The Women of NOW*; Yarrow, *90s Bitch*.
50 Yarrow, *90s Bitch*.
51 Yarrow, *90s Bitch*; Katelyn Burns, "The Rise of Anti-Trans 'Radical' Feminists, Explained," *Vox*, September 5, 2019; Solnit, "Trans Women Pose No Threat to Cis Women."
52 Solnit, *Men Explain Things to Me*, 9–10.
53 Manne, *Down Girl*, 52.

54 Manne, *Down Girl*, 57.
55 Jessica Bennett, "The Joy of Communal Girlhood, the Anguish of Teen Girls," *New York Times*, December 22, 2023; "Taylor Swift: The *Eras* Tour," BoxOfficeMojo, accessed July 25, 2025.
56 Bennett, "The Joy of Communal Girlhood."
57 Sarah Marshall, host, *You're Wrong About*, "Phones Are Good, Actually, With Taylor Lorenz," June 25, 2024, 60 minutes.
58 Aaratrika Ball, "Diddy Conspiracy Theory Suggests Jay-Z and Beyoncé Are Involved in Aaliyah's Death," *SportsSkeeda*, October 4, 2024; Craig Jenkins, "The Diddy Discourse Has Lost the Plot," *Vulture*, October 7, 2024.
59 Nicole Sperling, "'Barbie' Was Supposed To Change Hollywood For Women. Why Didn't It?" *New York Times*, July 22, 2024.
60 Beckwith, "Why Would Anyone Date Taylor Swift?"; Dave Rubin (@ daveclips), "Dave Rubin Clips II (Parody) - Retired Jan.20/2025," X; Conservative commentator Dave Rubin, in response to Swift's endorsement of Kamala Harris for president, tweeted, "Taylor Swift, you are a young pretty girl, do you know what gang members from Venezuela do to young pretty girls? It ain't pretty."
61 Hannah Grabenstein, "Are the 2024 Paris Olympics Gender Equal? That Depends How You Measure It," PBS, July 26, 2024.
62 Rhea Nayyar, "What Are Those Giant Painted Heads Floating in the Seine?" *HyperAllergic*, July 30, 2024.
63 Ann Fessler, *The Girls Who Went Away: The Hidden History of Women Who Surrendered Children for Adoption in the Decades before Roe* v *Wade* (Penguin Books, 2006), 115–16.
64 Fessler, *The Girls Who Went Away*, 115-16.
65 Zeisler, *We Were Feminists Once*.
66 Yarrow, *90s Bitch*, vxi.
67 Sophie Gilbert, *Girl on Girl: How Pop Culture Turned a Generation of Women Against Themselves* (Penguin Press, 2025).
68 Jodi Kantor and Megan Twohey, "Harvey Weinstein Paid off Sexual Harassment Accusers for Decades," *New York Times*, October 5, 2017.
69 *Striptease*, directed by Andrew Bergman (Columbia Pictures, 1996); Manohla Dargis, "Demi Moore and the Subversive Politics of The Naked Body," *New York Times*, September 9, 2024.
70 Dargis, "Demi Moore."
71 Walter Tevis, *The Queen's Gambit* (Random House, 1983). *The Queen's Gambit*, written and directed by Scott Frank, television series (Netflix, 2020).
72 Louisa Thomas, "Queenside," *New Yorker*, August 2, 2021, 28–33.
73 *Mrs. America*, showrun by Davhi Waller (FX on Hulu, 2020).
74 Elizabeth Flock, *The Furies: Women, Vengeance, and Justice* (Harper Collins, 2023).
75 Anna Motz, *If Love Could Kill: Myths and Truths of Women Who Commit Violence* (Knopf, 2024), xii.
76 *Lorena*, directed by Joshua Rofé, television series (Amazon Prime Video, 2019); *Monster*, directed by Patty Jenkins (Denver and Delilah Productions, 2003). Popularly and publicly known as Bobbitt, Gallo shifted back to her maiden name to reclaim a semblance of privacy.
77 Phyllis Chesler, *Patriarchy: Notes of an Expert Witness* (Common Courage Press, 1994).

78   Zeynep Tufekci, "Kate Middleton's Story Is About So Much More than Kate Middleton," *New York Times*, March 13, 2024.

79   Tufekci, "Kate Middleton's Story Is About So Much More than Kate Middleton."

80   Christine Blasey Ford, *One Way Back: A Memoir* (St. Martin's Press, 2024), 35.

81   Monica Lewinsky, "Shame and Survival," *Vanity Fair*, June 2014.

82   Lewinsky, "Shame snd Survival."

83   Mattie Kahn, "Gisele Bündchen on Healthy Eating and Unhealthy Relationships," *New York Times*, March 23, 2024.

84   Allyson McCabe, *Why Sinéad O'Connor Matters* (University of Texas Press, 2023), 71–72.

85   Caster Semenya, *The Race to be Myself: A Memoir* (WW Norton, 2023), 6.

86   Rachel Louise Snyder, "Chrystul Kizer Got 11 Years in Prison for Killing Her Abuser. This Is Justice?" *New York Times*, August 22, 2024; Rachel Louise Snyder, "Who Gets to Kill in Self-Defense?" *New York Times*, September 4, 2024.

87   Laura Stewart, "Missing and Murdered Indigenous Women and Girls: A Crisis Hiding in Plain Sight," *Cultural Survival*, June 1, 2023.

88   Jessica McDiarmid, *Highway of Tears* (Atria, 2019), 135.

89   McDiarmid, *Highway of Tears*, 136.

90   McDiarmid, *Highway of Tears,* 139.

91   David Brock, *Blinded by the Right: The Conscience of an Ex Conservative.* (Crown Books, 2023).

92   Nina Totenberg, host, "David Brock Interview Transcript," NPR, July 7, 2001.

93   Townhall.com, "Don Lemon: 'Nikki Haley isn't in her prime'"; Michael M. Grynbaum and John Koblin, "Uproar Hits CNN as Don Lemon Is Rebuked for Comments About Women," *New York Times*, February 17, 2023.

94   Tiffanie Turnbull, "Olympics Commentator Axed over Sexist Remark," BBC, July 29, 2024.

95   Turnbull, "Olympics Commentator Axed over Sexist Remark."

96   Allison Butler, "CNN's Don Lemon Still Gets It Wrong. His Non-Apology for Sexist Comments Is What Not to Do," *USA Today*, February 22, 2023.

97   Nicholas Kristof, "The Online Degradation of Women and Girls That We Meet With a Shrug," *New York Times*, March 23, 2024.

98   Hanna, *Rebel Girl*, 183.

99   McCabe, *Why Sinéad O'Connor Matters*, 72.

100 Jason Zinoman, "'Saturday Night Live' and the Underappreciated Influence of Carol Burnett," *New York Times*, October 13, 2024.

101 Tiffany Hsu, "Kate Middleton, Britney Spears and the Online Trolls Debating Their Existence," *New York Times*, March 20, 2024.

102 Gina Cherelus, "Bumble to Users: You Need Sex. Users to Bumble: Get Lost," *New York Times*, May 14, 2024.

103 *Below Deck, Season 2: Ohana*, produced by Mark Cronin et al., television series (Bravo, 2014).

104 *Kevin Can F**k Himself*, produced by Valerie Armstrong, Rashida Jones, Will McCormack, and Craig DiGregorio, television series (AMC, 2021–2022).

105 Patricia Aufderheide, *Media Literacy–A Report of the National Leadership Conference on Media Literacy* (The Aspen Institute, 1993).

106 Douglas Kellner and Jeff Share, "Critical Media Literacy, Democracy, and the Reconstruction of Education," in *Media Literacy: A Reader*, ed. Donaldo Macedo and Shirley Steinberg (Peter Lang, 2007).
107 Solnit, *Men Explain Things to Me*, 13.
108 Gilbert, *Girl on Girl*.

49 *THE JUDGMENT OF GENDER*

CHAPTER ONE

THE CONTEXT OF WOMANHOOD

EXCLUDING WOMEN

During an archeological excavation of a burial site, bones were found buried alongside weapons; because of the proximity to the weapons, the bones were believed to be male. When they were tested and proved to be female, the assumption was that she was buried with her man's weapons, not that there were cultures with women warriors.[1] This type of thinking has been so ingrained as part of human evolution that when presented with stories (and evidentiary data) to the contrary, it is easier to believe them to be a mistake than to adjust one's (erroneous) thinking. Philosopher Judith Butler's exploration of gender notes the "power of language to subordinate and exclude women."[2] By referring to "people," or "subjects," one may reasonably assume this means men and women, but British journalist and activist Caroline Criado Perez observes, "The lives of men have been taken to represent those of humans overall," negating women by not naming them, not including them, or not being clear about their exclusion.[3]

This ignorance is not limited to the (mis)understanding of tenth-century burial mysteries. The world's fastest-growing language is emoji, also a source for understanding how women have been minimized and ignored. Early human-image emojis were all male, even though the search terms were not gender specific. For example, if one wanted to insert the image of a runner into their text, what automatically appeared was a male runner. Unicode, the company that developed emojis, re-coded the humanoid emojis, and one can now insert male or female emojis. In addition, there are LGBTQ+ and trans icons available.[4]

This language and visual exclusion happen in multiple locations and serve to frame women as outsiders. For example, most sports are understood to be male and their pinnacle competitions—the Grand Slam, the World Cup—go unqualified, while women's sports and competitions are qualified: Women's Grand Slam, Women's World Cup. By extension, sports bars are not gender-specific, yet they commonly show male sports almost exclusively.[5]

In scientific research, even when language is gender-neutral, the subjects are almost exclusively male. Women have been ignored in all areas of research, and this act of ignoring is "a kind of not thinking" that invites men/maleness to serve as proxies for all of humanity.[6] Admittedly, scientific research on women carries a host of ethical quandaries connected to women's hormonal health and wellbeing. The tragic reality of countless women prescribed Thalidomide during difficult pregnancies is a valid warning that research into women's bodies needs to proceed cautiously and with great care. However, there is language readily available to clarify who, exactly, is studied and how, so that at the very least, those attempting to glean information or understand a broader context may know more thoroughly what data are included and excluded.

This chapter begins from this premise of willful ignorance. When women are not named, one must look closer to see if, or even how, they are present. One of the easiest ways to subjugate and oppress a body is to act as if that body does not exist or that it only exists with certain qualifications. This chapter discusses the context of womanhood, including what it means to ignore women, to leave them out of a larger conversation, which then dictates how they operate in the world and what it means to blame women for how they operate—or are perceived to operate—in the world. This chapter provides a rough timeline of how women have been covered in popular culture, from the paparazzi of the mid-twentieth century to contemporary social media. An exploration of the intersections of gender with race, class, and the body illustrates how women's multiple identities are parsed and compartmentalized.

IGNORING WOMEN

Women are easily ignored or bypassed in society, despite their obvious and increasing presence. Women represent the largest growth in employment, with 78 percent of women aged 25–54 part of the labor force in 2024. Since 2015, women represent more of the labor market, though it is not surprising that mothers of young children represent the slowest growth.[7] Young women are more likely to be enrolled in college than young men and of those over the age of 25, women are more likely than men to have a four-year college degree.[8] This increase in women's presence in public places may be seen as threatening, so a means to constrict and limit women must be exercised.

This constriction is painfully evident in the world of women's health, which illustrates how women are simultaneously centered and silenced. In order to maintain the perception of traditional femininity, including "being perpetually pleasant, self-sacrificing, and emotionally in control," displaying the virtues of "agreeability, extreme selflessness, and suppression of anger," women may ignore their own health concerns.[9] Psychologist and author Maytal Eyal notes, "For many women, it feels easier—beneficial, even—to silence their needs at the expense of their own health, rather than swim against the prevailing cultural current."[10] Simultaneously, when women do present specific health concerns, these are often ignored by medical professionals due to the unconscious bias of sexism (women's complaints must be emotional, not physical) and systemic gaps in medical research.[11] Owing to what is known as the "gender pain gap," many women's health issues are treated as emotional or psychological, rather than physical.[12] This gender pain gap is more severe for women of color, whose health concerns are often dismissed by health care providers.[13] When women complain of pain, they are more likely to receive sedatives or antidepressants than pain medication.[14]

When women are ignored or not taken seriously, their health suffers. In her study of how women have been left out of larger social conversations, Criado Perez explores how "the facts have been lying to us," owing to unclear language choices.[15] Through imprecise language, maleness has been constructed as universal. This model is both inaccurate—women are approximately 50 percent of the population—and irresponsible. Health concerns have long been constructed as universal when, in actuality, women have unique health parameters, coupled with traditional social expectations and assumptions that have an impact on health. For example, something as seemingly universal as sleep (all humans need sleep, some humans benefit from more or less sleep) can be understood as neglecting women's particular concerns. Women at various life stages, including those menstruating, pregnant, in perimenopause, or postmenopausal, may need different amounts of sleep. Because most sleep research subjects are men, it is not clear if women need more sleep at all, need more sleep because they are women, or are relatively sleep-deprived, compared to men, because of social pressures, such as greater responsibility for child care.[16]

Girls and women suffer from particular medical maladies that long go undiagnosed or brushed off as part of the cost of being female. For example, young women with acne, excessive hair, and menstrual abnormalities may be going through a particularly rough patch of adolescence, or they may have Polycystic Ovary Syndrome (PCOS) (or, something else entirely, of course.)[17] Medical professionals can easily dismiss young women's complaints about cosmetic concerns, or, more insidiously, advertisers can convince them to consume products— which will ultimately do them no good—in an effort to make them more appropriately feminine. Young women with potentially significant medical concerns may carry, in isolation, the weight of not being pretty enough. Because young women are often dismissed when expressing health-related concerns, any supportive diagnoses may be ignored.

This silencing of one's own experiences, coupled with a lack of formal knowledge, has made the conversation of menopause one that further centers and silences women. Since ancient times, "uterine melancholy" has largely been either ignored or misunderstood. The disease of "hysteria" was "believed to start in the uterus and travel around the body."[18] In 1821, a French physician named Charles-Pierre Louis de Gardanne named "menopause," combining the French word for moon (meno) and the definition of pause (to stop), to label what was understood as the cessation of a woman's menstrual cycle.[19] Far from being constructed as a newfound freedom for women, menopause was thought to make women both insane and worthless. Menstrual blood was thought to be evil and poisonous, and menstruation was a way for women's bodies to purge the toxins; once she stopped menstruating, the belief was that the toxins would overtake her body, causing her to go mad.[20] In 1966, gynecologist Robert A. Wilson called menopause a "serious, painful, and often crippling disease," and determined that "all post-menopausal women are castrates" because a woman could no longer reproduce.[21]

In 1923, two American chemists, Edgar Allen and Edward Doisy, isolated the estrogen hormone and identified its role in endocrine regulation.[22] In 1942, the first hormone replacement therapy (HRT), extracted from horse estrogen and sold under the name Premarin, was released with high hopes that it would bring an end to the "disease" of menopause.[23] The promise, often made to husbands, was that HRT would restore a woman's femininity and interest in sex. However, Premarin soon proved dangerous because it depended entirely on the manipulation of estrogen, which is not how the body naturally works. Hormone replacement therapy, comprised of the combination of estrogen and progestin, proved beneficial until widely-published misreporting of research into estrogen-progestin HRT indicated elevated risks for cancer.[24] This misinformation prevailed for years, resulting in an understanding of menopause as an inevitably miserable condition for which there was no safe medical support.

All humans with a uterus who live long enough will experience menopause, which means that as life expectancy expands, so too will the number of people who experience menopause. In some ways, menopause is an indicator of social and cultural privilege: In normative development, to live long enough to experience menopause is to live a long life. Yet there is precious little medical school training or knowledge about the process. Menopause is often dismissed as a "woman's issue," one rarely taken seriously or well-understood by doctors, with the result that "very real-life, and health-altering, symptoms are dismissed as emotional and psychological in nature, or are categorically dismissed as mood swings that a patient should just tolerate or tough out."[25] Even those pursuing obstetrics and gynecology who, one presumes, have very particular training in endocrinology and reproductive organs, have very little training in menopause.[26]

What is quite prevalent is the increased commodification of menopause. Women of a certain age are a prime target for a near infinite quantity and quality of products that promise to aid the transition from menses to menopause.[27] Menopause is now a topic of conversation in pop culture, one that destigmatizes biological reality and capitalizes on the lack of medical knowledge and attention by promising people easy and accessible solutions. While it is refreshing that, on some level, women's aging bodies are no longer seen exclusively as shameful vessels to be shuttled to the sidelines, this centering is entirely focused on capital. What healthcare providers cannot or will not understand is seized and promoted by the market.

When doctors ignore women's health issues, much of what is understood about health, more generally, is only partially understood. In her groundbreaking study on women's depression, psychologist Dana Crowley Jack argues, "Since no existing theory adequately explains the complex phenomenon of female depression, a return to depressed women's own descriptions of their experiences and feelings becomes critically important as a means to gain new insights."[28] That is, by listening to women, we gain a better understanding of the context of their health and well-being. By extension, constructing diagnoses without women's consent or participation perpetuates generational cycles of harm inflicted by dismissing or ignoring women's perspectives on their own health. Crowley Jack notes, "As [a] female, one inherits an ancestral, collective feeling of vulnerability that is linked with centuries of economic dependence and physical violence against women."[29]

Narratives constructed by men about women, repeatedly and over time, construct the dominant message that women are less than, frail, in need of supervision, and only viable as human beings for a limited time. If, for example, the ability to foster and grow human life is sacred, then one way to reduce women's power is to construct a narrative where this is their only purpose. Any role beyond that becomes a threat. Nineteenth-century psychiatry saw female independence as a form of madness, and so-called mad women were sent to asylums for disrupting families and defying their domestic responsibilities.[30] Assertive women were seen as "unnatural, and therefore sick."[31] Women's identities were linked to their reproductive systems and so (proper) women were expected to be fulfilled by performing the roles of wives and mothers.[32] This perspective is not one confined to the nineteenth century. With the passing of the Dobbs decision, and the second election of Trump, there is a stronger platform for greater control over women's bodies, including, but not limited to, the pronatal movement, fights for the human rights of fertilized cells, and plans to reward women for having more babies.[33]

Patriarchy has long owned the narrative of women's bodies, whether that narrative was supported by any evidence or not.

In her study of female evolution, scientist Cat Bohannon tells the story of the fifteenth-century physician Bartholomäus Metlinger, who wrote the first European textbook on pediatrics.[34] Metlinger argued that new mothers should not feed their babies for the first two weeks because their milk was not yet nutritious; instead, babies should suckle from another woman. He provided no evidence for this assertion. Sure, it was the 1400s and science, as we know it, was not sophisticated. So, I wonder, how did he assert, with conviction, that early breastfeeding was unhealthy? He did note that the new mother "should have her breast sucked by a young wolf," presumably implying that it is safer to attempt to feed a wild animal than to breastfeed one's own child.[35]

The lack of scientific evidence about the nutrition of breast milk had a larger political purpose: The use of wet nurses helped population growth; poor and enslaved women would feed wealthy women's babies. Wealthy women who did not feed their own babies were not protected from the natural birth control associated with the release of breast milk.[36] Healthy, wealthy women could make more babies more quickly when they did not have to feed their own children, while poor, enslaved women bore the burden of feeding their own and another's child. To some extent, population growth and all that entailed—greater labor sources, more powerful civilizations, better defenses—may be traced to the enslavement of women. Rather than seeing a woman's body as powerful because of its ability to build new lives, her body became a tool to serve the patriarchy.

When we ignore women, we ignore half of humanity, and through that ignorance, may forget that women are complex and complicated beings. In large part because the stereotypical narrative of women values modesty and demure compliance, women who live counter to that narrative are hard to comprehend. In her study of female violence, psychologist Anna Motz notes, "To look away from violent women," including abuse and trauma, is to ignore the context that foments violence, that sees women as helpless or without agency.[37] As a society, we cannot seem to handle when women commit violence because "people don't want to believe that women are capable of terrible things."[38] Even less comprehensible, and therefore more salacious, are pregnant women with drug use disorder or teen girls who commit violence.[39] When examined closely, violence committed by women (probably, violence committed by all people) has complex and complicated origins, which often involve a prior history of violent acts committed against them.[40] This lateral violence, a term that comes from Indigenous scholars to understand peer oppression within Indigenous communities, "happens when people who have been oppressed for a long time feel so powerless that rather than fighting back against their oppressor, they unleash their fear, angers, and frustration against their own community members."[41] Those who commit lateral violence may do so without full awareness of their actions because it "often provides individuals who hurt others with a false sense of power or influence."[42] In writer Rebecca Godfrey's exploration of the murder of a teen girl by her peers, some of the perpetrators said they did not fully understand why they participated in the beating, but that on some level, it made them feel connected.[43]

Another way of looking at violence committed by women is as narratives of vengeance, of women fighting back against years and generations of oppression. Journalist Elizabeth Flock's *The Furies: Women, Vengeance, and Justice* profiles three women who "handle matters on their own because the cops, courts, and state had failed to safeguard them."[44] It is not that what these women did was right, per se, but rather that their actions exist in a broader, more complicated context. Women's violence, particularly violence that seems unforgivable, such as killing a child, needs to be understood in a historical context that includes violence done to women over time. Motz notes, "the reality of women's violence is a truth too uncomfortable to take seriously; a taboo that offends the idealized notion of women as sources of love, nurture, and care."[45] Violent women and women's violence make law-abiding citizens uncomfortable. Female violence is largely private, often taking place within domestic spheres, which makes it even harder to understand; violent women are often "treated as less than fully human."[46] Violent women are ultimately "hypervisible in their status as violent offenders and almost invisible as human beings with human needs."[47] When women are centered for their violence, the messy history and larger context of that violence is silenced.

Maybe another reason why female violence is so shocking is because it proves that women have agency (however misguided). A woman who commits violence is often doubly blamed, first for the act and second for not making different (read: better) choices to prevent or avoid the act. When a woman is violent in response to domestic violence, a first reaction is often to question why she stayed with her abuser.[48] A particular irony faced by women, who statistically commit fewer crimes than men, is that they are typically more harshly punished. Because there is more male-perpetrated violence, and therefore more crowded prisons, there are incentives for men accused of violent crimes to negotiate and agree to plea bargains for lesser charges. In contrast, because women's prisons are not as crowded, there is less incentive for courts to accept plea bargains by women.[49]

Women are ignored in places where we might not even know to look for them or to parse their presence by naming them. Despite our everyday reliance on digital technologies for work and entertainment, most of us know little about how these technologies were developed or how they are maintained. Sociologist France Winddance Twine's analysis of racism and sexism in the tech industry reveals a toxic work environment where "women endured sexual harassment, systematic pay discrimination, and racism."[50] Google spokespeople blame the education pipeline, arguing that there are not enough women with computer science degrees for them to hire.[51] Sociologist Safiya Noble argues, "Institutional relations predicated on gender and race situate women and people of color outside the power systems from which technology arises."[52] The irony is that early computing work was feminized, with women working as "human computers," a job that was seen as subordinate.[53] These "human computers" were women "trained in math or a related field and tasked with performing the calculations that determined everything from the best wing shape for an airplane to the best flight path to the moon."[54] The most popular iteration of this is found in the book, and subsequent film, *Hidden Figures*, which told the tale of Black female computers who developed the formulas that made it possible for the first US spacecraft (crewed by the story's male hero John Glenn) to orbit the Earth.[55] The women were treated as "unskilled temporary workers," overseen by male engineers who "never even bothered to learn the computers' names."[56] Noble contends that "the very notion that technologies are neutral must be directly challenged as a misnomer."[57] Only when computing grew more complex did men step in, take over, and exclude women wherever possible. To this end, feminist data scholars Catherine D'Ignazio and Lauren Klein introduced data feminism, "a way of thinking about data, both their uses and their limits, that is informed by direct experience, by a commitment to action, and by intersectional feminist thought."[58] Data feminism is a way to explore power, who has it and who does not, where, in our current digital environment, data is power."[59] For example, the Google spokespeople may very well be correct that there are fewer women with computer science degrees for them to recruit. But do the folks at Google pause to think about the classroom environment where these young women learn whether they belong or not? Do they pause to consider that an imbalanced classroom or work space may not be a battle that many women want to fight?

BLAMING WOMEN

While society is loath to give women credit for much of anything—unless, that is, the woman occupies a traditional space—blaming women for men's failures is a tale as old as time. In 2024, when Supreme Court Justice Samuel Alito was critiqued for having a "stop the steal" flag in the yard of his home (thereby, one assumes, calling into question any impartiality in his rulings on cases arising from the January 6, 2021, insurrection on the US Capitol, or in any of the myriad felony cases against Trump) he blamed his wife, Martha-Ann, saying that it was her idea to hang the flag upside down as a part of a dispute with a neighbor.[60] In 2024, Senator Bob Menendez's (D-NJ) lawyer blamed his wife, Nadine, for her participation in a bribery scheme for which he was found guilty.[61] And of course, Hillary Clinton was regularly attacked for being a dangerous and manipulative threat to her husband's presidency.[62] One subversive way of looking at wife-blaming is that, when a wife is blamed for some infraction that a man cannot or will not take responsibility for, his transfer of blame subtly acknowledges that his wife is capable of independent thought and action.[63] Isn't this the one thing that made Hillary Clinton so hated as First Lady, Senator, and presidential candidate? She operated on her own, had her own opinions, and acted on her own agency. One may disagree with her policies and her approach to governing, but it seems indisputable that much of the animus directed at her was spurred by her independence.

During the tumultuous 2023–2024 academic year, when students at college campuses across the country protested the Israel-Palestine war as well as campus complicity feeding the military-industrial complex that made it so easy for other countries to drop bombs, some college presidents and chancellors were brought before Congress to testify to the work their campuses were doing to quell tensions. Not every campus rocked by student protest was held accountable by Congress. Instead, the presidents held most publicly accountable were all women: Elizabeth Magill of the University of Pennsylvania, Claudine Gay of Harvard University, Sally Kornbluth of the Massachusetts Institute of Technology, and Minouche Shafik of Columbia University. Dr. Nancy

Andrews, the first female Dean of Duke University School of Medicine, mused,

> Four women presidents, all new in their roles, far too new to have shaped the culture of their campuses, called before Congress? Of course there's a pattern. The question is, What's the agenda? Is it to take down women leaders? To attack elite universities through a perceived vulnerability? To further a political purpose?[64]

As Andrews documents, none of the campus leaders brought before Congress had been in their positions long enough to craft the culture of their respective campuses. Evidently, however, they had been there long enough to take the blame for the tumult. This exclusion, ignoring, and blaming of women is all made possible, in part, by a media environment that constructs women as objects, which, in turn, feeds a culture's confusion about how to approach women.

WOMEN IN POP CULTURE: FROM THE PAPARAZZI TO SOCIAL MEDIA

The year 1964, when Elizabeth Taylor left Eddie Fisher (her fourth husband) to marry Richard Burton (her fifth and, subsequently, sixth husband), marked a shift in how the press treated celebrities, especially celebrity women. When Taylor captured the attention of the world, photographers began to chase her and other celebrities "to get a juicy shot they could sell."[65] The paparazzi constructed an environment where they had full access to celebrities, no matter the location or pleas for privacy.[66] Furthermore, they contributed to, and bolstered, negative terms associated with female celebrities, such as "difficult, erratic, vain, narcissistic."[67]

Through the early twenty-first century, the paparazzi and tabloid media followed celebrities around and, in a time of print and broadcast TV dominance, audiences had multiple sources for soapy, gossipy stories. Celebrities themselves had little recourse to push back or be directly involved in the crafting of their own images. For example, in 1985, in what seemed both an egregious invasion of privacy and a juicy coup, paparazzi in helicopters surveilled and photographed the wedding of ascendant pop star Madonna and actor Sean Penn. Their wedding was a private affair, held at the edge of a cliff, overlooking the Pacific Ocean.[68] While paparazzi on foot or invading private property may be compelled to leave, how does one kick someone out of airspace?

This all changed with the rise of the internet, especially the ease with which it allowed people online to tell their own stories (or to craft the perception that they are telling their own stories). Prior to social media, the rise of the internet as we know it today was still heavily reliant on written text, especially evident in the development of "weblogs" or blogs. For a brief time in the early 2000s, blogs reigned as one of the most popular spaces where users gathered online. The arc of blogging—which started as a grassroots, independent movement that soon became co-opted and monetized as part of corporate culture—is notable specifically because of the early work done by women. Some of the earliest popular blogs were by women who wrote about struggling with the pressures of motherhood, including postpartum depression, balancing work and family life, and stress over raising their children while trying to find time and space for themselves and their marriages. Motherhood became a "lively public conversation" with the development of blogs on the newly popular internet.[69]

In her analysis of the internet, journalist Taylor Lorenz pays close attention to "mommy blogs," especially the community they built and the ire they produced. New mothers' concerns and interests were not addressed in the legacy media, which "pushed an idealized, often misogynistic version of motherhood that was less and less relevant to modern mothers."[70] Domestic life, especially post-partum life, was coded as private and women were not to talk (frankly) about their struggles, especially their struggles with their bodies, in the public sphere. Within the isolation of new motherhood, women had limited opportunities for connection. The burgeoning internet became a place where women gathered virtually, "either as readers, or writers, or both," of blogs that served as "a needed outlet for their creative energy as well as a way to connect with others like them."[71] Similar to the radical shift in perspective of what it meant to be a wife and mother cracked open by Friedan's *The Feminine Mystique*, blogs helped women see they were not alone in their struggles. They could speak to and have a direct audience with each other.[72] In part because blogging was so novel, there were no codified rules or expectations; women "wrote deeply personal, raw, and unfiltered accounts of the sides of motherhood not found in parenting books."[73] In general, women were not compensated for blogging, even though the work required time and energy. By contrast, most of the male authors of tech and politics blogs were either paid or supported by commercial endorsements. When women started accepting compensation for their work, via advertisements or endorsements, "people became blind with rage."[74] Mothers themselves are a multi trillion dollar market and control nearly 80 percent of household spending, yet paradoxically, they cannot profit from blogging about their knowledge, expertise, or experiences without being punished.[75]

Despite the rage, endorsements and paid posts became more common and the text-heavy internet became more visual, which made racial divisions in who was blogging more obvious and clear. The majority of successful mommy bloggers were "attractive, thin, white women. Black mothers and mothers representing other marginalized identities were not granted the most lucrative brand deals."[76] Sponsored mothers and mothers with endorsement deals started to lose independence; content "needed to be pre-approved" as advertisers preferred an aspirational story to a messy truth.[77] Once again, motherhood was compartmentalized and contained.

Mommy blogs illustrate how, for a brief moment in time, women were in charge of a space on the internet and crafted it to their needs—only to have it ripped away by the enforcers of patriarchal capitalism. As the internet grew more agile, the development of social media dramatically shifted the online landscape for both celebrities and regular people. The development and popularization of Facebook (2004), YouTube (2005), Twitter (2006), Instagram (2010), Snapchat (2011), and TikTok (2016) changed the face and the use of the internet. All of these sites relied on brief visual stories, with limited word counts. To compete with each other and either secure or maintain dominance, each platform added more visual capabilities, and in some cases, bought the competition (Facebook acquired Instagram; Google bought YouTube; Elon Musk bought Twitter and renamed it X).

While the paparazzi and tabloids still held sway over the images and stories of celebrities, the rise of social media helped create the influencer: A savvy user and content creator of social media who made generous use of endorsements and advertisements to cultivate a personal brand. Influencers create short and elaborate videos for social media that highlight their self-constructed brand, such as dancer, parent, fashion icon, or cultural critic. Oftentimes, influencers' presentation of self includes some sort of external or self-created drama, which serves to engage their followers and encourages them to share other influencers' posts, to attract even more attention. Using social media to become famous, or even notorious, influencers often live by the show business adage that "there is no such thing as bad publicity." Even when influencers behave badly (and, in some cases, especially when they behave badly), or are excoriated for their actions, they receive a great deal of attention. For example, conservative political commentator Candace Owens was fired by the Daily Beast for alleged anti-Semitic comments, which led directly to a massive increase of her TikTok and YouTube subscribers.[78] The Wilking sisters, Melanie and Miranda, became famous on TikTok for their dance routines and, ultimately, even more famous for alleged connections to a cult, which led to a Netflix docuseries.[79] Married couple Matt and Abby Howard documented their entire relationship (dating, marriage, and the birth of their children) on YouTube and TikTok, as they promoted traditional Christian and gender values, which resulted in significant online flogging and millions of followers.[80] This documentation of everyday life, including the pecuniary reward for questionable or bad behavior, cultivated a sense of intimacy between influencers and followers. Once again, women are at the forefront: While there are several male social media influencers, women pioneered the influencer phenomenon, which includes those whose online brand revolves around being partnered with men.

These examples illustrate how contemporary pop culture continues to manipulate women and girls. Influencer content may feel as though it provides women more control because they can represent themselves online as spontaneous, personal, and highly intimate. In reality, their posts are carefully crafted, planned, and released. Their content may appear casual and messy, like early mommy blogs, but the contrived representations of spontaneity and authenticity are the larger meta-message of social media. Women have gone from being able to be genuinely messy to selling a cute-messy visage in a relatively short amount of time.

GENDER AND ITS INTERSECTIONS

In her 1851 response to the *Declaration of Sentiments*, the document that grew out of the 1848 women's rights convention at Seneca Falls, New York, which codified women's rights, Sojourner Truth asked, "That man over there says that women need to be helped into carriages and lifted over ditches, and to have the best place anywhere. Nobody helps me into carriages, over mud-puddles or gives me any best place! Ain't I a woman?"[81] While the term "intersectionality" and its implications for understanding how, for example, race and gender overlap, would not be part of the lexicon for more than a hundred years, Truth anticipated the point of the term in this speech: Yes, women are understood to possess protected status, but specifically which women and protected how?

In *Can We All Be Feminists?*, June Eric-Udorie comments that, as a journalist, she was regularly faced with White, female editors who identified as feminists but nevertheless ignored or bypassed stories of women of color:

> It quickly dawned on me that their feminism didn't care about a black, queer, disabled young woman like me. Their feminism was entirely focused on the experiences of women who were white, wealthy or middle class, heterosexual, and able-bodied. Feeling powerless, I made the choice to ignore their blind spots and carried on accepting writing assignments.[82]

While there is a legitimate overarching argument that women are silenced, women is not an homogenous category. To combat the silencing, feminists must look inward, examine their own motivations, and look beyond their comfort zones, their own privilege, and their own preferred media choices. White women who identify as feminists, particularly White women in the public sphere, must reckon with their own behavior and choices and must look beyond their own privileges, however minimal, to better understand gender and its myriad intersections. A White feminism may be helpful in moving some issues forward, but it will always only be partial, and may even be regressive when women of color, disabled women, queer women, trans women, poor women, and other marginalized groups are ignored.[83] Feminism in the United States has all-too-often been equated with middle-class White women while women of color have all-too-often been ignored or marginalized.[84] Stories of White women's struggles receive more attention, and are generally more sympathetic, than stories of Black women's struggles, who receive both less attention and less sympathy.[85] Legal scholar Kimberlé Crenshaw notes, "Sexual harassment had been a common experience of Black women's work life since they arrived in America."[86] In order to make any change, to study the centralizing and silencing of women is to study women of color, queer women, women with disabilities, women of all ages, urban, rural, and suburban women, and so on.

Any feminism that excludes the multiple intersecting and conflicting identities of all women is, at best, an incomplete feminism. Novelist Alice Walker argued that the term and the work of feminism were not inclusive enough because of its exclusion of women of color.[87] This does not mean that all feminists must tackle all issues, but rather that all feminists should specify their central concern and acknowledge that their concern is part of a larger project of women's equality.

Gender and Race

Crenshaw coined the term "intersectionality" as a way to address the multiple worlds where Black women live and to address, in particular, the legal issues faced by women of color. She notes, "Because the intersectional experience is greater than the sum of racism and sexism, any analysis that does not take intersectionality into account cannot sufficiently address the particular manner in which Black women are subordinated."[88] Drawing from Crenshaw, Eric-Udorie notes that intersectionality "offers us a way to understand how multiple structures—capitalism, heterosexism, patriarchy, white supremacy, and so on—work together to harm women."[89]

An example of the tensions of these intersections is found in the wardrobe malfunction that happened to pop singer and actor Janet Jackson, for which she was squarely blamed. Jackson has arguably been famous since birth. Born into the musical Jackson family, she joined her brothers in their music careers, following the Jackson 5 and their various solo careers, including her most famous and notorious brother, Michael, with whom she collaborated on many projects. Jackson headlined the 2004 Super Bowl halftime show, performing a song with pop star Justin Timberlake. During their performance,

Timberlake stripped off Jackson's top in a planned "costume reveal," accidentally (or on purpose?) exposing Jackson's right breast to the world. After the incident, Jackson was subjected to major backlash from the media and the public; she was blamed for the reveal, even though it was Timberlake who grabbed her costume. She was investigated by the FCC because of about half a million complaints about her "indecent exposure."[90] Even as a well-known celebrity (arguably, more well-known than Timberlake at the time), Jackson carried the bulk of the punishment for the exposure, from which Timberlake was largely unscathed.

In the United States, Black women are doubly subjugated: as women and as women of color. This subjugation is rooted in the dueling oppression of patriarchy and the legacy of slavery. Angela Davis's analysis of Black women's history notes that "Black women were equal to their men in the oppression they suffered" within slave communities.[91] Former *Vibe* editor-in-chief Danyel Smith remembers having to behave in a particular way when on the job: "As a Black woman, I was in a no-win situation: to fail was to live up to my male bosses' low expectations, and to succeed was to invite their resentment."[92] While all Black bodies are in danger, Black women may be in more danger. In her discussion of slavery and its resistance, historian Kellie Carter Jackson notes that there was a limited frame for understanding Blackness, largely equated with maleness; Black feminine autonomy was unfamiliar.[93] For example, Black men harmed by police generally receive news attention; these may be terrible stories involving a great deal of violence, including death, but nevertheless, they are stories that are told. Black women's stories of state-sanctioned violence are largely sidelined.[94]

While women athletes receive treatment that calls out and centralizes their gender as a way to present them as less than, this is doubly true for women athletes of color. Black gymnasts Simone Biles, Betty Okino, Dominique Dawes, and Gabby Douglas challenged the White, lithe, blond, ponytailed image of the female gymnast and, immediately upon winning medals, press commentary focused on their hair and makeup.[95] At the 2024 Paris Olympics, Biles pushed back, posting a reel on her Instagram page, "don't come for me about my hair. IT WAS DONE but bus has NO AC & it's like 9,000 degrees" and "gonna hold your hand when I say this ... next time you wanna comment on a black girl's hair JUST DON'T."[96]

Women of color who commit crimes are also treated differently because of the intersection of their gender and race. There is a greater prevalence of mental health struggles that go undiagnosed and subsequently untreated and unsupported among women of color, in part because of systemic inequalities. Women of color who commit crimes are more harshly punished than White women.[97]

Indigenous people—in the United States, across North America, and around the globe—have long been the target of genocide, and Indigenous women occupy a very particular space for eradication. The entrenched racism of seeing Indigenous women as exotic, sexualized objects has long been part of the Western narrative of Indigenous bodies.[98] The Disney version of Pocahontas, for example, was a whitewashed story of star-crossed lovers; the actual story involved the settler-sanctioned rape of a child, who died at age 21, likely of smallpox, after being paraded around as a "civilized savage."[99] As will be discussed in Chapter 5, colonizers knew that attacking Indigenous women and dismantling their roles as autonomous beings was the most effective step towards geographic, political, social, and economic control.

The end result of ignoring and maligning bodies of color is that people of color, and women of color in particular, become both victims of, and complicit in, White supremacy and the work of silencing.[100] The promise of assimilation, where one might not be seen as "other," is always just out of reach for women of color. While White women have a greater chance to fit in, the bodily presentation of their economic class may betray them from full assimilation.

Gender and Class

Women who appear to transgress norms, may actually uphold and enforce them.[101] For example, when former Facebook CFO Sheryl Sandberg encouraged women to "lean in," she implied that women who did not make it to the "top" had only themselves to blame.[102] Sandberg did not acknowledge the economic realities of poor women who may not have had access to child care or health care, or women who may not be interested in the corporate grind.[103] The assumption that more women occupying a particular space automatically equates to a better space, is unfair and unrealistic, and leaves out any critique of the corporate structure that engenders such hierarchies.[104] Champions of neoliberalism, such as Sandberg, ignore how the promise of financial reward, coupled with an emphasis on hyperindividuality, pits poor women against one another.

For example, even at the height of her athletic talent and popularity, ice skater Tonya Harding struggled with her public image, particularly around her lower-class status and, more egregiously, her apparent lack of effort to hide that she was poor. The intensity of attention paid to her body, which is perhaps to be expected of an athlete, also focused on her lower-class background, which was unusual among elite figure skaters. In a profile of Harding's fans in the *New Yorker*, Susan Orlean provides a lengthy discussion of the poverty of Clackamas County, Oregon, where Harding trained.[105] Orlean focuses on the lack of roots, the absence of community, and how all social activities were loosely organized around the mall where Harding practiced. To satisfy the requirement for town recreational facilities, there was an Olympic-size ice rink in the mall, surrounded by the food court. Orlean observes of Harding's practice, "Every contour of her body was outlined in black—her meaty back, her strong upper legs, with their blocky muscles ... For an hour, she practiced pieces of her program—a spin, a leap, a movement of her leg or hand. The pieces were never fused together into something fluid or pretty."[106] During training, are the pieces supposed to be fused together and pretty? Or, because she is practicing, maybe she repeats the same move over and over and over again in order to fuse it into her muscle memory? Orlean does not appear to approve of the other skaters either, whom she describes as girls who looked like Harding, "with long multi-level blond hair and a puff of bangs, eyes rimmed in black liner, and stocky bodies in inexpensive clothes."[107] As will be discussed in Chapter 6, it is not out of the ordinary within the confines of patriarchy for women to harm other women. Why is Orlean so fascinated with the poverty of Harding and her community? What role does that fascination with poverty play in further silencing women?

Harding was known for her aggressive, athletic skating, and especially for landing the triple axel in 1991, a notoriously difficult skating move that involves launching from the front foot, spinning three times, then landing in reverse, skating immediately into the next move. Harding struggled after that achievement, never landing it in competition again.[108] She spent years working on her skating, competed in many events, but was always dogged for her appearance, which was connected directly to her childhood poverty.

Harding did not fit the model of what it meant to be a figure skater, and her treatment in the elite skating community was almost always spiteful. In writer and podcaster Sarah Marshall's deep-dive into Harding's career and interpersonal struggles, she argues that Harding's mere presence, including the fantastical tales told about her, was problematic:

> Her mother had been married six times to six different men, or maybe seven, depending on the journalist's sources. Tonya owned her first rifle, a .22, when she was still in kindergarten, and had moved thirteen times by fifth grade. She dropped out of high school at fifteen. (In fact, she later obtained a GED.) She drank beer and played pool and smoked even though she had asthma. She raced cars at Port-

land International Raceway, and was involved in a much-hyped traffic altercation in 1992, when she brandished a Wiffle-ball bat at another driver ... Her sister was a prostitute. Her father was largely unemployed, as was her mother, as was her ex-husband.[109]

Harding made her own costumes, which were brightly colored, bedazzled, and definitely not in line with the pastel and muted color expectations of the time. At the 1994 Nationals, she was ordered to change her costume "because the judges deemed it too risqué."[110] Harding was also married, then separated, then reunited, then divorced, which meant there was no delusion of her virginity, which violated the image of the demure, docile skater.

Harding was undeniably an excellent skater. However, her victories were short-lived and overshadowed by her personal crises, including, but not limited to, the attack on fellow skater Nancy Kerrigan. In an unprovoked attack, Shane Stant, a friend of Harding's husband Jeff Gillooly, struck Kerrigan on the thigh with a collapsible baton with the intent to eliminate her from competition, ostensibly to clear the way for Harding to win. A court of law found Gillooly and co-conspirator Shawn Eckardt guilty of conspiracy to plan the attack. While Harding maintained that she did not know about the attack ahead of time, she accepted a plea agreement that stated she helped cover up the attack after the fact. Although the attack on Kerrigan was terrible and grossly unfair, the media made it even more so by exploiting both Kerrigan and Harding to suit an invented narrative. Immediately after the attack, cameras captured Kerrigan crying, repeatedly saying, "Why?" This later became "Why me?" in the popular press.[111] It was reported and repeated that Kerrigan had been hit on the knee with, depending on the misreporting, either a crowbar, wrench, or lead pipe.[112] The assertion that Harding had hit Kerrigan's knee made for a more dramatic story because a serious joint injury could end an elite skater's career, and one inflicted by one's closest competitor was a perfect match for sensationalized tabloid reporting.[113] An attack on the thigh, by someone only tangentially connected to the competition, was less enticing. Kerrigan recovered in six weeks, in time to win the silver medal in the singles competition at the Olympics in Lillehammer.[114]

Harding had been heavily criticized prior to the attack as a favorite punching bag of the press and the US skating federation. Because of her poverty and reputation as "white trash," the press was primed to see Harding as a villain and a perpetrator, and the journalists covering her "seemed to reveal the same motive: Tonya was going nowhere fast, and she had decided to take Nancy with her."[115] While they were not best friends, Harding and Kerrigan did spend a fair amount of time together (the world of women's figure skating is small and they were often in the same competitions) and respected each other's skills.[116]

Harding and Kerrigan were formidable competitors; each had a dramatically different skating style, with Kerrigan's more fluid and artistic one preferred by the judges. Harding often earned high scores for her technique, but low scores for artistry. While technical scores may be close to objective—falls and stumbles are clear and obvious deductions—"artistry" is more subjective. It is entirely possible that judges award or detract points based on their own preferences. One Olympic judge referred to Kerrigan as a "lovely lady" who was "raised as a lady. We all notice that."[117]

The irony is that both Harding and Kerrigan grew up poor. Somehow, Kerrigan was the right kind of poor. Her costumes were simple and unadorned, made by fashion designer Vera Wang. She hid her crooked teeth (before later getting them fixed) with a demure, closed-mouth smile. She appeared to have no competitive savvy. Most importantly, she was appropriately feminine, "beautiful without being sexual, strong without being intimidating, and vulnerable without being weak."[118] Kerrigan was subjectively more attractive and had a more stable family structure, including a present and employed father.[119] The figure skating community preferred diminutive skaters with a princess look, which "Nancy Kerrigan delivered."[120] Harding was punished, in part, because she did not disguise or appear ashamed by her poverty. In many ways, her body and its presentation flaunted her poverty; this highlights the risks that women face when their bodies don't follow an expected norm.

Gender and the Body

Despite generations of female athletes performing their chosen sport with great physical prowess and courage, these athletes are still othered and ignored. Women athletes receive particular physical scrutiny that demands they prove they are female. In the mid-twentieth century, sex testing for the Olympics followed the "nude parade" policy: Female athletes were to get naked in front of a doctor, who would determine if their body was, in fact, female. In the late twentieth century, with the increased sophistication of the study of genetics, Olympic officials tested women's chromosomes; anyone who "passed" the test was issued a card of certification that they needed to carry with them to be allowed to compete. All these tests were abandoned at the start of the twenty-first century, which in some ways is more respectful (both tests were invasive, and the chromosome test could be inaccurate) and in other ways, is more problematic (decisions about who is eligible to participate as female vary across different organizing bodies).[121] All athletes' bodies are on display for their physical prowess; female athletes' bodies are under an even more severe microscope as they must repeatedly prove their sex.[122] South African runner Caster Semenya, born with difference in sex development (DSD), more commonly understood as intersex, recalls that "sports and entertainment commentators discussed my facial features, the size of my arms and legs and breasts, the muscles in my abdomen. They would zoom in on pictures of my crotch and wonder what could possibly be going on between my legs."[123]

When women athletes are centered, it is often in ways that minimize them. When basketball phenom Caitlin Clark held a press conference after her team's 2024 NCAA March Madness run, a reporter for the Indianapolis Star, Gregg Doyel, made a heart with his hands, a gesture that Clark would often make to her family during games. When Clark noted that the gesture was a family communication, he stated, "OK, well start doing it to me and we'll get along just fine."[124] Doyel apologized right away; nevertheless, this slip revealed the normalization of seeing women as less than. It is hard to imagine any reporter making that kind of comment to a male athlete. Gymnast Suni Lee, gold medal winner from the 2020 Tokyo Olympics, struggled in college because of stalkers who followed her across multiple state lines and because of the overwhelming attention she got as a medalist. She resorted to taking her classes online and rarely leaving her room.[125] American rugby-7s player Ilona Maher helped secure her team a bronze medal at the 2024 Paris Olympics, the first ever for an American rugby team. As a muscular athlete, Maher faced online scorn for being fat, including one social media post, "I bet that person has a 30-percent BMI," to which Maher responded, "I do have a BMI of 30, I am considered overweight. But alas, I'm going to the Olympics. And you're not."[126] When champion gymnast Simone Biles felt "the twisties," a disorientation where an athlete suffers from something akin to vertigo and cannot find a safe focal point, at the 2020 Tokyo Olympics, and subsequently dropped out, she was protecting her mental and physical health; one slight error in any of her routines could easily lead to serious injury or death. However, the social media response instantly framed her as a quitter and a traitor to her country.[127] Never mind that Biles was also struggling with the aftermath of speaking out against athletic director Larry Nassar and the sexual assault she endured.

Attention to the body and judgments about whose bodily appearance is most appropriate are upended when the body is fat. Fat women are a particular threat because their bodies do not match what is expected of women. Fat women who embrace their bodies are doubly threatening because they may have given up any effort at conventional notions of self-improvement. French DJ Barbara Butch, who opened the 2024 Paris Olympics, was swiftly castigated for being a fat DJ. Butch is aware that her image is bothersome, saying, "My mere existence is political."[128] Butch notes that being a woman is difficult and "for fat people, it's even worse because we are constantly told that the moment we will be happy is when we are thin."[129] Butch was attacked for her openly female, fat, LGBTQ+ presentation on an international stage, including death and rape threats.[130] I wonder, why does the bodily presentation of a DJ matter? And in what possible way are death and rape threats a reasonable reaction to a person whose body departs from idealized norms about desirable body types?

Feminism can combat patriarchy, and therefore, combat the silencing of women, but it must be more inclusive. Performance artist and writer Selina Thompson notes, "Unless we build a feminism that starts from the needs of the most vulnerable and most maligned—those furthest from what historically has been the default body—our feminism will always be a shadow of what it could be."[131]

In her essay on women's reproductive rights, Rebecca Solnit writes, "There are other things I'd rather write about, but this affects everything else."[132] The context of womanhood has an influence and an impact on every facet of society, and until that is seriously and consistently considered, women will always be prone to compartmentalization in ways that minimize them. Chapters 2 through 6 will explore, via case studies of particular women, how women have been minimized, including generational harm, women who act out, women who occupy a space that is not theirs, women who are physically harmed for being women, and women who harm other women.

NOTES

1. Caroline Criado-Perez, *Invisible Women: Data Bias in a World Designed for Men* (Abrams Press, 2019).
2. Judith Butler, *Gender Trouble: Feminism and the Subversion of Identity* (Routledge, 1999), 35.
3. Criado-Perez, *Invisible Women*, xv.
4. Criado-Perez, *Invisible Women*.
5. For a counter-narrative, see Mekahlo Medina, "First Women's Sports Bar in California Officially Opens," NBC Los Angeles, July 27, 2024; and Hannah Goldfield, "The Portland Bar That Screens Only Women's Sports," *New Yorker*, June 23, 2025; both about the rise of sports bars focused on women's sports. Even in non-physical competition, such as chess, where no one can tell the gender of a player from the moves made, women are othered as less than; see Louisa Thomas, "Hou Yifan and the Wait for Chess's First Woman World Champion, " *New Yorker*, July 26, 2021.
6. Criado Perez, *Invisible Women*, xvi.
7. Lauren Bauer and Noadia Steinmetz-Silber, "Prime-Age Women Are Still Driving the Labor Market Recovery," Brookings Institution, July 26, 2024.
8. Kim Parker, "What's Behind the Growing Gap Between Men and Women in College Completion?" Pew Research Center, November 8, 2021.
9. Maytal Eyal, "Self-Silencing Is Making Women Sick," *Time*, October 3, 2023.
10. Eyal, "Self-Silencing is Making Women Sick."
11. Stacey Colino, "Women Are Still Under-Represented in Medical Research. Here's Where the Gender Gap Is Most Pronounced," *Time*, November 1, 2024.
12. Mary Claire Haver, *The New Menopause: Navigating Your Path Through Hormonal Change with Purpose, Power, and Facts* (Rodale Books, 2024).
13. Haver, *The New Menopause*.
14. Haver, *The New Menopause*.
15. Criado-Perez, *Invisible Women*, 21.
16. Erica Schwiegershausen, "Do Women Really Need 10 Hours of Sleep?" *The Cut*, May 3, 2024.
17. Theresa R. Weiss and Sandra M. Bulmer, "Young Women's Experiences Living with Polycystic Ovary Syndrome," *Journal of Obstetric, Gynecologic & Neonatal Nursing* 40, no. 6 (2011): 709–18.
18. Haver, *The New Menopause*, 9–10.
19. Haver, *The New Menopause*.
20. Niki Bezzant, "'She Will Not Become Dull and Unattractive': The Charming History of Menopause and HRT," *The Guardian*, January 18, 2022; Haver, *The New Menopause*.
21. Bezzant, "'She Will Not Become Dull and Unattractive'."
22. Haver, *The New Menopause*.
23. Bezzant, "'She Will Not Become Dull and Unattractive'"; Haver, *The New Menopause*.
24. Bezzant, "'She Will Not Become Dull and Unattractive'"; Haver, *The New Menopause*.
25. Haver, *The New Menopause*, 9.
26. Haver, *The New Menopause*.

27 Even a cursory glance at social media illustrates the strength of this market. As a woman of a certain age, I am bombarded with advertisements disguised as advice for products, tips, recipes, recommendations, vitamins, supplements, exercises, meditations, tinctures, and so on and so forth.

28 Dana Crowley Jack, *Silencing the Self: Women and Depression* (William Morrow, 1991), 2.

29 Crowley Jack, *Silencing the Self*, 139.

30 Phyllis Chesler, *Patriarchy: Notes of an Expert Witness* (Common Courage Press, 1994); Kate Moore, "Declared Insane for Speaking Up: The Dark American History of Silencing Women Through Psychiatry," *Time*, June 22, 2021.

31 Elinor Cleghorn, "Medical Myths About Gender Roles Go Back to Ancient Greece. Women Are Still Paying the Price Today," *Time*, June 17, 2021.

32 Cleghorn, "Medical Myths About Gender Roles," 2021.

33 Hannah Jocelyn, "Motherhood in the Age of Reproductive Surveillance," *New Yorker*, April 25, 2025; Caroline Kitchener, "White House Assesses Ways to Persuade Women to Have More Children," *New York Times*, April 21, 2025, updated April 23, 2025. Despite wanting women to have more babies, Trump 2.0 backed out of a campaign promise to help fund IVF; see Riley Beggin and Jeff Stein, "White House Has No Plan to Mandate IVF Care, Despite Campaign Pledge," *Washington Post*, August 3, 2025.

34 Cat Bohannon, *Eve: How the Female Body Drove 200 Million Years of Human Evolution* (Knopf, 2023).

35 Bohannon, *Eve*, 34.

36 Bohannon, *Eve*.

37 Anna Motz, *If Love Could Kill: The Myths and Truths of Women Who Commit Violence* (Knopf, 2024), xvii–xviii.

38 Alexandra Schwartz, "When Women Commit Violence," *New Yorker*, February 5, 2024.

39 Rebecca Godfrey, *Under the Bridge: The True Story of the Murder of Reena Virk* (Gallery Books, 2005); Reena Roy, "Teen Convicted, Sentenced to Life in Prison for Killing Mother, Attempted Murder of Stepdad," ABC News, September 23, 2024; Jan Hoffman, "Pregnant, Addicted and Fighting the Pull of Drugs," *New York Times*, June 16, 2024.

40 Elizabeth Flock, *The Furies: Women, Vengeance, and Justice* (Harper Collins, 2023); Motz, *If Love Could Kill*.

41 "Lateral Violence," We R Native, accessed September 5, 2025, via Wayback Machine.

42 "Lateral Violence."

43 Godfrey, *Under the Bridge*, 2005.

44 Flock, *The Furies*, 3.

45 Motz, *If Love Could Kill*, xi–xii.

46 Motz, *If Love Could Kill*, xiv.

47 Motz, *If Love Could Kill*, xiv.

48 Chesler, *Patriarchy*.

49 Chesler, *Patriarchy*.

50 France Winddance Twine, *Geek Girls: Inequality and Opportunity in Silicon Valley* (NYU Press, 2022), 5.

51 Safiya Umoja Noble, *Algorithms of Oppression: How Search Engines Reinforce Racism* (NYU Press, 2018); Winddance Twine, *Geek Girls*.

52 Noble, *Algorithms of Oppression*, 108.
53 Winddance Twine, *Geek Girls*, 31.
54 Catherine D'Ignazio and Lauren F. Klein, *Data Feminism* (MIT Press, 2020).
55 *Hidden Figures*, directed by Theodore Melfi (20th Century Studios, 2017); Margot Lee Shetterly, *Hidden Figures: The American Dream and the Untold Story of the Black Women Mathematicians Who Helped Win the Space Race* (William Morrow, 2016).
56 D'Ignazio & Klein, *Data Feminism*.
57 Noble, *Algorithms of Oppression*, 108.
58 D'Ignazio & Klein, *Data Feminism*.
59 D'Ignazio & Klein, *Data Feminism*.
60 Rebecca Davis O'Brien and Reid J. Epstein, "Take My Wife, Please: For Political Damage Control, Just Blame Your Spouse," *New York Times*, May 17, 2024, updated May 20, 2024.
61 Jonathan Dienst and Erica Byfield, "Sen. Menendez Found Guilty on All Counts in Federal Corruption Trial," NBC News New York, July 16, 2024.
62 Davis O'Brien and Epstein, "Take My Wife, Please."
63 Jennifer Weiner, "Justice Alito's Blame-the-Wife Defense Never Goes Out of Style," *New York Times*, May 20, 2024.
64 Kate Zernike, "The Campus Wars Aren't About Gender ... Are They?" *New York Times*, January 28, 2024.
65 Alissa Wilkinson, "'Elizabeth Taylor: The Lost Tapes' and the Moment Star Worship Curdled," *New York Times*, August 2, 2024.
66 Mary Gabriel, *Madonna: A Rebel Life* (Hatchette Books, 2023).
67 Dina Gachman, "Sympathy for the Diva: Why We Love 'Difficult' Stars," *New York Times*, July 24, 2024.
68 Gabriel, *Madonna*.
69 Kathryn Jezer-Morton, "Did Moms Exist Before Social Media?" *New York Times*, April 16, 2020.
70 Taylor Lorenz, *Extremely Online: The Untold Story of Fame, Influence and Power on the Internet* (Simon and Schuster, 2023), 20.
71 Lorenz, *Extremely Online*, 20.
72 Jezer-Morton, "Did Moms Exist Before Social Media?"
73 Lorenz, *Extremely Online*, 20.
74 Lorenz, *Extremely Online*, 22.
75 Lorenz, *Extremely Online*.
76 Lorenz, *Extremely Online*, 29.
77 Lorenz, *Extremely Online*, 26; Jezer-Morton, "Did Moms Exist Before Social Media?"
78 Todd Spangler, "Candace Owens Is Out at Daily Wire, CEO Says," *Variety*, March 22, 2024; Rachel Leishman, "Fine, We Can Talk About the Fever Dream That Is Brett Cooper's 'Daily Wire' Show," *The Mary Sue*, October 23, 2023.
79 Gabrielle Bluestone, "Dancing in the Name of the Lord," *The Cut*, June 3, 2024; *Dancing for the Devil: The 7M TikTok Cult*, directed by Derek Doneen, television series (Netflix, 2024).
80 Leigh Blickley, "TikTok Couple Matt and Abby Howard's Most Controversial Parenting Moments," *US Weekly*, June 9, 2024; "The Worst TikTok Husband? Matt & Abby," posted November 14, 2023, by Dani Green, YouTube, 21:06.

81 Sojourner Truth, "Ain't I a Woman?" Fordham University, accessed August 4, 2025.
82 June Eric-Udorie, "Introduction," in *Can We All be Feminists?* ed. by June Eric-Udorie (Penguin Books, 2018), xi–xii.
83 Eric-Udorie, "Introduction."
84 bell hooks, *Feminist Theory: From Margin to Center* (Routledge, 1984).
85 Deirdre Cooper Owens, "Listening To Black Women Saves Lives," *The Lancet* 397, no. 10276 (2021): 788–89.
86 Kimberlé Williams Crenshaw, "Black Women Still in Defense of Ourselves," *The Nation*, October 5, 2011.
87 Katie Rogers, *American Woman: The Transformation of the Modern First Lady, from Hillary Clinton to Jill Biden* (Crown Books, 2024).
88 Kimberlé Crenshaw, "Demarginalizing the Intersection of Race and Sex: A Black Feminist Critique of Antidiscrimination Doctrine, Feminist Theory, and Antiracist Politics" *University of Chicago Legal Forum* 1989, no. 1 (1989): 138–67, 140.
89 Eric-Udorie, "Introduction," xvi–xvii.
90 Kim Renfro and Charise Frazier, "An Essential Timeline of the Fallout from Janet Jackson and Justin Timberlake's Super Bowl Halftime Show," *Business Insider*, January 30, 2022.
91 Angela Davis, *Women, Race and Class* (Vintage Press, 1981), 23.
92 Danyel Smith, "I Knew Diddy for Years. What I Now Remember Haunts Me," *New York Times*, July 12, 2024.
93 Sarah Marshall, host, *You're Wrong About*, "Revolutions and Resistance With Kellie Carter Jackson," October 12, 2024, 65 minutes.
94 Andrene Taylor, "Our Patriarchal Society Doesn't Always Tell the Stories of Black Women," *Andscape*, July 22, 2020.
95 *Simone Biles Rising*, directed by Katie Walsh, television series (Netflix, 2024).
96 Simone Biles (@simonebiles), Instagram, July 31, 2024.
97 Motz, *If Love Could Kill*.
98 Mona Gable, *Searching for Savanna: The Murder of One Native American Woman and the Violence Against Many* (Atria Books, 2023).
99 Brooks Barnes, "What 'Pocahontas' Tells Us About Disney, for Better and Worse," *New York Times*, December 16, 2023.
100 Smith, "I Knew Diddy For Years"; Eric-Udorie, "Introduction."
101 Anne Helen Petersen, *Too Fat, Too Slutty, Too Loud: The Rise and Reign of the Unruly Woman* (Plume, 2017).
102 Sheryl Sandberg, *Lean In: Women, Work, and the Will to Lead* (Alfred A. Knopf, 2013).
103 Charlotte Shane, "No Wave Feminism," in *Can We All Be Feminists?* editor June Eric-Udorie, 1–15 (Penguin Books, 2018).
104 Shane, "No Wave Feminism."
105 Susan Orlean, "The Tonya Harding Fan Club," *New Yorker*, February 14, 1994.
106 Orlean, "The Tonya Harding Fan Club."
107 Orlean, "The Tonya Harding Fan Club."
108 Sarah Marshall, "Remote Control: Tonya Harding, Nancy Kerrigan, and the Spectacles of Female Power and Pain," *The Believer*, January 1, 2014.
109 Marshall, "Remote Control."
110 Marshall, "Remote Control."
111 Marshall, "Remote Control."

112 Marshall, "Remote Control."
113 Marshall, "Remote Control."
114 Sarah Marshall, "Making an Ice Queen," *The Baffler*, December 11, 2017.
115 Marshall, "Remote Control."
116 Michael Hobbes and Sarah Marshall, hosts, *You're Wrong About*, "Tonya Harding," July 18 and 26, 2019, 74 minutes.
117 Marshall, "Remote Control."
118 Marshall, "Making An Ice Queen."
119 Allison Yarrow, *90s Bitch: Media, Culture, and the Failed Promise of Gender Equality* (Harper Perennial, 2018).
120 Yarrow, *90s Bitch*, 250.
121 Brittany Luse, host, "Olympic Hurdles For Women Athletes; Plus, Big Trucks and Big Questions," *It's Been a Minute*, July 26, 2024, 32 minutes.
122 Women are to perform in pain *and* be pretty. In the 1996 Atlanta Olympics, gymnast Kerri Strug tore two ligaments in her ankle during her first vault, then vaulted *again*, at the insistence of her coaches, in a (successful) attempt to wrest the gold medal from the Russian team. Strug was expected to compete while in pain because of the event's double significance as a chance to beat the Russians at the Olympics. Meanwhile, Strug was critiqued for not *appearing* tough enough. It turned out that the US team did not need her second successful vault to win; the team score was already high enough for the team victory. See Rick Weinberg, "Kerri Strug Fights Off Pain, Helps U.S. Win Gold," ESPN, July 19, 2004.
123 Caster Semenya, *The Race to be Myself: A Memoir* (WW Norton, 2023), 5. See also the story of Algerian boxer Imane Khelif, who was mis-gendered as trans or male *because* of her brute strength and because she beat an opponent in less than 45 seconds; see Megan Janetsky, "Vitriol About Female Boxer Fuels Concern of Backlash Against LGBTQ+ and Women Athletes," *Associated Press*, August 2, 2024.
124 Ryan Young, "Indianapolis Star Columnist Gregg Doyel Apologizes After Awkward, Uncomfortable Interaction with Caitlin Clark," *Yahoo Sports*, April 17, 2024.
125 Because of COVID-19, the Tokyo Olympics were held in 2021, but are generally still referred to as the 2020 Olympics. Juliet Macur, "Stalkers, Disease and Doubt: A Gymnast's Hard Road Back to the Games," *New York Times*, July 29, 2024.
126 Kavitha A. Davidson, "What Olympics Star Ilona Maher Doesn't Have to Explain to You About Her Body," MSNBC, July 31, 2024; Ilona Maher (@ilonamaher), TikTok, July 29, 2024.
127 Juliet Macur, "Simone Biles is Done Being Judged," *New York Times*, July 28, 2024; *Simone Biles Rising*, directed by Katie Walsh, television series (Netflix, 2024).
128 Catherine Porter and Ségolène Le Stradic, "A 'Love Activist' D.J. Opened the Olympics. Then Came a Wave of Hate, " *New York Times*, August 2, 2024.
129 Porter and Le Stradic, "A 'Love Activist' D.J. Opened the Olympics."
130 Porter and Le Stradic, "A 'Love Activist' D.J. Opened the Olympics."
131 Selina Thompson, "Fat Demands," in *Can We All Be Feminists?* editor June Eric-Udorie (Penguin Books, 2018), 32.
132 Rebecca Solnit, *Men Explain Things to Me* (Haymarket Books, 2014), 35.

CHAPTER TWO

A GENERATIONAL LINEAGE OF HARMING WOMEN

GENERATIONAL SILENCING

In 1981, Lady Diana Spencer married Prince Charles, heir apparent to the British throne. Just twenty years old at the time of her marriage to Charles, twelve years her senior, Diana, Princess of Wales, became a global icon and the subject of intense press scrutiny. Diana was understood to be virginal and pure, a good look for the royal family.[1] Mostly loved by the British public, Princess Diana became a problem for the royal family, particularly Charles, who did not like being upstaged by his wife.[2] The marriage, largely arranged by the royal family, was not one known for its love or mutual understanding. Prince Charles was in love with Camilla Parker-Bowles, who was married and the mother of two children. The royal marriage was rocky, at best, and, with much wrangling, in 1996, Princess Diana and Prince Charles were able to convince Queen Elizabeth that a divorce was in the best interest of themselves, their children, and the royal family. A divorce that might have rendered Diana obsolete instead made her more popular.

The publication of Andrew Morton's *Diana: Her True Story* introduced a larger world to Diana's behind-the-scenes marriage and misery.[3] Known as the "people's princess," in 1997, Diana and her partner, Dodi Fayed, died in a tragic car accident in Paris while chased by paparazzi. Decades after her death, Diana occupies an incredibly popular place on social media and is the subject of numerous documentaries, biopics, and podcast series and episodes.[4] While Princess Diana's story is important as a clear illustration of the centering and silencing of women, it is her generational legacy that is of particular interest to this text. Princess Diana was mother to both heir apparent Prince William and Prince Harry, whose wives have inherited pop culture's fascination with— and destruction of— women within the British royal family.

Crown Prince William and his wife, Catherine, the Duchess of Wales, have long been treated kindly by the British and global press. However, similar to its treatment of Diana, the press have roundly ignored the couple's—and especially Princess Kate's—requests for privacy. In 2024, Princess Kate withdrew from public events, setting off a wave of rumors and gossip about her health and standing in the royal family. In an ill-fated attempt to thwart the press, her staff published a family picture, which was later discovered to have been doctored.[5] When she ultimately went public with her cancer diagnosis and invited the public into her journey to recovery, press-fueled vitriol diminished to invasive kindness. Since she shared her cancer diagnosis publicly, Princess Kate has generally been well treated by the press, even as they continued to encroach on what, for many of us, would be a time of retreat and increased privacy. Like their treatment of her mother-in-law before her, the press seem incapable of leaving Kate alone.

The press treatment of Kate contrasts sharply with its treatment of her estranged sister-in-law, Meghan Markle, wife of Crown Prince William's younger brother Harry. While Kate has generally been regarded with "extreme deference," Markle received a "thrashing."[6] Princess Kate was cast "as an 'English rose'—beautiful, noble, white," while Markle was cast as "a dangerous, trashy newcomer."[7]

Markle, who married Harry in 2018, became the first American, Black, divorcée, with a professional acting career, to marry into the royal family. While many Americans viewed Markle as a college-educated woman, an entrepreneur devoted to public service, and a popular actress, the Monarchy saw her as divorced, biracial, and raised Catholic, identity markers that violated their expectations of proper demographics and family structure.[8] In large part because of the royal family's long-standing racism—including family members' comments about Harry and Megan's son, Archie, looking like a monkey—and the extreme racism of the British press—which ran news headlines such as "Harry to Marry Into Gangster Royalty?" and quips about, "the royal's future mother-in-law" living "in Crenshaw, surrounded by bloodbath robberies and drug-induced violence"—Harry and Meghan excised themselves from the royal family and moved to the United States to live and raise their children.[9] To the best of their ability, Harry and Meghan took control of the narrative, via his memoir *Spare* and their Netflix documentary *Harry and Meghan*.[10]

Among the countless things these three women represent, one of particular concern is the generational harm passed down from Diana. Diana's death, squarely blamed on the hordes of photographers chasing her and Fayed through the streets of Paris, offered a moment of reflection: Chasing this woman around the globe had serious repercussions. And yet, several decades on, the paparazzi, the press, and numerous social media accounts relentlessly attack both Middleton and Markle, centering and silencing each of them in ways that ominously echo the treatment of their famous mother-in-law. Princess Kate and Meghan Markle occupy a great deal of space in pop culture, which is, for many, part of the *job* of being royal; yet they are silenced because, for the most part, they have limited means to minimize or manage their exposure. The press seem to have taken to heart few if any lessons from their treatment of Diana.

This chapter explores the generational harm inflicted on women through the damning legacy of ignoring sexual harassment as exemplified by the experiences of Anita Hill and Christine Blasey Ford; the intersection of fame and infamy for female pop stars, as seen through Madonna; and the current social media trend that promotes the lifestyles of tradwives, who illustrate one logical (if erroneous), response by women who conclude that, despite generations of struggle for material change, very little has shifted.

FIGHTING SEXUAL HARASSMENT: ANITA HILL AND CHRISTINE BLASEY FORD

In 1991, Anita Hill, then a law professor at the University of Oklahoma College of Law, was asked to provide background information for Supreme Court nominee Clarence Thomas as part of his nomination and confirmation process.[11] Hill worked for Thomas between 1981–1983, first in the Office for Civil Rights, then for the Equal Employment Opportunity Commission (EEOC). In what she believed was a confidential conversation as a professional reference, Hill described his treatment of her, including his propositioning her repeatedly, despite her saying no; his attempts to discuss pornography with her, including comments on bestiality and penis size; and his comments about a pubic hair on a soda can—all of which occurred at work.[12] Leaked at the last moment, her testimony sparked her participation in the Senate confirmation hearings.[13]

As a conservative Black man with limited judicial experience, Thomas's Supreme Court nomination was fraught from the beginning. He had only served as a judge for about two years and was thought to be too inexperienced to serve as a Justice. His originalist position on the Constitution was a point of concern for progressive and women's organizations, who protested his nomination. One of Thomas's advantages was that, as a public figure, there were more opportunities for him to craft his own story, contextualizing and addressing his shortcomings. Prior to the nomination as well as during the hearings, journalist Juan Williams wrote multiple, highly favorable profiles of Thomas, which, in hindsight, can only be seen as public relations pieces. Prior to the nomination, in 1987, Williams profiled Thomas for *The Atlantic*.[14]

He chronicled Thomas's poverty-stricken childhood in the segregated deep South, where he was raised primarily by his grandfather. Williams traced Thomas's conservatism to his early education. He attended an all-White Catholic boarding school where he was regularly mocked and isolated as the only Black student. He tried to adapt his behavior, but it did not work, and no one in any position of authority made any effort to stop the insults. When Thomas left school, "He held a conviction that he has carried since: there is nothing a black man can do to be accepted by whites," Williams wrote.[15] Through Thomas's college and law school experiences, he found that White students and professors would never see him as anything other than Black, which led him to believe that Black people should "prepare to do for themselves" by making their own schools, investing in Black businesses, investing in Black corporations, and living in Black neighborhoods.[16] Thomas opposed affirmative action, which he saw as "window dressing" that failed to integrate poor Black people into the mainstream economy.[17]

Williams repeatedly noted how Thomas kept quiet and worked to maintain a low profile because he did not want to be known as the token Black student, Black voice, or Black employee. According to Williams, Thomas has a strong belief in the individual, rather than the system; as director of the EEOC, he worked to eliminate class action suits or cases that alleged systemic discrimination and chose to focus on those brought by individuals. He supported Reagan's approach to civil rights, which involved ignoring racial injustices, refusing to meet with civil rights leaders, and accepting minimal support from Black voters.

In October 1991, Williams published a piece in the *Washington Post*, countering many of the critiques lobbed at Thomas during the nomination process.[18] Defending Thomas's evasiveness during the nomination process, Williams pointed out that Thomas had chosen not to answer the same questions that David Souter and Anthony Kennedy, two previous nominees, had also refused to answer. Defending Thomas's lack of judicial experience, he noted that Earl Warren, Felix Frankfurter, and William Rehnquist also had zero judicial experience before joining the Court.

Beyond the flattering profiles, the very structure of the hearing put Thomas and the Senate committee in charge. Thomas was invited to speak both *before* and *after* Hill, engendering multiple opportunities to defend himself and deny her accusations. It was in his self-defense that Thomas called the hearings a "high tech lynching," thereby taking control of the narrative.[19] Anyone who challenged Thomas would be accused of racism, and more particularly, racism against a conservative Black man. He announced that he had not listened to Hill's testimony, which "insulated him from having to deny any of the particulars, positioning him perfectly to take the offense."[20] Thomas's behavior illustrates how the centering and silencing of an individual can be manipulated in one's favor: As a nominee for the highest Court in the nation, Thomas was very much at the center of the conversation, and he used his penchant for quiet to his advantage. By opting not to listen and, by extension, to not speak, he weaponized his silence to his advantage in ways that Hill, and countless other women, could not.

Senators lobbed Thomas softball questions that enabled his evasion. Senator Orrin Hatch (R-UT) asked Thomas, "Did you ever have lunch with Professor Hill at which you talked about sex or pressured her to go out with you?"[21] Who determines pressure? Also, if the alleged conversations about sex took place at a time other than lunch, Thomas could have truthfully responded "no" to Hatch's question. What if the topic of sex came up before lunch? Or after lunch? Thomas's opportunities to split hairs were plentiful. He was never asked a more direct question, such as "did you ever ask Hill to go out with you," which would have required a yes or no answer; he may have genuinely believed, or been comfortable asserting, that there was no pressure involved.

In contrast, the committee used Hill's self-imposed silence at the time of the alleged harassment against her during the hearing, where much of the conversation focused on why she had not come forward sooner with her claims and why she accepted a second job with Thomas. What the Senate Judiciary Committee could not seem to grasp was that there were precious few alternatives for Hill to consider as a young, Black, female lawyer in the 1980s. As a subordinate in her early twenties, she may have come to the logical conclusion that this was the way work was. For generations, women, and especially women of color, had been treated as objects in the workplace. Why would her experience be any different? In her essay on Anita Hill, Solnit points out that when Hill declined Thomas's advances, it was "as though *no* were not itself valid."[22]

The senators conducting the hearing seemed to have no understanding, or did not care, that their deeply personal questions posed to Hill were offensive and that the actions Thomas was accused of could be problematic. In a particularly uncomfortable exchange, Senator Arlen Specter (D-PA) commented that talking about a woman's breasts "is not too bad—women's large breasts. That is a word we use all the time."[23] Hill countered that what was bad were the specific scenes from pornography films, including bestiality, that Thomas talked about. Specter indicated that this conversation was not a problem, but, as Hill later observed, his beliefs "ignored the fact that the workplace is rarely a place where women go to discuss their own anatomy or the anatomy of other women, particularly when the discussion is of a sexual nature."[24] Senator Patrick Leahy (D-VT) wanted to know both what had happened and why it was wrong. Senator Alan Simpson (R-WY) referred to Hill's testimony as "this sexual harassment crap," implying that not only was she lying but also that her concerns did not amount to the severity of "real harassment."[25]

This questioning—why talking about a woman's breasts is "not too bad," wondering why what Thomas did was so wrong, and making a distinction between "real" and "crap" harassment—is reflective of the all-White, all-male committee and its complete lack of awareness about how to engage professionally with women, especially around questions of inappropriate or uncomfortable conversations and interactions. As most women did at that time, Anita Hill endured the conversations because that was the only viable option. Hill worked and testified at a time when she had no significant legal protection, and the responsibility to prevent, ignore, or capitulate to Thomas's unwanted, vulgar conduct was solely hers. Sexual harassment in the workplace was not acknowledged as an actual civil rights offense before the mid-1980s. At that time, public understandings of sexual harassment or sexual assault were extremely limited, and public discussion of these topics was even more so. We now know that survivors of sexual assault often do not speak about their assault immediately, and it may be much later, in a safer space or as experiences trigger memories, that conversation becomes viable.[26]

During her nine hours of testimony, Hill realized that she could not show any physical response to the questions, that any reaction would reflect poorly on her. So she vowed to stay completely still: "I had to be impervious to the lights and to the heat as well as the natural reactions of my body. Though I felt each one of the Senators' attempts to humiliate me, I vowed not to so much as twitch."[27] In order to be the "perfect" witness, Hill could not in any way appear uncomfortable; to not be seen as unstable or untrustworthy, she (once again) needed to self-silence. The pressure of being the sole woman—the sole Black woman—in front of the panel of powerful White men limited her ability to be human. No such pressure weighed on any of the men, including Thomas.

While Hill was the most prominent subject of public scrutiny, other women were also called to testify at Thomas's nomination hearing. As Hill later explained,

> We were all roughly the same age at the time of the incidents—all younger than Thomas. We were all single women and thus could be easily viewed

> as vulnerable. We were all from Southern or rural backgrounds with relatively few connections to power in Washington. And we were all Black.[28]

At the time, these credible testimonies meant nothing to the senators conducting the hearing. Rather than framing the quantity of corroborated stories as evidence of wrongdoing by Thomas, the narrative instead reinforced the notion that Hill and other women were attacking Thomas.

Since the 1991 public testimony at the confirmation hearing, Hill's participation and presentation have been dissected, detailed, deliberated, and ultimately re-told and revisited multiple times. At the time, and in the intervening years, the image of Anita Hill—a Black woman, previously unknown to the American people, sitting alone, confronting an all-White, all-male Senate committee—tells a story of the power of patriarchy in which she was simultaneously centered and silenced. The story pitted race against gender; Hill was accused of vilifying not only a specific Black man but Black manhood, more generally. By speaking out against Thomas, Hill was seen as betraying Black people and Black professional development.[29] Writing at the time of the hearing, journalist Rosemary Bray noted, "Hill put her private business on the street, and she downgraded a Black man to a room filled with White men who might alter his fate."[30]

Published three years after the hearing, David Brock's racist and misogynistic attack on Hill served to discredit both her testimony as well as her character in order to prop up Thomas.[31] As a well-known conservative columnist, Brock had a platform that Hill did not. Employing propaganda tactics, Brock recast the testimonies of Thomas and Hill, observing, "The two accounts, sworn under oath, were ultimately irreconcilable. Thomas's denial was categorical. No dates, no movies, nothing. For her part, Hill had drastically raised the ante by transforming Thomas from a garden-variety workplace harasser into a sexual savage."[32] Brock defended Thomas as someone punished for poor communication, rather than sexual harassment, belittling Hill for misunderstanding Thomas's intentions and thus discrediting her experience, "The testimony seemed to rule out the most likely explanations of what had really happened—mixed signals, miscommunication, or even an affair gone sour between two young, attractive, single people in the workplace."[33] It is possible that aspects of Brock's interpretations are plausible. Notoriously silent, Justice Thomas may very well be a poor communicator. However, it was *not* "two ... single people," as Brock asserted. When Hill worked for Thomas, he was still married to his first wife, Kathy Ambush. There was no evidence that Thomas and Hill had had an affair. And even if Thomas was only a "garden-variety workplace harasser," that would *still* have been entirely inappropriate in any work setting. Hill never characterized Thomas as a "sexual savage." Instead, she dispassionately detailed uncomfortable questions and conversations. Brock further defended and empathized with Thomas for having been forced by the committee to "prove a negative," which is categorically false.[34] Senator Joe Biden (D-DE) opened the Senate Judiciary Committee hearing by stating that Thomas "would at all times be given the benefit of the doubt."[35] For anyone who did not watch the hearing or seek counter sources, Brock's portrait of Thomas as the victim and Hill as the aggressor played into the long and uneven "he said, she said" dynamic embedded in the fabric of patriarchy.

Brock manipulated Hill's testimony when she acknowledged that it might have been a mistake not to speak up immediately, but that, at the time, she could not fully appreciate the reality of the situation: For Brock that meant nothing bad actually happened.[36] Brock also tapped into the sensitivity around the intersection of race and gender, using Hill's very identity against itself as evidence of her predilection for making up situations that did not exist.

Brock repeatedly asserted that Hill's public persona as a quiet, straight-laced young woman with deep religious faith and family connections was a ruse. Meanwhile, in a perplexing contradiction, he lauded Thomas's calm demeanor and family history, which were to be respected. He skewed Hill's alleged innocence and naiveté to call her judgment into question, specifically as a woman who "saw evidence of sexist and racist hostility and prejudice where often none existed."[37] Brock tapped into racist tropes of Black women, skewering Hill as aggressive and emasculating, for which there was no evidence.[38] He further attacks Hill, asserting that she conflated sexual harassment and racism, writing, "Indeed, the 'pattern' in the Thomas-Hill story seemed not to be a pattern of sexual harassment by Thomas, but of sexual harassment or racial discrimination claims by Hill."[39] That small word—claims—was enough to construct an environment of distrust of Hill.

What is beyond the pale about Brock's skewering of Hill is that, eight years after his book's publication, he acknowledged that he had lied throughout it. To protect and support Thomas, he destroyed Hill's supporters without any primary evidence, and he "consciously lied" in defense of Thomas, particularly regarding Thomas's reputation for enjoying hard-core pornography.[40] Brock confessed his lies in service of Thomas just prior to the release of his 2002 book, *Blinded by the Right: The Conscience of an Ex-Conservative*, in which he denounced his past as a conservative pundit.[41] In 2024, Brock referred to his attack on Hill as his "original sin," and claimed that he has worked since then to correct his errors.[42] He has done so through a similar pattern: Attack, apologize, and then support the person he attacked. In 2004, he started the progressive advocacy group Media Matters for America, which tracks press accuracy.[43] And, in 2024, he published *Stench: The Making of the Thomas Court and the Unmaking of America*, a denunciation of Clarence Thomas.[44] Brock profited from spreading, and subsequently recanting, deliberate misinformation; attacking Hill gave Brock a prominent platform and, in part, legitimized Thomas's role on the Court. That Brock later apologized for lying is almost irrelevant when one considers that Supreme Court appointments are lifetime positions and that, to this day, Hill lives with the ripple effects of Brock's lies.

Eight years after her testimony, Hill shared her account of the nomination hearing and the event leading up to it in her memoir. Particularly valuable is the portrait Hill paints of the Senate Judiciary Committee's utter lack of understanding of sexual harassment and sexual assault. Quickly, questions of Thomas's competence shifted to Hill's credibility as she became the target. The task at hand for the senators was to show either that Hill was lying and had fabricated her statement or that Thomas's alleged conduct was inoffensive.[45] Hill noted, the "committee had no experience in or rules for evaluating a claim of sexual harassment … had no rules for conducting the proceedings and chose instead to make the rules on an ad hoc basis, as the hearing evolved."[46] To alleviate any concerns about her honesty, Hill agreed to a polygraph test, which found no indication of lying. Subjecting Hill to a polygraph test linked her to the long line of women who have submitted to psychological testing after having been deemed crazy for reporting harassment.[47] Under Biden's direction, the message was sent that Thomas was to be believed, which meant, Hill explained, that "if it were a case of my word against his, his would always be better."[48]

The intersection of race and gender in this hearing pitted two people of color against each other and elevated Thomas's conservatism as a shield. According to Hill, Thomas did not see race or racism as an obstacle; instead, as Hill characterized Thomas's beliefs, "the real barriers to economic and political achievement were a lack of industry and initiative and a reliance on remedial programs."[49] His conservative position garnered the support of Republican senators, giving them "something akin to a spiritual boost—a platform of righteousness," Hill later recalled, noting that she was accused of racism for attacking such a prominent and public Black man.[50] Senator Ted Kennedy (D-MA) defended Hill against the accusations of racism, stating, "The issue isn't discrimination and racism, it's about sexual harassment. And I hope we can keep our eyes on that particular issue."[51]

The power imbalances were painfully obvious. The

White, male senators had no familiarity with what it felt like to be powerless, especially the powerlessness of being Black and female.[52] Though she was subpoenaed to testify, Hill bore the responsibility of her presence and was accused of bringing "bedroom politics" to a public conversation (even though she made clear that she had no intimate relationship with Thomas and that all their interactions took place at work).[53] Hill was unmarried, did not have children, and was "portrayed as stiff, frigid, and sexually unavailable."[54] The Senate ultimately confirmed Thomas to the Supreme Court, despite the credibility of Hill's frank testimony. The ease with which Hill was belittled and the ways in which her testimony was questioned were, themselves, forms of abuse.

Nevertheless, by speaking out in such a public forum and withstanding the attacks against her person, Hill made it safer for women to push back. She suffered a humiliating ordeal, Thomas got appointed to the Supreme Court, *and* workplace sexual harassment became a national conversation. As Solnit notes, "Hill is often credited with launching a revolution in recognition of and response to workplace harassment."[55] And yet, even with greater awareness of and sensitivity to workplace sexual harassment, patriarchal power imbalances remain firmly rooted.

As of this writing, Clarence Thomas remains on the Supreme Court, though there are calls for his impeachment and criminal investigations.[56] By law, Justices are to fill out financial disclosures at the end of each year; Thomas does not always do this.[57] Thomas has *declared* $4 million in gifts, exponentially greater than any other Justice.[58] He has failed to disclose additional private travel provided by conservative donor Harlan Crow.[59]

Anita Hill testified in 1991 and opened up a conversation on sexual harassment in the workplace. Twenty-seven years later, in an eerily similar situation, another woman was thrust into the spotlight to testify against an extremely powerful man, with sadly similar results. Similar to Anita Hill before her, Christine Blasey Ford is not a woman who sought fame or notoriety. She is a law professor, wife, mother, avid surfer, and, prior to 2018, not a public figure. In 2018, when Trump nominated Brett Kavanaugh to the Supreme Court, Blasey Ford recognized him as the man who assaulted her at a party in the 1980s, when they were both in high school. She had not spoken publicly about the assault, having discussed it only in a couples counseling session with her husband and in a spontaneous comment to a friend. However, when it looked as though Kavanaugh would be nominated, Blasey Ford confided in some close friends about her memories of being assaulted by him at a summer party in suburban Maryland. In consultation with friends and legal representation, Blasey Ford decided to come forward with her allegations, with the hope that the information shared might shed light on Kavanaugh's character. In July 2018, she left a voicemail on the *Washington Post* tip line, stating that Kavanaugh had assaulted her and that she was willing to share therapy records to support this, and, while she did not want remain silent, she was also not willing to put her family in Washington, DC, and California under the stress of an intense spotlight.

At the time, the nation was moving through the MeToo movement, with a variety of powerful public figures, across a range of professions, publicly called out for their heretofore private behavior. Blasey Ford was part of a cultural movement acknowledging and reckoning with sexual assault in public. Blasey Ford hired lawyers to help her through the process of her accusation, and, between August and September 2018, she submitted a letter to California Senator Dianne Feinstein (D-CA) and Iowa Representative and conference hearing chair Chuck Grassley (R-IA). Both senators ignored her letter. At that point, her lawyers recommended that she *not* pursue the charges. However, a *Washington Post* reporter broke the story and named Blasey Ford in the article.[60] Once her story went public, she started receiving death threats and had to hire a security team.

Kavanaugh was nominated, and Blasey Ford was called to testify at his hearing. She and her husband decided that he would stay at home with their sons in an effort to keep their lives as normal as possible; however, this decision made her look isolated and alone, as if her husband and sons did not support her. Conversely, Kavanaugh's wife and daughter attended the hearings, bolstering the facade of having women's support, including, especially, those closest to him.

The confirmation hearing played out much like Thomas's, with one pointed difference. During cross-examination, the Republican senators employed a female sex crimes prosecutor to pose their questions. While this acknowledged a certain awareness of the topic's sensitivity—unlike the blatant disregard for any sensitivity or compassion afforded to Anita Hill—it also let the Republican senators off the hook. Unlike Thomas's hearing, any egregious lack of awareness on their part would not be on display. This structure also meant that, unlike during Thomas's nomination hearing, there would be no visuals in the news of an all-male panel attacking a lone woman.

One role that hardly differed at all between hearings was that of Republican Senator Orrin Hatch (R-UT). Still presiding in the Senate at 82 years old when Kavanaugh was nominated, Hatch released a statement after Blasey Ford's testimony characterizing her as an "attractive, good witness."[61] Hatch's deputy chief of staff had to defend his boss, saying that what the senator *meant* was that Blasey Ford's *personality* was attractive, a compliment Hatch had bestowed upon women *and* men.[62]

Kavanaugh vehemently denied the assault accusations and repeatedly referenced all the women with whom he was close. He noted that he had many close female friends, that one of his closest friends was a woman who had been sexually assaulted, and that he had witnessed his mother, a lawyer, battle workplace sexual harassment. (As if this proximity somehow made him incapable of bad behavior?) Trump supported his nominee by mocking Blasey Ford at an October 2018 rally and complaining, "A man's life is in tatters. A man's life is shattered."[63]

It is plausible that Kavanaugh, and Thomas before him, genuinely believed their actions were not problematic. Given their proximate power, including the unearned privilege of being male, as well as the utter lack of conversation around sexual assault, they could easily rationalize (and therefore forget about) their behaviors.

The silver lining, if there is one, is that it took the opposition a week to mount its defense against, and attack on, Blasey Ford, indicating that her testimony was credible. In an attempt at due diligence, the FBI was tasked with reviewing Kavanaugh's background more thoroughly, and the message to the public was that they had free rein to conduct a deep investigation.[64] However, what has subsequently come to light, via a report from Senator Sheldon Whitehouse (D-RI), is that Trump directed the FBI to conduct an extremely limited investigation.[65] They interviewed just ten people, but *neither* Blasey Ford nor Kavanaugh, in part because investigators were unclear about the scope of their search based on differences between Trump's public statements and directives he made versus those made in private.[66] After the hearings, Blasey Ford reflected, "Once the nomination was confirmed anyway, it was clear that I, and Anita Hill before me, hadn't solved the problem ... It felt like I had been believed, but then the response was a proverbial shrug."[67]

Blasey Ford's testimony against Kavanaugh renewed interest in Anita Hill's testimony against Clarence Thomas and the topic of confronting workplace sexual harassment. Reviewing the Thomas hearing decades later, anthropologist Victoria Massie wrote that "the cards were stacked against Hill from the beginning because she was a woman," but her testimony ultimately revealed a secret "so many women felt pressured to bear privately."[68] Even though it failed to keep an alleged serial sexual harasser from the highest court, Hill's testimony irrevocably changed how Americans viewed sexual harassment in the workplace.[69] In the year after her testimony, the EEOC registered a 71 percent increase in sexual harassment claims (filed, ironically, with the very office that

Thomas had gutted); by 2000, the total number was 15,836 claims.[70] Launched in 1985, Emily's List, the nonprofit that supports and funds women running for political office and focuses on women's issues in elections, tripled its roster of donors within six months of the Thomas nomination hearing.[71] Law professor Patricia Williams notes, "Twenty years later, if some men's behavior has not changed as much as one might have hoped, the collective women's response has undergone seismic change."[72] In a public letter to Hill, journalist Letty Cottin Pogrebin wrote,

> Thanks to your brave, frank testimony and your stately comportment in the face of hostile interrogation and vilification, we no longer laugh off unwanted sexual advances; we file charges. We no longer protect our attackers from humiliation; we name names. We demand that our employers be accountable to their policies against harassment and that the offender be punished. We may still be risking our jobs, but more and more of us are telling the truth.[73]

If one thinks of Supreme Court confirmation hearings as public job interviews, the performances of Thomas and Kavanaugh ought to have been disqualifying. In 1991, Thomas accused his interviewers of performing a lynching, and, in 2018, Kavanaugh broke down in tears about his love of beer. Both men eluded credible sexual assault claims, conceivably committing perjury during their interviews and testimonies.[74] If any "regular" person, particularly any non-male candidate, behaved like Thomas or Kavanaugh during a job interview, they would be very unlikely to land the job. *Any* woman who cried during a job interview would not only forfeit the job but also reinforce the trope of the hysterical woman, who is unfit for professional responsibilities.[75] Yet, propelled by patriarchy, these two men were appointed to lifetime positions of extraordinary power.

MADONNA AND EVERY FEMALE POP STAR SINCE

It is impossible to overstate the trailblazing influence of Madonna on multiple entertainment industries, on the hyphenate careers of numerous actor-dancer-singers, and on women in the music industry. She became globally famous at a time when the paparazzi and tabloid media had almost full control over crafting celebrity images, but well before social media enabled celebrities to participate in crafting their own images. While Madonna was not well known beyond the New York City art and dance scene of the early 1980s, by her mid-twenties, she became, arguably, the most well-known female artist in the world. For many artists, including the next generation of young female pop singers, Madonna serves as a model and an indirect mentor.

Madonna became a global phenomenon in the mid-1980s, launched via her song and performance of "Like A Virgin," which debuted at the 1984 MTV Video Music Awards:

> In mocking the social covenant that traditionally codified a woman's status as lesser, she declared liberation not in the language of feminist politics but in the language of sex. Madonna in her wedding attire claimed that power as her own ... Madonna showed that for women of her generation, [the sexual revolution had not] even begun.[76]

Critics panned the "Like A Virgin" album, with some arguing that "any music that appealed to an audience of girls and young women was inherently valueless."[77] Meanwhile, Madonna was selling out arenas in record time and was often forced to add additional dates because of audience demand. The teen girls and young women who bought her music, merchandise, and tickets may have been mocked as frivolous, but they were making Madonna a cultural icon and an economic power-house, and, in so doing, her young fans were invited to see themselves in new and different ways.

Over the years, Madonna has endured controversy not just in the music industry but also in the academy and across cultural criticism. Like the lore of Barbie discussed in the Introduction, the mythos of Madonna, including the commodification of all things connected to her, cuts across a variety of fields. But have Madonna, her presence, and her very public actions, substantively changed anything for female pop singers? There is no denying her talent, her longevity, or her genre-expanding and genre-shifting contributions to the intersecting industries of music, film, dance, and fashion. But has it gotten any easier for women pop artists to be in the spotlight without also being attacked? Has anything materially been learned from Madonna's unique professional position? Or, like Princess Diana and Anita Hill before her, has Madonna shifted the conversation without actually shifting the conclusion?

Upon Madonna's global stardom, sex-positive feminist cultural critic Camille Paglia penned an op-ed for the *New York Times* defending the pop star's very public sexual expressions. Paglia lamented *Ms.* magazine's choice of Cyndi Lauper as its woman of the year in 1985, arguing that it rightly belonged to Madonna, who "grew, flourished, metamorphosed and became an international star of staggering dimensions. She is also a shrewd business tycoon, a modern woman of all-around talent."[78] In praising Madonna's video for "Justify My Love," which featured a variety of sexual fantasies filmed in black and white, Paglia pushed back against Madonna's critics who saw her as either sexually exploited or a dangerous influence on children. For Paglia, the accusations of pornography were actually what made the video great. Madonna's willingness to take such risks was an illustration of the success of sex-positive representation.[79]

According to Paglia, Madonna's self-awareness and her embrace of sexual provocation and artifice were what made her so profound. Twenty years later, Paglia defended her 1985 endorsement of Madonna, remembering that she was lambasted for her "fantastical utterance" that Madonna was the future of feminism.[80] Madonna's sexuality was, in Paglia's estimation, going to "liberate an entire generation of women to learn how to be able to handle their own sexuality."[81] While it does not appear that women's sexuality was fully liberated by 2010 (or by today, for that matter), Paglia believed her "sentence was prophetic."[82] Madonna centered her sexuality and her sexual expression, manipulating the expected intersections between sexual expression and gender, which, while it worked for her, did not mean that it worked for *other* female pop stars. Miley Cyrus, the Disney child-actor-turned-singer, was blasted in the press for her 2013 Video Music Award performance with Robin Thicke to his song "Blurred Lines" (whose lyrics condone date rape), being overt and explicit about her sexuality, and not maintaining the sanitized Disney image (even though she was no longer employed by Disney).[83] Similarly, pop star Sabrina Carpenter went viral for her lyrics' use of sexual innuendo, leading her 2024 album *Short N' Sweet* to be nicknamed the "ovulation album of the year."[84] Carpenter ended her concerts with her song "Nonsense," where she acted out different sex positions after singing, "Have you ever tried this one?"[85] Cyrus and Carpenter echo Madonna's sexually provocative lyrics and stage performances, and still must defend their sexuality in ways that their male counterparts do not.

Madonna cuts across musical genres, disallowing anyone to box her into a musical type and, in so doing, maintains control of her music. This control is not afforded to women in Madonna's wake. While it is hard to deny the power of Taylor Swift, she, too, has had to fight back against a music industry that berates and belittles women. Like Madonna, Swift has crossed genres, beginning in country and crossing over to pop and folk. She positions herself as a songwriter who creates songs relatable to a wide audience.[86] She began her career signed to the Big Machine Label Group, then switched, in 2018, to Universal Music Group's Republic Records. One year later, her original label was acquired by

Scooter Braun, who refused to sell the masters of her first six studio albums back to her. After failing to gain ownership of her music, Swift began re-recording and re-releasing those six albums.[87] Any of her songs labeled "Taylor's version" means she owns the rights to master recordings.[88] Swift may be, in part, known for her string of celebrity boyfriends (and the threat that she will most likely profit off of any break-up), and her nascent political engagement in her endorsement of Kamala Harris, but she is also a woman and artist who had to fight for control over her creative work.

Each iteration of Madonna's oeuvre came with different personae and costuming, which made her difficult to categorize. Madonna capitalized on her shape-shifting tendencies, spinning any criticism into a proud embodiment which, in turn, made her both more famous and more wealthy. For example, Madonna manipulated blondness, including an entire global tour in the 1990s, "Blond Ambition," that challenged the expectations of female pop stars' physical presence. This celebration and promotion of blondness is not extended to other, less-savvy artists. Jessica Simpson, a singer-actress-designer, suffered in the public eye in part because no one in the music industry quite knew how to market her as separate and distinct from Britney Spears or Christina Aguilera.[89] Over the years, Simpson was publicly shamed for gaining weight and getting Botox.[90] Where Madonna was aggressive (for which she was criticized), Simpson tried to be diplomatic (for which she was also criticized); there was no space for her to be "herself." Like Madonna, she did not "fit" in the space reserved for female artists. Unlike Madonna, Simpson was swiftly branded as stupid. Her blondness did not reflect ambition as much as it proved a stereotype. At the height of her popularity, she was best known as a "dumb blonde," in large part because of her MTV reality show, *The Newlyweds*, which focused on her marriage to boy-band singer Nick Lachey.[91] The most iconic moment of *The Newlyweds*, for which Simpson received relentless mockery (from audiences as well as from her husband), centered on a brief scene where she and Lachey are eating together, and she expressed uncertainty about whether "Chicken of the Sea" was chicken or tuna fish. Viewers found her ignorance inane, using it as a way to bolster themselves, such as one person who reported in an online post, "Whenever I find myself going through some troubling times, and start to grow weary of the world's ways, I try to remember this scene. Because it always reminds me that while life is hard, it's also much, MUCH harder if you're stupid."[92] In fact, the scene of *The Newlyweds* where Simpson expresses her confusion is actually about her not knowing why the *brand* of tuna is called "Chicken of the Sea," which is a fair question. After repeatedly rolling his eyes at her, Lachey explains the brand name, "A lot of people eat tuna, a lot of people eat chicken, so it's like the chicken of the sea," a both obnoxious and uninformed response to her confusion.[93] It is nearly impossible to imagine that Madonna would have stood for such mockery and if it did happen, she would have swiftly found a way to work it to her advantage.

While Madonna clearly set the stage for young female pop stars, maybe more precisely, she set the stage for young, *White,* female pop stars. Though Madonna challenged much of what it meant to be a singer-dancer-actor-performer, she did so with the protection and privilege of being White, particularly at a time when corporate media rejected many Black female artists. Extremely popular at the time, the cable television station MTV focused almost exclusively on White artists; MTV's executives defended themselves against accusations of racism, saying that Black music and Black artists did not fit the new cable TV channel's focus on rock music.[94] It must be noted that while Madonna's music was incredibly popular, it was never categorized as *rock*. While Madonna was often credited with supporting Black and queer artists, including her back-up dancers on multiple tours and those featured in her concert film *Truth or Dare*, cultural critic bell hooks argues that Madonna's artistry and sexual rebellion were heavily reliant on her Whiteness.[95] Whereas Paglia praises Madonna's artifice as evidence of her power, hooks sees it as an abuse of power: "The socially constructed image of innocent womanhood relies on the continued production of the racist/sexist sexual myth that black women are not innocent and never can be."[96] The *Truth or Dare* documentary highlights "a cast of characters from marginalized groups—non-white folks, heterosexual and gay, and gay white folks," who Madonna described as "emotional cripples."[97] While Madonna may have challenged the patriarchy and centered bodies that were largely ignored at the time, hooks argues she was actually endorsing the White supremacist status quo.[98] This White supremacist status quo continues to be seen in pop culture, specifically in Taylor Swift's video for her 2014 song "Wildest Dream," which takes place on the African continent and appropriates African culture.[99] What does it mean that a video, with over half a billion views on YouTube, by a White artist, borrows from Black culture without commentary or acknowledgment? This cognitive dissonance illustrates another lesson not learned in the generational lineage of White artists' co-optation of Black culture.

As of this writing, Madonna is in her mid-60s and no less influential or controversial. She is intimately familiar with why she remains controversial. Accepting her 2016 award for Woman of the Year, Madonna said, "People say that I am controversial, but I think the most controversial thing I've done is to stick around."[100] In large part because of her fame and notoriety, Madonna is one of the few women who can grow old in the public eye, and though she has, of course, been slammed for obvious plastic surgery, it has not made her any less famous or any less well-regarded by her legions of fans.[101] Mary Gabriel and Kristin Lieb's review of Madonna's 2023–2024 *Celebration* world tour observed,

> Older men are considered wise, but older women are often ignored or discounted. Thanks to the intervention of the pharmaceutical industry, men are encouraged to have an active sex life into their 80s. The idea of older women having sex remains,

for many, repellent.[102]

Based on her age, one presumes Madonna has gone through menopause, which, as discussed in Chapter 1, makes her largely irrelevant *as a woman*. But because she is Madonna, she largely escapes that critique. Despite her success, despite her refusal to be silenced in any capacity, it seems likely that any number of female pop stars in her wake will still need to fight for their autonomy. While Madonna was certainly not the first female singer to receive popular and critical acclaim, she represents a female talent who broke barriers while also reinforcing certain conventions of gender, race, and class. In so doing, she and her fame expanded the conversations on women in popular music, especially about embracing a robust sexuality and profiting from it, which simultaneously highlighted the strict compartments within which women live. Yes, Madonna's notoriety blazed the trail for countless female artists since, and yet, it remains quite easy to center and silence female pop stars.

RESULT: TRADWIVES AND STAY-AT-HOME GIRLFRIENDS

When we live in a culture with a generational lineage of harming women, the logical endpoint is not surprising: The rise of the tradwife and stay-at-home-girlfriend (SAHG). The tradwife is a "TikTok-fluent married woman who keeps house, extols 'traditional' values and yields to her husband," while the SAHG's day is "filled mostly with home care and self-care—elaborate skin, fitness and food routines that keep their bodies beautiful and their lives serene for their boyfriends who are, after all, funding the whole shebang."[103] These trends reflect and renew the rise of the cult of motherhood, as promoted by the popular press in the nineteenth century, in which "the perfect woman was the perfect mother."[104] Looking back to an idealized past, tradwife influencers "specifically preach the gospel of rigid gender roles and biblical submissiveness, glamorizing a 1950s housewife aesthetic while calling for some variation of a 'return to tradition.'"[105]

The twenty-first-century tradwife and SAHG may make life choices that resemble mid-twentieth-century lifestyles (or even earlier ways of living), but she does so in distinctly modern ways by virtue of the simple fact that she *has the choice* to stay at home (whereas many wives and mothers in generations past lacked that freedom). She also has a wider technological and mediated landscape by which to highlight and promote her life choices. In her dissection of women's labor, Black feminist activist Angela Davis observes that a woman's place had long been in the home,

> but during the pre-industrial era, the economy itself had been centered in the home and its surrounding farmland ... When manufacturing moved out of the home and into the factory, the ideology of womanhood began to raise the wife and mother as ideals.[106]

A woman's place may have been in the home, but until industrialization, so, too, was a man's place. The social construction of the ideal wife/mother, one who was largely homebound and happy about it, arose as an ideal in concert with industrialization. The expectation that women were to stay home was crafted to differentiate women from men as the economy shifted from household-based agriculture to corporate-based industry.

The tradwife and the SAHG embody a modern iteration of Phyllis Schlafly, embracing a power connected to the domestic sphere.[107] The 1950s American housewife led a largely private life, confined to the domestic space, and, in the 1970s, many housewives wore their domesticity as a source of pride in opposition to late-twentieth-century feminism and the political campaign to pass the Equal Rights Amendment (ERA). Estee Williams, an influencer living in Virginia, first became viral on social media for promoting the tradwife movement. "We believe our place ... our purpose is to be homemakers," she said in a video defending her lifestyle after receiving countless critiques online.[108] Her TikTok page consists of videos of her dressing up in 1950s attire, doing her make-up, and cooking and cleaning for her husband. Although she has stated in previous videos that she respects a woman's right to choose her lifestyle, critics say that her promoting women's "submission to their husbands" has serious implications, especially considering most women cannot financially attain the idealized lifestyle portrayed in her videos.[109] Still, her content continues to be popular with women commenting on how badly they want to lead a life like hers and men commenting on how they want to find a wife like her. The tradwife movement may express not only a woman's desire for a simpler life in which she is no longer disappointed by promises of independence and autonomy but also a man's desire for a submissive woman, relationship roles endorsed and sanctioned with increasing urgency by the ascendancy of the so-called manosphere and the policies of Trump 2.0.[110]

While this concept may raise the hackles of generations of women who have fought so hard for equality, the outcome is, sadly, not surprising. Tradwives and SAHGs may see liberation as "overrated," where they have been "sold a bill of goods. Yes, we are allowed to have successful careers. But nobody has decreased the amount of laundry or errands that still needed to be run. Nobody had added any more hours onto the clock."[111] Young women may justifiably see the slog of previous generations and conclude that it is not worth the fight.[112] Achieving true independence and autonomy is hard and still may fall short of its promises. In the past, White, economically stable women had no choice but to stay at home. When White women started working outside the home but were still, for the most part, responsible for housework and childcare, the luster of independence in the workplace dulled for many. The problem may not be the dangers of feminism, "but capitalism—specifically the American version, where work-life balance is a punchline."[113]

In her widely-read essay on the benefits of being a tradwife, Grazie Sophia Christie detailed her route to a more traditional life. While a student at Harvard University, she saw her youth as a superpower and used it to harness an older, wealthier husband, questioning,

> Why assume the burdens of womanhood, its too-quick-to-vanish upper hand, but not its brief benefits at least? Perhaps it became easier to avoid the topic wholesale than to accept that women really do have a tragically short window of power, and reason enough to take advantage of that fact while they still can.[114]

For Christie, snagging a handsome, wealthy, older man—she spent time around Harvard Business School functions and the library in order to meet desirable types of men—meant that she would not have to train or teach her man how to be an adult (previous girlfriends presumably had already done that), and she could write when and how she wanted without having to worry about paying bills. She acknowledges that her arrangement comes with the burden of a lack of independence; she knows that her husband is in charge, and that is the price she pays for a life of relative ease. "I live in an apartment whose rent he pays and that shapes the freedom with which I can even be angry at him. He doesn't have to hold it over my head. It just floats there, complicating usual shorthands to explain dissatisfaction like, *You aren't being supportive lately*."[115] Of the 550 comments on her article, the vast majority are critical of her choices, with many commenters expressing dismay that she is taking women and womankind backwards.

Importantly, tradwives are, for the most part, White and exclusively in heterosexual relationships. Tradwifery is not the provenance of women of color, which reflects a larger history of women of color working outside the home. As Davis notes, "Proportionately, more black women have always worked outside their homes than have their white sisters. The enormous space that work occupies in black women's lives today follows a pattern during the very earliest days of slavery."[116] Black women who stay at home typically eschew the "tradwife" label and its White connotations, instead referring to themselves as "Black housewives" and extolling the virtues of traditional marriage as alleviating the pressures of economic insecurity born of a racist labor structure.[117]

In the history of Western marriage, "the laws defining marriage made the husband essentially an owner and the wife a possession. Or the man a boss and the woman a servant or slave," Rebecca Solnit has observed.[118] Much of this can be seen in the history of American slavery and how Black women were the property of their slavemaster, a man who exercised his physical and economic power through sanctioned rape, which served to keep women controlled and to make more slave labor.[119] Young women today may feel they have been sold a rotten bill of goods and therefore choose to opt out of the fight for greater equality; they have seen their mothers and grandmothers campaign for equality, with little change, little advancement, and—possibly worse—little protection or support when efforts at emancipation go wrong.

The cruelty of tradwifery, like the cruelty of so much fascination with celebrity lifestyles, is that the projected image of the tradwife and SAHG is one that can only be secured by a select few. While many tradwives and SAHG's promote the virtue of homelife, this promotion is often *a paid job*, not just a life of leisure enabled by a wealthy partner. Tradwives "spend their days taking care of their homes and families and documenting their activities on social media," and, like mommy blogs discussed in Chapter 1, their domestic labor is often sponsored.[120] Tradwives have distinctly twenty-first-century jobs: selling both merchandise and a lifestyle via short-form social media. Tradwives work "the hustle of the anti-hustle, the opt-out from job dissatisfaction and economic insecurity."[121] The tradwife may announce an economic security enabled by her man, but she is the one at work, admittedly, work that keeps her homebound or, at least, close to home. For example, the women centered in *The Secret Lives of Mormon Wives*, the Hulu reality show that grew from their TikTok notoriety, acknowledge *they* are the breadwinners, via product endorsements and sales of their own branded products, in their otherwise traditional marriages.[122]

The tradwife and SAHG have tapped a broader societal desire for greater rest and opportunities to peer into the work of parenting without having to experience it. To be a tradwife or a SAHG is to hack into a perceived life of ease, "to move forward by moving backward."[123] As fewer and fewer children are born around the world, "content about children is surging" online.[124] In a social media environment premised on an economy whose benefits are not available to all, *watching* other people care for children is less expensive and burdensome than bearing and rearing them oneself. In a post-*Roe* environment, where unplanned or unwanted pregnancies are considerable risks, watching tradwives and SAHGs serves as one way to conceptualize an unknowable and precarious future.

Who is an authority on whether the tradwife is liberated or oppressed? A widely read—and widely criticized—essay on Hannah Neeleman, a wife and mother of eight who lives on a farm in Utah and competed in a Mrs. World pageant twelve days postpartum, reveals fault lines in the often one-sided story of tradwifery.[125] Neeleman is one of the most popular social media influencers, depicting her family's farm life and child rearing to nearly 10 million followers.[126] In her profile of Neeleman, journalist Megan Agnew asks whether Neeleman's participation in the Mrs. World pageant was the "ultimate act of empowerment … or the ultimate demonstration of oppression?"[127]

Neeleman grew up in Utah and moved to New York City to study ballet at Juilliard. When she met Daniel, they quickly married, and she was pregnant within three months of the wedding. She continued to pursue dance through the birth of her first three children. When Daniel decided he wanted to be a farmer, she agreed to give up dance. Neeleman claims that her husband gave up some of his dreams as well, but Agnew is openly skeptical of this in her profile. She notes that they live on the farm he wanted, go on dates that he chooses, have no nannies, and what was once Neeleman's home dance studio is now the classroom where she homeschools their children.

Upon publication of the initial profile, Agnew was criticized by readers for inserting her own skepticism into the piece. Who was she to judge Neeleman's choices? In her defense, Agnew pointed out the ironies of the tradwife lifestyle, including children who are "not allowed screens, but who are reality characters online for millions. A stay-at-home mother who has made a career out of being so. An analogue, old-fashioned farm, only working because it is underwritten by social media cash."[128]

According to Agnew, Daniel leads the brand while Hannah is the face, which fulfills his plans as he "had always imagined this enormous, daring life for himself, despite growing up in the Connecticut suburb without a single animal, the son of an airline founder."[129] Though Daniel has no background or training in agriculture, as the son of the founder of JetBlue Airlines and the husband of an incredibly popular and lucrative influencer, he is able to pursue farm life without fear of economic stress.

Maybe we just know too much about people these days? While we are arguing over the progressive/regressive politics of tradwifery, capitalism and the shine of patriarchy are winning. British journalist Sarah Ditum asks whether the families promoting their return-to-simplicity lives really do want to encourage people to have more children or maybe are just "more interested in influencing them to purchase some branded homeware or ready meals."[130] Not unlike the structures of the mid-twentieth-century housewife, the narrative of the tradwife and SAHG may pander more to image than reality.

The multigenerational harm bestowed upon women creates situations in which any action deemed "different" or abnormal severely limits women's opportunities. The next chapter discusses women who violate norms of expected behavior and, in so doing, challenge deep-rooted assumptions about womanhood.

NOTES

1. *The Princess*, directed by Ed Perkins (Lightbox Productions, 2022).
2. *The Princess*, Perkins; Amanda Spence, "Why Princess Diana Was Seen as 'a Problem' to the Royal Family," *Royals*, October 10, 2019.
3. Andrew Morton, *Diana: Her True Story* (Michael O'Mara Books, 1992).
4. *The Queen*, directed by Stephen Frears (Pathé Renn Production, 2006); Michael Hobbes and Sarah Marshall, hosts, *You're Wrong About*, "Princess Diana," September 28; October 5, 12; and November 2, 9, 2020, 60 minutes; *The Crown*, produced by Andy Stebbing et al., television series (Left Bank Pictures, 2016–2023). *The Princess*, Perkins.
5. Zoe Magee and Kevin Shalvey, "Kate Middleton Apologizes for 'Confusion' Caused by Edited Photo," *GMA*, March 11, 2024.
6. Zeynep Tufekci, "Kate Middleton's Story Is About So Much More than Kate Middleton," *New York Times*, March 13, 2024.
7. Tufekci, "Kate Middleton's Story."
8. Sophie Gilbert, "What Meghan Markle Means for the Royal Family," *The Atlantic*, November 27, 2017.
9. Maeve McDermott, "BBC Host Danny Baker Fired After Tweet Depicting Royal Baby as a Monkey," *USA Today*, May 9, 2019. Louise Berwick, "Harry to Marry Into Gangster Royalty? New Love from 'Crime-Ridden Neighbourhood'," *Daily Star*, November 3, 2016. Helen Lewis, "Harry and Meghan Won't Play the Game," *The Atlantic*, January 9, 2020.
10. Prince Harry, The Duke of Sussex, *Spare* (Random House, 2023); *Harry & Meghan*, produced by Ashley B. Carey et al., television series (Netflix, 2022).
11. Allison Yarrow, *90s Bitch: Media, Culture, and the Failed Promise of Gender Equality* (Harper Perennial, 2018).
12. Anita Hill, *Speaking Truth to Power* (Anchor Books, 1997).
13. Hill was *not* invited to provide "dirt," but rather was subpoenaed to speak as a former employee. See Michael Hobbes and Sarah Marshall, hosts, *You're Wrong About*, "Anita Hill," May 26, 2018, 60 minutes. Yarrow, *90s Bitch*.
14. Juan Williams, "A Question of Fairness," *The Atlantic*, February 1987.
15. Williams, "A Question of Fairness."
16. Williams, "A Question of Fairness."
17. Williams, "A Question of Fairness."
18. Juan Williams, "Open Season On Clarence Thomas," *Washington Post*, October 10, 1991.
19. "User Clip: Clarence Thomas Lynching." C-SPAN, October 11, 1991.
20. Hill, *Speaking Truth to Power*, 201.
21. Hill, *Speaking Truth to Power*, 204.
22. Rebecca Solnit, *Men Explain Things to Me* (Haymarket Books, 2014), 110.
23. Hill, *Speaking Truth to Power*, 179–80.
24. Hill, *Speaking Truth to Power*, 179–80.
25. Hill, *Speaking Truth to Power*, 215–216.
26. "Myths And Facts About Sexual Violence," Georgetown Law, accessed July 25, 2025. Shara Kaszovitz, "5 Reasons Why Victims Wait to Disclose That They Were Sexually Assaulted," Jackson Women's Health System, accessed August 4, 2025.
27. Hill, *Speaking Truth to Power*, 187.
28. Hill, *Speaking Truth to Power*, 233.

29 Rosemary L. Bray, "Taking Sides Against Ourselves," *New York Times*, November 17, 1991. Victoria M. Massie, "How Racism and Sexism Shaped the Clarence Thomas/Anita Hill Hearing," *Vox*, April 16, 2016.
30 Bray, "Taking Sides Against Ourselves."
31 David Brock, *The Real Anita Hill: The Untold Story* (Free Press, 1993).
32 Brock, *The Real Anita Hill*, 3.
33 Brock, *The Real Anita Hill*, 4.
34 Brock, *The Real Anita Hill*, 4.
35 Hill, *Speaking Truth to Power*, 171.
36 Brock, *The Real Anita Hill*.
37 Brock, *The Real Anita Hill*, 346–47.
38 Lisa Rosenthal and Marci Lobel, "Stereotypes of Black American Women Related to Sexuality and Motherhood," *Psychology of Women Quarterly*, 40, no. 3 (2016): 414–27.
39 Brock, *The Real Anita Hill*, 338.
40 Alex Kuczynski and William Glaberson, "Book Author Says He Lied in His Attacks on Anita Hill in Bid to Aid Justice Thomas," *New York Times*, June 27, 2001.
41 David Brock, *Blinded by the Right: The Conscience of an Ex Conservative* (Crown Books, 2023).
42 Jennifer Szalai, "First He Went After Anita Hill. Now He's Coming for Clarence Thomas," *New York Times*, September 16, 2024.
43 Media Matters for America, which is, admittedly, utilized in this text.
44 David Brock, *Stench: The Making of the Thomas Court and the Unmaking of America* (Penguin-Random House, 2024). Szalai, "First He Went After Anita Hill."
45 Hill, *Speaking Truth to Power*.
46 Hill, *Speaking Truth to Power*, 170.
47 Phyllis Chesler, *Patriarchy: Notes of an Expert Witness* (Common Courage Press, 1994).
48 Hill, *Speaking Truth to Power*, 171.
49 Hill, *Speaking Truth to Power*, 202.
50 Hill, *Speaking Truth to Power*, 203–4.
51 Hill, *Speaking Truth to Power*, 229.
52 Bray, "Taking Sides Against Ourselves."
53 Patricia J. Williams, "The Legacy of Anita Hill, Then and Now," *The Nation*, October 5, 2011.
54 Yarrow, *90s Bitch*, 52.
55 Solnit, *Men Explain Things to Me*, 112.
56 Maya C. Miller, "Democrats Seek Criminal Investigation of Justice Thomas over Travel and Gifts," *New York Times*, July 9, 2024.
57 Abbie VanSickle, "Justice Thomas Failed to Reveal More Private Flights, Senator Says," *New York Times*, August 5, 2024.
58 Rhiannon Hamam, Michael Liroff, and Peter Shamshiri, hosts, *5-4*, "Garland v Cargill," Prologue Projects, June 25, 2024, 45–60 minutes. Next is Antonin Scalia, who declared just around $200,000 prior to his death.
59 VanSickle, "Justice Thomas Failed To Reveal More Private Flights."
60 Emma Brown, "California Professor, Writer of Confidential Brett Kavanaugh Letter, Speaks Out About Her Allegations of Sexual Assault," *Washington Post*, September 16, 2018.

61 Mahita Gajanan, "Sen. Orrin Hatch Calls Christine Blasey Ford an 'Attractive' Witness," *Time*, September 27, 2018.
62 Gajanan, "Sen. Orrin Hatch."
63 Maggie Haberman and Peter Baker, "Trump Taunts Christine Blasey Ford at Rally," *New York Times*, October 2, 2018.
64 Shawn Musgrave, "Trump White House Got in the Way of Brett Kavanaugh Sexual Assault Investigation," *The Intercept*, October 8, 2024.
65 Sheldon Whitehouse, "Unworthy of Reliance: The Flawed Supplemental Background Investigation Into Sexual-Assault Allegations Against Justice Brett Kavanaugh," *Sheldon Whitehouse*, October 2024.
66 Musgrave, "Trump White House Got in the Way"; Whitehouse, "Unworthy Of Reliance."
67 Christine Blasey Ford, *One Way Back: A Memoir*. (St. Martin's Press, 2024), xvi.
68 Massie, "How Racism and Sexism."
69 Massie, "How Racism and Sexism."
70 Massie, "How Racism and Sexism."
71 Williams, "The Legacy of Anita Hill"; Sara Marcus, *Girls to the Front: The True Story of the Riot Grrrl Revolution* (Harper Perennial, 2010).
72 Williams, "The Legacy of Anita Hill."
73 Letty Cottin Pogrebin, "A Thank You Note to Anita Hill," *The Nation*, October 5, 2011.
74 Sarah Marshall, host, *You're Wrong About*, "Has the Supreme Court Always Been This Terrible? With Mackenzie Joy Brennan," July 22, 2024, 60 minutes.
75 Chesler, *Patriarchy*.
76 Mary Gabriel, *Madonna: A Rebel Life* (Hatchette Books, 2023), 156.
77 Gabriel, *Madonna*, 158.
78 Camille Paglia, "Madonna—Finally, a Real Feminist," *New York Times*, December 14, 1990.
79 Paglia, "Madonna."
80 Camille Paglia, "Madonna — Finally, a Real Feminist," *New York Times*, video, September 24, 2010, 02:32.
81 Paglia, "Madonna — Finally, a Real Feminist."
82 Paglia, "Madonna — Finally, a Real Feminist."
83 "Controversies," *Miley Cyrus Wiki* (Fandom), accessed July 25, 2025.
84 viki_g23 (@viki_g23), TikTok. unfabled.co (@unfabled.co), TikTok.
85 luffyfathom (@luffyfathom), TikTok.
86 *Taylor Swift vs. Scooter Braun: Bad Blood*, produced by Kate Siney, television series (Optomen Productions, 2024).
87 Constance Grady, "The Taylor Swift/Scooter Braun Controversy, Explained," *Vox*, July 1, 2019.
88 Heili Potgieter, "Swift Justice: The Tale of Copyright Cat-and-Mouse in Taylor's Version," *Spoor-Fisher*, April 11, 2024.
89 Chelsea Devantez, host, Glamorous Trash, "Jessica Simpson's Open Book." October 28, 2020, 1hr, 23 minutes; and Michael Hobbes and Sarah Marshall, hosts, *You're Wrong About*, "Quarantine Deep Dive: Jessica Simpson's *Open Book*," May 7, 14, 28; June 8, 2020, 60 minutes.
90 Hobbes and Marshall, "Quarantine Deep Dive."
91 *The Newlyweds: Nick and Jessica*, produced by Greg Johnston, Lois Curran, and Rod Aissa, television series (MTV, 2003–2005).

92 "Jessica Simpson (Tuna? Chicken?)," posted April 29, 2010, by Jandro Meza, YouTube, 01:16.
93 Fishermen referred to albacore tuna as "chicken of the sea" because of its white meat and mild flavor.
94 Nadra Kareem Nittle, "How MTV Handled Accusations of Racism and Became More Inclusive," *LiveAbout*, January 14, 2020.
95 *Madonna: Truth Or Dare*, directed by Alek Keshishian and Mark Aldo Miceli (Miramax Films, 1991); bell hooks, "Madonna: Plantation Mistress or Soul Sister?" in *Gender, Race and Class in Media*, ed. Gail Dines and Jean M. Humez (Sage Publications, 1995).
96 Paglia, "Madonna"; hooks, "Madonna," 29.
97 hooks, "Madonna," 31.
98 hooks, "Madonna."
99 Afua Hirsch, "Imperial Feminism," in *Can We All Be Feminists?* ed. June Eric-Udorie (Penguin Books, 2018).
100 "Madonna Woman of the Year Full Speech," posted May 22, 2016, by Billboard, YouTube, 10:29.
101 Alexandra Del Rosario, "Madonna Blames 'Ageism,' 'Misogyny' for Remarks About Her Face: Some Fans Don't Agree," *LA Times*, February 8, 2023.
102 Mary Gabriel and Kristin J. Lieb, "The Nerve of Madonna to Pull It Off, Again," *New York Times*, May 16, 2024.
103 Monica Hesse, "Tradwives, Stay-at-Home Girlfriends and the Dream of Feminine Leisure," *Washington Post*, April 10, 2024.
104 Angela Davis, *Women, Race and Class* (Vintage Press, 1981), 31.
105 Olivia Little, "Tradwife Influencers are Quietly Spreading Far-Right Conspiracy Theories," Media Matters, May 1, 2024.
106 Davis, *Women, Race and Class*, 32.
107 "About," *The Real Mrs. America*, accessed August 4, 2025.
108 Estee Williams (@esteecwilliams), TikTok.
109 Jack Ramage, "Who Is Estee Williams? Meet the Gen Z Tradwife Taking TikTok by Storm," *Screenshot*, April 2, 2024.
110 Jessica Grose, "'Tradwife' Content Isn't Really for Women. It's for Men Who Want Submissive Wives, " *New York Times*, May 15, 2024. Rachel Louise Snyder, "We Underestimate the Manosphere at Our Peril," *New York Times*, March 28, 2025.
111 Hesse, "Tradwives, Stay-at-Home Girlfriends."
112 Andi Zeisler, *We Were Feminists Once: From Riot Grrrl to Covergirl®, the Buying and Selling of a Political Movement* (Public Affairs, 2016).
113 Hesse, "Tradwives, Stay-at-Home Girlfriends."
114 Grazie Sophia Christie, "The Case For Marrying an Older Man," *The Cut*, March 27, 2024.
115 Christie, "The Case For Marrying an Older Man."
116 Davis, *Women, Race and Class*.
117 Nylah Burton, "Black 'Tradwives' Say Marriage is the Key to Escaping Burnout," *Refinery29*, December 21, 2022.
118 Solnit, *Men Explain Things to Me*, 56.
119 Davis, *Women, Race and Class*.
120 Sophie Elmhirst, "The Rise and Fall of the Trad Wife," *New Yorker*, March 29, 2024.
121 Elmhirst, "The Rise and Fall of the Trad Wife."

122 *The Secret Lives of Mormon Wives*, composed by Max Beck (Hulu, 2024). Most notably, the women debate if it is worth it to endorse a brand of vibrators, a product decidedly in opposition to Mormon values on sexual behavior.
123 Hesse, "Tradwives, Stay-at-Home Girlfriends."
124 Sarah Ditum, "For Most Women, Tradwives Are a Freak Show," *The Times*, July 22, 2024.
125 Meagan Kohler, "Unfair Media Portrayals—Not a Rich Family Life—Are Erasing Hannah Neeleman's True Identity," *Deseret News*, August 2, 2024.
126 Megan Agnew, "Meet the Queen of the 'Trad Wives' (And Her Eight Children)," *The Times*, July 20, 2024. Ballerina Farm (@ballerinafarm), Instagram.
127 Agnew, Megan, "Meet the Queen of the 'Trad Wives'."
128 Megan Agnew, "My Day with the Tradwife Queen and What It Taught Me," *The Times*, July 29, 2024.
129 Agnew, "My Day with the Tradwife Queen."
130 Sarah Ditum, "For Most Women."

CHAPTER THREE

WHEN WOMEN ACT OUT

THE DANGER OF DUPLICITOUS WOMEN

Anna Sorokin, popularly known as Anna Delvey, a self-proclaimed trust-fund child from Germany, established herself in New York City and built connections with famous artists, athletes, and CEOs. She plotted the launch of elite social clubs in the world's wealthiest cities until it was discovered that she had no trust fund, no money, and would not be paying back any of the individuals or banks from which she had borrowed. *New York Magazine* detailed her story, which served as the basis for the Netflix miniseries *Inventing Anna.*[1] Audiences were captivated by how she deceived America's most powerful elite and, for a while, lived a luxurious lifestyle despite her own lack of wealth.

Elizabeth Holmes, the former CEO of biomedical firm Theranos, which had reached a value of $9 billion, claimed that her minimally invasive blood tests could detect health issues ranging from high cholesterol to cancer. Her appearance and demeanor, inspired by her hero Steve Jobs, helped her convince investors that her invention would revolutionize the medical industry.[2] After multiple accusations of consumer deception, she was removed from her company and endured an arduous trial. A jury later convicted Holmes of four counts of fraud relating to the blood-testing device.[3] In her defense, she claimed that she had been sexually assaulted in college and that Sunny Balwani, her former boyfriend and COO of Theranos, emotionally abused her, which led to her "pouring on to her business." Holmes's explanations did not inspire the sympathy of the jury or the media, which pivoted from depicting her as a powerful entrepreneur to a lying criminal.[4]

Martha Stewart, a self-made billionaire who monetized housewifery and weaponized divorce, also branded herself, selling numerous Martha Stewart Living products—including home goods, garden care and maintenance, and cookbooks and cookware—and hosting a reality show.[5] Soon after her company, Martha Stewart Living Omnimedia, went public, she was accused and convicted of lying about a stock trade with another company, for which she served five months in prison. Prosecutors could never prove insider trading—an offense with a much stiffer penalty—but did prove that she had lied (by omission) about a conversation with her broker.[6]

Sorokin, Holmes, and Stewart were all women involved in business ventures typically pursued by men—con artists, med-tech development, and stock trading. Men who con others for large sums of money are not expected to apologize on behalf of their gender, and men who build companies with the intention of disrupting an industry are never expected to apologize for accidentally or willfully deceiving the public.[7] These three women responded to the accusations against them in a masculine fashion: They expressed no remorse.[8]

The media responses to Sorokin, Holmes, and Stewart illustrate a public largely in awe of women behaving badly. Social media posts lauded how Sorokin conned bankers and financiers, in part because it was so rare to see any person, let alone a woman, best the establishment. For example, one YouTube video that provided a timeline of Sorokin's cons included comments such as, "This broke ass girl had the guts to walk into a bank & ask for a $22 million loan lmfao. I need her confidence;" and "Scamming wealthy hotels out of cash: Nice girl;" and "Just goes to show you, if you scam the poor you're a bank, if you scam the rich, you go to jail;" and "she didn't even have to marry a rich man. Iconic."[9] A TikTok page following Sorokin's trial featured comments from users, saying, "I'm okay with it. These rich people got scammed, it is good for them," and, "The reason she [is] in jail is because she was this close to scamming banks/elites ... Makes you question how banks/elite really have more power over people."[10] Many users posting about the Theranos scandal on social media believed Holmes was lying about her sexual abuse to gain sympathy with the jury, with commenters writing, "This is just about as disgusting a case of sexual assault as a shield that I could imagine. She's spitting in the eye of actual survivors here."[11] Critics' reviews of the documentary *Martha* described Stewart as "unrepentant" in regard to her marriage, career, and stock manipulation, and claimed that Stewart was targeted for stock trading because, as a woman, she was too successful.[12]

This chapter focuses on the media representation of, and response to, women who act out and challenge the expectation of their "place" in society, with a focus on two very different pop stars whose actions brought them more notoriety than their music, Sinéad O'Connor and Britney Spears. O'Connor used her platform as a pop singer to talk back to the abuses of the Catholic Church, the music industry, and ignorance about mental health care. During this time, O'Connor was branded as "crazy," and effectively banished from the public sphere. Spears moved from child actor to teen pop star and sex symbol to gossip culture target when she experienced multiple public breakdowns. In 2021, when it was revealed that Spears had lived for thirteen years under the confines of a legal conservatorship that controlled her every move, a decades-long tabloid narrative of the pop star began to unravel.

Both O'Connor and Spears released memoirs about their roles as public figures and used their platforms to tell their stories about how pop culture constructed distorted images of them. O'Connor's memoir, *Rememberings*, provides unashamed insight into her personal struggles and political passions.[13] Spears's memoir, *The Woman in Me*, tells a clear and wrenching narrative of the multiple abuses and exploitation she suffered, while her social media presence indicates the trauma of that treatment is not yet fully healed.[14] This chapter further explores what it means for women to act out and what it means for audiences and the media to revisit and reconsider those actions.

WHEN WOMEN SPEAK OUT: SINÉAD O'CONNOR

In 1991, O'Connor announced that she would refuse any awards bestowed by MTV because the channel ignored Black artists. Also in 1991, she refused an invitation to perform on *Saturday Night Live* (*SNL*) because the scheduled host, comedian Andrew Dice Clay, often disparaged women in his routines. In 1992, she asked that the Star Spangled Banner not be played before a scheduled New Jersey performance because she felt it clashed with her music's larger message.[15] And finally, in 1992, she appeared on *SNL* to sing two songs, including her adaptation of Bob Marley's "War," whose lyrics she altered to reflect her concern with child abuse, particularly sexual abuse by Catholic priests. While singing, she tore up a picture of Pope John Paul II. With this one, seemingly salacious act, O'Connor catapulted to a type of fame far different from what her first two, commercially successful and critically acclaimed albums had brought her.

Within days, O'Connor was excoriated by the popular press and either praised or attacked for speaking out against the Catholic Church. She was called names and made the subject of a protest where her CDs were steamrolled, while Frank Sinatra and Joe Pesci both threatened her with violence, and *SNL* founder and showrunner Lorne Michaels patronizingly referred to her behavior as "inappropriate."[16] In the *SNL* episode following hers, as part of his opening monologue, host Joe Pesci commented that O'Connor was lucky he was not hosting the night she performed, saying, "If it was my show, I would have gave her such a smack." He then went on to visually demonstrate the smack to the audience's cheers and applause.[17]

Ripping up the picture of the Pope was not impulsive; O'Connor had planned it carefully as a protest against the abuse of children, which church administration had ignored or covered up for far too long. O'Connor used her voice and her platform as a public figure to speak out against the abuse in a carefully planned moment of activism. The picture of the Pope that she tore had been hanging in her mother's bedroom; upon her mother's death, O'Connor took down the photo, with the intention to destroy it because "it represented lies and liars and abuse," she wrote.[18] O'Connor was inspired by Bob Geldof who, in 1978, "ripped up a photo of Olivia Newton-John and John Travolta on *Top of the Pops* because their shit record 'Summer Nights' had been number one for seven weeks and finally Geldof's Boomtown Rats single 'Rat Trap' had taken over."[19] She conveys the message that because Geldof was male and because Newton-John and Travolta were not the heads of a global religion, *no one* remembers (or cares about) him tearing up that particular photo.

O'Connor was still a teenager—though she was never marketed as a *teen* pop star—when her first album, *The Lion and the Cobra*, was released in 1987. She became internationally known for the single "Nothing Compares 2 U," written for O'Connor by pop artist Prince, off her second album, 1990's *I Do Not Want What I Haven't Got*. While O'Connor was labeled a pop star, she never saw herself that way: "Everyone wants a pop star, see? But I'm a protest singer. I just had stuff to get off my chest. I had no desire for fame."[20] She wanted to be known as a protest singer, and while it was "totally cool for U2, Michael Stipe, and Sting to flaunt their activist bona fides," cultural critic Allyson McCabe observes that female artists were supposed to stick to "singing sexual come-ons, love songs, or songs about nothing, baby, baby, baby."[21] O'Connor's contemporaries, including Madonna, were not obviously political in their music, and feminist punk rock, which will be discussed in Chapter 5, scorned the Top 40 popularity that O'Connor had. There was little to no room for lyrically aggressive female activism on the pop charts.

O'Connor was a young Irish singer who had achieved global fame at a time when young, female pop stars were not meant to be edgy or political. With her shaved head, shy demeanor, and keening voice, she struggled in the limelight, where she was expected to be pretty, feminine, and demure. Introductions of O'Connor invariably mentioned her shaved head, with many assuming it expressed her defiance of feminine beauty rather than being a political statement.[22] When the press seemed ill-equipped to imagine any other angle, discussing her shaved head was a way to talk about her body.

While O'Connor was roundly criticized for ripping up the picture of the Pope, the passage of time has revealed that *she was right*. If it was possible to turn a blind eye to the actions of the Catholic Church in the early 1990s, doing so became impossible when legacy news organizations began to report on the abuses.[23] When the *Boston Globe* published its Spotlight series on serial abuse and cover-up in the Catholic Church, what had previously been dismissed as isolated incidents of abuse were shown to be chronic and systemic. *The Globe* published eight hundred articles on the scandal, demonstrating not only that the documented instances of abuse were *in no way* isolated incidents, but also that Church leadership had known about and actively sought to cover up the abuse.[24] In 2003, the *Globe* was awarded the Pulitzer Prize in public service for this reporting.[25]

Decades later, as part of the public relations blitz for *SNL's* fiftieth anniversary, Lorne Michaels admitted, "There was a part of me that just admired the bravery of what she'd done, and also the absolute sincerity of it."[26] It is not surprising that an early alarm on a flashpoint issue was not only ignored, but also actively denied and castigated—especially when the messenger delivering it was a woman already deemed controversial for not fitting conventional standards for female celebrity.

O'Connor exemplifies the value, and the danger, of speaking out. As a woman, to speak first, or even early, in the effort to push against injustice or to expose an ugly truth, is to risk scorn and, almost certainly, to undergo scathing attacks. It took an entire team of investigative reporters at one of the most prestigious US newspapers to do what one woman had attempted to do on her own—alerting the public to abuse in an effort to stop it and secure justice for generations of survivors.

Over the years, O'Connor has been called many names—including, but not limited to, variations on crazy, mad, and insane—which, in her memoir, she accepts.[27] She concurs that she did "sensibly and truly lose her marbles," in part because she was so young when she started singing. The lesson learned, she observes, is that "after losing them, one finds them and plays the game better."[28]

O'Connor owned her story and did not shy away from her commitments to stopping child sex abuse by Catholic priests and to being open about her mental health struggles and honest about the physical, psychological, and sexual abuse she endured as a child. While the popular press framed O'Connor's tearing up the picture of the Pope as the end of her career, she saw it quite differently. She observes, "I feel that having a number-one record derailed my career and my tearing the photo put me back on the right track ... I wasn't comfortable with what other people called success because it meant I had to be as others wanted me to be. After *SNL* I could just be me. Do what I love. Be imperfect. Be mad, even."[29]

WHEN WOMEN ACT OUT: BRITNEY SPEARS

Pop singer Britney Spears rose to fame as a teenage dancer, singer, and actor. As a teen pop star, she was relentlessly pushed into the limelight, where she was mercilessly scrutinized. Interviews with Spears at the rise of her career clearly illustrate her surprise and confusion about questions focused on her body, her sexuality, and her public behavior.[30] In one press conference, when asked repeatedly if she was a virgin, Spears tried to sidestep the question by claiming (reasonably) that the topic was private; the reporter agreed with her, then pressed for an answer nevertheless.[31] In one interview, as a lead-up to a question, ABC anchor Diane Sawyer told Spears that the wife of the governor of Maryland threatened to shoot Spears because of how she dressed; she then asked Spears to defend her appearance. Not for a moment did Sawyer question the appropriateness of a prominent adult threatening a teenager with violence.[32]

As a young adult, Spears's relationships and public activities were regularly headline news. She withstood public criticism for a 55-hour marriage to childhood friend Jason Alexander, followed by her marriage to back-up dancer Kevin Federline, with whom she had two children before they divorced.[33] After she was photographed driving with her infant son in her lap (instead of a car seat), then-host of the *Today* show Matt Lauer asked her what she was thinking. Lauer all but ignored her defense that she was trying to protect her son from being attacked by the hordes of photographers following her.[34] While pregnant with her second child and holding her first, she stumbled on her way out of a coffee shop. What might be seen for any other woman as a literal misstep became fodder for public scrutiny of her mental well-being.[35] The press and paparazzi pounced on any flaw in her public presentation and used those flaws to frame her as an inadequate mother. Not unlike Princess Diana, discussed in Chapter 2, the paparazzi were criticized for, but rarely prevented from, relentlessly stalking Spears. Their actions were truly invasive, but public demand for salacious gossip and images made those invasions highly profitable.

Spears was, for many years, caught in a maelstrom of unfair and abusive expectations. Both spontaneous moments (such as trying to get coffee) and planned public appearances (such as awards shows) were places where she could be caught off guard. For example, after Spears performed "Oops! ... I Did It Again" at the 2000 MTV Music Awards in a sparkly, flesh-colored bikini top, thong, and bell-bottom tights, which gave the illusion of nudity, MTV chastised her for being too sexy. It seems a safe assumption that MTV staffers signed off on the performance or, at the very least, saw a dress rehearsal; her costume would in no way have been a surprise. Both the controversy and the demand that she respond to it meant more money for MTV; they could both center and silence her to their financial advantage. MTV, complicit in the treatment, brought her on to review footage of the complaints and demanded that she defend her presentation. MTV both punished her *and* profited from her appearance, securing "a piece of the backlash, too."[36] And even though they may have found her risqué enough to demand that she answer to her critics, they invited her *back* for the 2001 awards, where she performed "I'm A Slave 4 U," in a bikini, surrounded by caged wild animals, and adorned with a Burmese python. Media outlets, including, but not limited to, MTV, centered Spears by putting her on stage at every opportunity possible while simultaneously silencing her by shaming the very behavior and appearance from which they profited.

After a tumultuous few years, Spears appeared to have a breakdown. Over the course of a few days in 2007, she shaved her head, got a tattoo, and attacked a paparazzo's car.[37] The whole ordeal was repeatedly scrutinized publicly across multiple gossip and tabloid channels. After her public outbursts, Spears was involuntarily committed to a psychiatric ward and, while undergoing treatment, her parents and multiple lawyers crafted a conservatorship that took control of both her person and her finances. Between 2008 and 2021, Spears was legally prohibited from making almost any decision on her own; both her finances and her person were tightly controlled. During the enforced conservatorship, Spears released four albums, headlined a multi-million-dollar grossing global tour, and performed for four years in a Las Vegas residency.[38] For many years, the restrictions on Spears were kept quiet, especially as she continued to release albums, perform publicly, and endorse products. In this way, Spears was doubly silenced. Not only was she not in control of her own life, she was not allowed to publicly acknowledge—or protest—that lack of control. A grassroots fan campaign, #FreeBritney, helped raise awareness of her plight, and upon her legal release from her conservatorship, Spears re-emerged in a new, yet still conflicted, light.

During the conservatorship, many people profited from Spears's continued work and staked their own claims on her story. Spears's mother, Lynne Spears, published her memoir, *Through the Storm: A Real Story of Fame and Family in a Tabloid World,* detailing her side of the tumultuous public life of her famous daughter.[39] Britney is the middle of three children, including her older brother Bryan and her younger sister Jamie Lynn, who, for a time, had her own career as a singer and TV star. Lynne Spears described the family's surprise at Britney's success. "It's really a story of one simple, Southern woman whose family got caught in a tornado called fame," Lynne Spears wrote, slickly reframing what most everyone understood to be Britney's story as the story of *her own* struggles.[40]

Lynne Spears repeatedly asserts that she was only on her daughter's payroll early in her career, when she managed Britney's website and fan club. "Britney was building me a big, beautiful home, prettier and more grandiose than anything I ever imagined I would have," Lynne Spears acknowledged, "The two of us had traveled to some fantastic exotic locations and had such wonderful times together."[41] There was no need to be *on* payroll when houses were custom-built and luxury vacations were made possible because of Britney Spears's income. Lynne Spears denied being a typical stage mom, "I simply did not have the huge ambitions for her that I have been accused of having. If a door opened, we walked through it," she explained.[42]

Lynne Spears makes only fleeting references to the conservatorship, defending the choices she and her ex-husband, Jamie Spears, made: "We—Jamie and I, Larry [Rudolph, Britney Spears's manager], and other members of her team—felt she needed to check in somewhere and just chill."[43] That may well have been true. After having two babies in quick succession, Britney Spears had effectively been abandoned by her husband and was fighting for custody of her children, while financially supporting her *entire* family. These dramas played out in full public view, leaving one of the most famous women in the world with no time to "just chill." Lynne Spears recounted that all eyes were on Britney, who was "living in a fishbowl, and every false move she made was duly noted by millions of people all over the world. She could run, but there was no place on earth my child could hide."[44] Clearly, not even from her own parents.

For all her "concerns" about protecting her daughter, it appears that Lynne Spears is the one who exploited Britney the most. "Lynne Spears was supposed to be her defender and advocate," blogger Lindsay Ferrier wrote. "Clearly, she failed miserably in that role. How devastating it must be to have a mom who sells you out over and over and over again."[45] Lynne Spears clearly views her two famous daughters in very different ways. In her memoir, Lynne excuses or brushes aside the life choices made by Jamie Lynn. While Lynne Spears shamed Britney for her lack of faith in God, and for experimenting with sex (outside of marriage), drugs, and alcohol, she describes Jamie Lynn as "always conscientious," rarely missing curfew, aware of fame's dark side, and, most importantly, "close to the Lord, and to her family and friends."[46] Lynne Spears treated Jamie Lynn's pregnancy at age sixteen differently from Britney's sex outside of marriage: The family rallied around the pregnancy, praising Jamie Lynne's commitment to her boyfriend (although they eventually broke up) and her decision not to seek an abortion.

For thirteen years, from age 27 to 40, Spears lived under the court-ordered legal supervision of her parents in a conservatorship that controlled her professional, her personal life, and even her body; it effectively dictated her every waking moment, rendering her incapable of making her own decisions. Such a restrictive conservatorship is generally reserved for people with severe disabilities or dementia who cannot, under any circumstance, care for themselves.[47]

Meanwhile, Spears was still touring globally, making millions of dollars for herself and others, conveying a public image of freedom and success. The legal team tasked with maintaining the conservatorship, against Britney's wishes, was paid with money she earned from her records, concert performances, and endorsements.[48] In June 2021, Spears appeared in court to argue against the conservatorship. It was the first time in thirteen years that the public heard her speak about it. "I'll be honest with you," Spears testified, "I haven't been back to court in a long time because I don't think I was heard on any level when I came to court last time."[49] Spears criticized the California legal system for perpetuating her misfortune, including restrictions on her finances and seeing her boyfriend, contracts that had been negotiated and signed without her participation, and constant psychiatric scrutiny. Spears also described not being allowed to remove her IUD because her conservators did not want her to have another child—an extreme example of symbolic silencing, an adult woman restricted from autonomy over her own body.[50] Commenting on the conservatorship's control of her reproductive choices, journalist Jan Hoffman observed, "The specter it raises—forced sterilization—does have a grim, extensive history in the United States, especially against poor women, women of color, and inmates."[51] As an incredibly wealthy White American, Spears does not fit any of those categories, and yet her copious privileges did not protect her from this extreme degree of bodily control.

While it may very well be true that Spears was financially irresponsible and probably had mental health struggles that compromised her independence, given her public presence as a performer, and her cogent public testimony about her treatment while living as a conserved person, it is hard to imagine she was wholly debilitated.

In 2023, two years after the dissolution of the conservatorship, Britney Spears released her memoir, *The Woman in Me*, which shed light on her understanding of her career and the legal restrictions that had constrained her.[52] The memoir covers her childhood, introduction to performing, small-town life in Kentwood, Louisiana, family and financial struggles largely due to her father's alcoholic volatility, her catapult to global fame, and all the repercussions of that, as well as her perspective on the conservatorship. In the *New York Times* review of the book, media critic Leah Greenblatt described Spears's prose as "chatty and confiding and occasionally salty," and concluded, "it's nearly impossible to come out of it without empathy for and real outrage on behalf of Spears."[53]

With the dissolution of her conservatorship and the release of her memoir, whose content was largely drawn and refined from her journals, Britney Spears was finally able to be seen as a complex human being. In taking control of her narrative, Spears presented herself as a pop star *and* as a person with potentially significant mental health issues whose chaotic life may have been dramatically exaggerated by the media's narratives about her. The memoir provided an opportunity for Britney Spears to (finally) tell her own story and to address many of the stories that had been told about her, without her consent. Revisiting some of her most notorious public moments, Spears invited audiences to reconsider what they thought they knew about her, including her breakup with pop singer Justin Timberlake, and her experience during her years-long conservatorship.

Despite the drama of their breakup, Britney Spears remembered her time with Justin Timberlake as sweet, young love. She described their relationship's significant public-private divide: Although they were sexually active and lived together, her public image at the time was crafted to emphasize her virginity (though, of course, his never was). Her memoir, and much of the press about it, made public that she had an abortion, which was, at the time, a source of disagreement between her and Timberlake. She wanted to keep the baby, but he thought they were not ready. Upon their breakup, she was cast as the villain, which was "proven" by the video for his song "Cry Me a River," which showed a Britney look-alike in bed with another man. Spears defended herself against

Timberlake's passive attack, writing,

> There's always been more leeway in Hollywood for men than for women. And I see how men are encouraged to talk trash about women in order to become famous and powerful ... The thought of my betraying him gave the album more angst, gave it a purpose: shit-talking an unfaithful woman. ... Getting revenge on women for perceived disrespect was all the rage at the time.[54]

Timberlake's video centered on and silenced Spears. Her *fictional* doppelgänger makes poor choices for which the *actual* Britney must answer. She recalled an interview where Diane Sawyer grilled her about her behavior with Timberlake, berating her:

> "He's going on television and saying you broke his heart. You did something that caused him so much pain. So much suffering. What did you do?" I didn't want to share anything private with the world. I didn't owe the media details of my breakup. I shouldn't have been forced to speak on national TV, forced to cry in front of this stranger, a woman who was relentlessly going after me with harsh question after harsh question. Instead, I felt like I had been exploited, set up in front of the whole world.[55]

Sawyer's "gotcha" questions seemed doubly unfair. Not only was Spears forced to explain the breakup in a way that Timberlake was not, but she also used *a music video* as proof of Timberlake's version of the story. Even if Britney Spears *had* cheated on Timberlake, how was any of this anyone's business? Why does the public deserve to know the angst arising from a *teenage* relationship, even if those teens are celebrities? As discussed earlier, this was not the only time that Sawyer hounded Spears without also addressing other, possibly more pertinent details. Maybe Spears did dress provocatively as a teenager, and maybe she did break Timberlake's heart, but in no way is Sawyer's lurid curiosity anything other than unethical.

Spears pointed out the double standard imposed on her. Constructed as a virgin well into her twenties, and contrary to her real life (she acknowledged having been sexually active since her teens), she was publicly shamed for being too sexual and, therefore, a bad role model for young girls. But she never asked to be that person. "Why did my managers work so hard to claim I was some kind of young-girl virgin, even into my twenties?" Spears asked. "Whose business was it if I'd had sex or not?"[56]

Spears reflected deeply on the actions that led to the conservatorship. Going through a very public divorce and custody battle—for which she was both shamed and wholly financially responsible—Spears recalled, "Nobody seemed to understand that I was simply out of my mind with grief."[57] Spears was flummoxed by the structure of the conservatorship. As she understood it, conservatorships were reserved for those with extremely limited mental and physical capacity, whereas, "I was highly functional. I'd just done the best album of my career. I was making a lot of people a lot of money, especially my father who I found out took a bigger salary than he paid me," paying himself $6 million.[58] Her erratic behavior, or maybe more accurately, behavior that was presented as erratic, was tabloid fodder. Spears's pain lined the pockets of those around her, entirely at her expense. The subject of countless media images and constant tabloid speculation, her family, handlers, and the media amplified her music but silenced her voice, leaving her few opportunities to narrate her own story, much less to speak out in her own defense.

While she was closely monitored, her two most famous exes, Kevin Federline and Justin Timberlake, were free to do what they wanted without significant repercussions. Federline had effectively abandoned her while he was on tour, but he remained relatively unscathed during the divorce and custody hearings. The double standard of their freedom was not lost on Spears, "Justin and Kevin were able to have all the sex and smoke all the weed in the world and no one said one word to them. I came home from a night at the clubs and my own mother tore into me."[59]

It was not lost on Spears that, during her conservatorship, her mother was profiting from her misery while simultaneously punishing her for her bad choices, via the publication of Lynne's memoir. "The book was huge for her," Britney wrote, "and all at my expense. The timing was un-fucking-believable ... I look at the worst things I did during that time and I don't believe the sum total of them is anywhere near as cruel as what my mother did by writing and promoting that book."[60] Spears displayed remarkable insight in reflecting on her previous life. She has suffered so much trauma, on top of a largely insecure childhood; it is no surprise that she fell apart.

The juxtaposition of the private conservatorship with Britney Spears's very public life meant that she had to behave in public as if everything was fine. The conservatorship dictated her every move, yet she could not speak of it. As a public figure since childhood, Spears's body was always on display, always controlled for some carefully constructed presentation. Then, when her world began to unravel, her body became a way for her to push back:

> I'd been eyeballed so much growing up. I'd been looked up and down, had people telling me what they thought of my body, since I was a teenager. Shaving my head and acting out were my ways of pushing back. But under the conservatorship I was made to understand that those days were now over. I had to grow my hair out and get back into shape. I had to go to bed early and take whatever medications they told me to take.[61]

The conservatorship capitalized on Spears's public presence while simultaneously silencing her. She notes, "It was always incredible to me that so many people felt so comfortable talking about my body. It had started when I was young. Whether it was strangers in the media or within my own family, people seemed to experience my body as public property: something they could police, control, criticize, or use as a weapon."[62] The conservatorship was the ultimate control of her body, leaving little to no room for her to act independently.

As in the cases of women declared insane, any struggle Spears expressed was taken as evidence of a further breakdown. Spears recalled, "The hardest part was that I believed that, in front of the doctors or visitors, I had to pretend the whole time I was okay. If I became flustered, it was taken as evidence that I wasn't improving. If I got upset and asserted myself, I was out of control and crazy."[63]

Upon public confirmation of the conservatorship, public opinion shifted squarely to Spears's defense, and many people revisited how she had been treated.[64] It became clear that she had never been able to live on her own terms. However, is the reimagining of Spears too little, too late? Are the press kinder to Spears because they learned a lesson? Or is it not kindness, but an absence of cruelty, because they have severely curtailed access to her and cannot foment much gossip because of her lack of public appearances? The conservatorship and all it entailed led to Spears's estrangement from her family and her retirement from recording and performing. Her only public presentation these days is her Instagram page, which she periodically deactivates, and is itself a site for much speculation.[65] On Instagram, she comments regularly about the press and her family's treatment of her over the years, but as of this writing, she no longer speaks to the press publicly or on record.[66] If her Instagram is to be believed, her life involves short dance videos that highlight her clothing, reminiscences of past times, or re-posts of older videos, and vacation pics. She regularly makes cryptic posts about the abuse she suffered from her family. Is Britney Spears living her best life? Maybe, maybe not. But it does *appear* that she is finally living life on her own terms, even if those terms are problematic. What seems so clear in hindsight is how she has rarely, if ever, been publicly treated like a human being. In her memoir, she asked, "Why was it so easy for everyone to forget that I was a human being—vulnerable enough that these headlines could leave a bruise?"[67]

Given the media climate at the time of the conservatorship's onset, it is surprising that it was kept quiet for so long by so many. For *thirteen years*, it was rarely discussed. The significant number of people on Spears's payroll clearly had a lot to gain from keeping their mouths shut. It was only when Spears walked away from an elaborate introduction to what would have been her next Las Vegas residency, *Domination*, that the depth and breadth of the conservatorship became of interest again.[68] Long ogled, admired, and critiqued, Spears was finally able to use her body in a simple, clear way to express her own desires: She walked offstage. She later announced, via her Instagram account, that she would not perform the residency because of her father's declining health.[69]

Both Sinéad O'Connor and Britney Spears, two female pop stars with very different public images, illustrate the threats of speaking and acting out. Both were called names and mocked for their public behaviors. O'Connor leaned into her own mental health struggles, being public about them, while Spears's health struggles were shrouded from the public, hidden behind a smothering legal conservatorship that tightly controlled her life. They both illustrate that revisiting women who were previously deemed problematic may cast new light on stories and identities once believed to be incontrovertible truths.

WHEN WOMEN ARE SILENT/CED

In the haunting film *The Assistant*, the story unfolds over the course of one day in the life of Jane, the eponymous assistant, who works for a powerful film magnate. She overhears the abuse he hurls at everyone who enters his office, and she witnesses the disheveled women who leave.[70] While the film's setting is based on the office of disgraced film producer and convicted sexual predator Harvey Weinstein, *The Assistant* is a condemnation of so many powerful men in leadership roles who are able to hide their nefarious acts in plain sight.

One of the most effective ways to silence a woman is through non-disclosure agreements (NDAs), which are often designed to protect a company's proprietary information and which also serve a different purpose when used in private settlements of alleged harassment. In part because NDAs restrict public conversations about mistreatment or proprietary information, many people do not know about them or understand their use. Although NDAs may result in large payouts for those who agree to them, they are still very much a tool of control for those who initiate them. Journalists Jodi Kantor and Megan Twohey detailed how Fox News, on behalf of commentator Bill O'Reilly, relied on settlements with confidentiality clauses and NDAs to "pay victims to keep quiet" about the misconduct of the popular conservative commentator and host.[71] In 2017, Fox forced O'Reilly to resign because of multiple, credible allegations of sexual assault, including a $32 million settlement. The Fox company was aware of allegations made over the years and participated in *six* settlements before finally forcing O'Reilly out.[72] According to Kantor and Twohey's analysis, the deals Fox made look like cover-ups, with a host of restrictive clauses, including terms that required signers to turn over anything that might be considered "evidence" and to refrain from helping other women who might have similar claims. Women who might be subpoenaed to testify in *other* sexual assault cases were required to notify O'Reilly's legal team so that they could prepare to preemptively discredit their testimony.

In cases of alleged harassment, NDAs typically back women into corners, often proving to be more beneficial to corporations or their male executives. If a woman needed money, could not afford a lengthy legal battle, wanted to protect her privacy, or did not want to be publicly shamed, name-called, or doxed, an out-of-court settlement based on an NDA imposes a certain logic. Although NDAs may protect some women's privacy, they also leave many women with gaps in their resumes that, for legal reasons, they cannot explain. Many of the women profiled by Kantor and Twohey were forced to change careers and find new jobs in different fields because of the negative treatment and relatively spineless responses to their credible accusations.

The shroud of NDAs shifted dramatically and publicly in the lead-up to the 2020 presidential election when, in an early Democratic debate, Senator Elizabeth Warren (D-MA) called out business tycoon and former NYC Mayor Michael Bloomberg for his treatment of women and his history of using NDAs to silence them.[73] Warren comments that when she asked Bloomberg about women's claims of a hostile work environment, he responded that his company and his foundation "employed lots of women ... and he took great pride in the fact that his company had received an award for being a great place to work."[74] A company can employ lots of women, *and* it can be a great place to work, but this does not mean these two claims are connected or causal; it can be a great place to work for those who are not women but a terrible place to work for those who are. Bloomberg did not specify which jobs, at what levels, the women in his company and his foundation held. On the debate stage, Warren asked Bloomberg, "Mr. Mayor, are you willing to release all of those women from those nondisclosure agreements, so we can hear their stories?"[75] Warren mused,

> Yes, the fifteenth richest man in America thought he knew exactly what he could get away with. He thought he could silence any woman who'd ever worked for him while he ran for the highest office in the land. He thought no one would seriously challenge him. He thought his money and power insulated him from ever having to talk about the

unacceptable things he had done.[76]

Bloomberg responded,

> None of them accused me of doing anything, other than maybe they didn't like a joke I told. And let me just—and let me—there's agreements between two parties that wanted to keep it quiet, and that's up to them, they signed those agreements, and we'll live with it ... they decided when they made an agreement that they wanted to keep it quiet for everybody's interests. They signed the agreements, and that's what we're going to live with.[77]

Bloomberg's disjointed defense portrays *him* as the victim of the NDAs. The women may have opted for NDAs because, in a confrontation with a man as wealthy and influential as Bloomberg, any other course of action would have led to lengthy, public battles that they could not afford, financially, emotionally, or professionally. Bloomberg's defense echoes the attacks on Anita Hill and Christine Blasey Ford, discussed in Chapter 2: Women cannot take a joke, *and* take things too seriously.

Probably the most notorious case of silencing and its ramifications can be found in the very public take-down of serial sexual assaulter, film producer Harvey Weinstein. A few very brave women risked their careers, any semblance of privacy, and relentless criticism when they spoke out against Weinstein. Like Anita Hill and Christine Blasey Ford, by *not* being silent, they made it safer for women to both speak out and be believed.

To speak out, especially against someone as powerful as Weinstein, means taking a huge risk. The first women to speak out against Weinstein had less to lose in terms of their careers because they were older, their careers were well-established, or they had moved out of the public sphere; these women could afford the risk in a way that young, newly hired, less powerful women could not. Even so, some women with extraordinary power, notably Gwyneth Paltrow, were scared to go on record, but encouraged other women to do so.[78] What needs to be remembered when a case like Weinstein's blows up across major media outlets is that for years, several women kept their silence as a form of self-protection. When we read countless headlines and books, listen to podcasts, and follow social media accounts of people who, seeing Weinstein finally facing justice, speak out themselves, this might be the *beginning* of the story for us, as audiences, but it is the *middle*, and maybe, hopefully, close to the *end* of the story for the women assaulted, harassed, threatened, and cajoled by Weinstein and his team of protectors. The hashtag #MeToo may have opened the floodgates, but it also revealed how tightly protected many men were, and most likely still are.

In 2017, using her social media platform, actor Rose McGowan was one of the first people to publicly accuse Weinstein of sexual assault and hijacking her career. When McGowan first went public with allegations against Weinstein, a leaked memo illustrates how his team of lawyers drew on the centuries-old notion of women's madness to construct "a plot to make her seem 'increasingly unglued.'"[79] McGowan, who struggled with mental health issues, was not seen as a credible witness and was easily lambasted by the press and Weinstein's support team.

Within three years of public documentation of his years of attacks on women, including actors and staffers, Weinstein was found guilty on all charges in both a New York court and a Los Angeles court.[80] When Weinstein was first publicly accused in the *New York Times* and the *New Yorker*, it opened the floodgates for women to speak up and speak out against abusers in multiple high-profile and low-profile workplaces.[81] What became obvious with the repeated and credible claims against Weinstein, and the revelation of how long they had been kept under wraps, is the strength of patriarchy's grip.

Writer Anne Helen Petersen observes,

> The charges against Weinstein—coupled with the veritable flood of allegations against other men in Hollywood that followed, and the millions of women who proclaimed they'd also been subject to sexual harassment or assault—doesn't just *suggest* that society values women less than men. It *announces* it as truth.[82]

The testimony by courageous women that led to Weinstein's convictions is incredibly important and undoubtedly made conversations of workplace sexual harassment, especially by prominent men, part of the public conversations across industries. High-profile White women, including Ashley Judd, Rose McGowan, Gretchen Carlson, and Megyn Kelly, did indeed come forward in ways that helped make women who are neither White nor famous safer. Their actions made it more palatable for audiences to see these "ideal" victims as spokeswomen of the movement. When actor Alyssa Milano started the hashtag #MeToo in the fall of 2017, it went viral within 24 hours, with twelve million posts.[83] However, this is only part of the story.[84] The "me too" conversation began much earlier in a world before social media and before "going viral" was part of the lexicon. What must be made clear and centered is that the phrase "me too" was started by a Black female activist working with sexual assault survivors, a *decade* before Milano popularized the phrase as a hashtag.

Tarana Burke began the MeToo movement via her own public acknowledgement of being sexually assaulted as a child. In her social justice work since the early 2000s, she had used the short, succinct phrase "me too" as a way for survivors of sexual assault to connect and share in empathy and understanding.[85] In conversation with Monica Lewinsky, on her podcast *Reclaiming*, Burke details the value of the phrase "me too" as a

> way for survivors to communicate with each other in short form, in short hand, to say, it doesn't really matter what happened or how it happened, or what the details were. But if it happened to you and it happened to me, I know who you are.[86]

In her memoir, Burke details the shock she felt at seeing her phrase become a hashtag and go viral on the internet, and her concern over whether its rapid-fire popularity would diminish the labor she had dedicated to constructing a safe space for women to speak about their hardships. As it became trendy, did the hashtag #MeToo lose some of its power? Or did it become more powerful because famous White women had adopted it? Either way, even a movement that centered women *also* silences them by ignoring, and perhaps inadvertently erasing, the non-famous, non-celebrity Black woman who started the conversation.

REVISITING WOMEN WHO ACT OUT

I was inspired to revisit women deemed problematic via their media representations in part by Sarah Marshall's podcast, *You're Wrong About*, where she chooses a person, topic, or event that the media painted in a particular way and questions the accuracy, fairness, and legitimacy of that representation.[87] With great empathy, humor, and superior pop culture knowledge, Marshall asks listeners to reconsider what they think they know or think they remember about a controversial topic or human being. What if what we think we know is wrong? What if we missed some key elements of a story or made assumptions that were unfair or misinformed? What if, at the height of the story or person's controversy, the press exaggerated or lied about certain aspects as a way to drum up greater attention?

To revisit women who act out is to attempt to redress a wrong and perhaps to prevent future misrepresentations. The first multi-chapter episode of *You're Wrong About* detailed the timeline, story arc, and grave misunderstanding of ice skater Tonya Harding, discussed in Chapter 1. Revisiting Harding many years later, it became clear that she was judged for being poor, not for her skating skills.[88] Lorena Gallo (FKA, Lorena Bobbitt) became a national public sensation in the mid-1990s when she amputated the penis of her then-husband, John Wayne Bobbitt. At the time, the media portrayed Gallo as a vengeful, crazy woman, and there were countless penis jokes made at her (and his) expense.[89] An arduous trial revealed the physical, emotional, and sexual abuse she endured in their marriage, which led to the jury finding her not guilty by reason of insanity.[90] As noted in Chapter 1, why must she be considered legally insane for defending herself against serial abuse?[91] When gymnast Simone Biles backed out of the 2020 Tokyo Olympics because of "the twisties," as discussed in Chapter 1, the narrative was that she was a selfish quitter and a traitor to her country.[92]

Context matters. As we see clearly in the cases of O'Connor and Spears, when new revelations about them or their past situations are taken into account, their previously unacceptable behaviors can be seen in a new, more empathetic light. These days, many skaters wear bright costumes, skate to rock music, and music with lyrics.[93] Films such as *I, Tonya* retell the story of her skating and the attack on Kerrigan from Harding's position, with a focus on the difficulties as she faced them.[94] With a greater understanding of spousal abuse, Gallo is now seen as a survivor of domestic violence who made a desperate choice for her survival. A TikTok compilation video of Gallo garnered supportive comments, including "goddess," "I don't blame her at all for what she did," "She's a QUEEN," and "It's the way the media minimized her abuse for me."[95] To revisit Biles is to look at her in a different way: As a woman protecting both her mental and physical health and as a woman who had endured years of sexual assault by her athletic doctor.[96] In reviewing social media comments about herself, four years after her departure from the 2020

Olympics, Biles shrugs off the hecklers as armchair complainers and questions whether any of them could even do a cartwheel (let alone her gravity-defying routines).[97] Although women who act and speak out may ultimately be revisited, reevaluated, and redeemed, they are still expected to operate in gender-appropriate spaces. The following chapters tackle how women operate in environments that actively work to exclude them.

NOTES

1. Jessica Pressler, "Maybe She Has So Much Money She Just Lost Track of It," *The Cut*. May 28, 2018; *Inventing Anna*, produced by Jess Brownell, Holden Chang, and Jessica Pressler, television series (Netflix, 2022).
2. Rebecca Jarvis, host, *The Dropout*, season 1, ABC News, 2019, 37–45 minutes.
3. Jarvis, *The Dropout*.
4. Jarvis, *The Dropout*.
5. *Martha*, directed by RJ Cutler (Netflix, 2024).
6. Cutler, "Martha."
7. See especially Lizzie Widdicombe, "The Rise and Fall of WeWork," *New Yorker*, November 6, 2019, which profiles the rise and fall of We Work and its founder Adam Neumann who, when kicked out of his own company, became a billionaire; and Mike Isaac, *Super Pumped: The Battle For Uber* (WW Norton, 2019), which profiles Travis Kalanick's deceptive development of Uber. The "fake it 'til you make it" ethos of male disruptors does not extend to women.
8. Libby Torres and Rebecca Cohen, "Anna Sorokin Acknowledges That Defrauding Banks Was Wrong but Doesn't Think She Owes Them an Apology," *Business Insider*, June 16, 2022. Jarvis, *The Dropout*. Cutler, "Martha."
9. "The Fake Socialite Who Scammed New York's Elite," posted June 12, 2019, by Cheddar, YouTube, 10:50.
10. Brut (@brutamerica), TikTok.
11. Rebecca Jarvis, "Elizabeth Holmes' Emotional Testimony at Theranos Trial," posted November 29, 2021, by ABC News, YouTube, 04:24.
12. Etan Vlessing, "Martha Stewart Dishes on 'Cookie-Cutter Life,' Insider Trading Scandal in 'Martha' Netflix Documentary Trailer," *Hollywood Reporter*, October 10, 2024; *Martha*, Cutler; Owen Gleiberman, "'Martha' Review: R.J. Cutler's Splendid Documentary Taps Into Everything We Love, and Don't, About Martha Stewart," *Variety*, October 30, 2024.
13. Sinéad O'Connor, *Rememberings* (Houghton-Mifflin-Harcourt Publishers, 2021).
14. Britney Spears, *The Woman In Me* (Gallery Books, 2023). Britney Spears (@britneyspears), Instagram.
15. Alan Light, "Sinead O'Connor Speaks," *Rolling Stone*, October 29, 1992. Allyson McCabe, *Why Sinéad O'Connor Matters* (University of Texas Press, 2023).
16. William Reilly, "Steamroller Crushes Sinéad O'Connor Recordings," *UPI*, October 21, 1992; Light, "Sinead O'Connor Speaks"; Joe Pesci, "Opening Monologue," aired on October 10, 1992, posted October 2, 2013, by Saturday Night Live, YouTube; Bob Guccione Jr., "Lorne Michaels Talks SNL, Sinead O'Connor, Wayne's World, and More in Our 1993 Interview," *Spin* (via *Yahoo Entertainment*), February 1993.
17. McCabe, *Why Sinéad O'Connor Matters*, 14.
18. O'Connor, *Rememberings*, 177.
19. O'Connor, *Rememberings*, 177.
20. O'Connor, *Rememberings*, 179.
21. McCabe, *Why Sinéad O'Connor Matters*, 62.
22. Will Millar, "Sinéad O'Connor: The Devastating and Dark Story Behind the Irish Singer's Shaved Head," *Edinburgh News*, July 27, 2023.

23   Aurelien Breeden, "Over 200,000 Minors Abused by Clergy in France Since 1950, Report Estimates," *New York Times*, October 5, 2021; James F. Clarity, "Ireland's Catholic Hierarchy Confronts Sex Abuse of Children," *New York Times*, October 19, 1995.

24   Jon Henley, "How The Boston Globe Exposed the Abuse Scandal That Rocked the Catholic Church," *The Guardian*, April 21, 2010.

25   "The Boston Globe," *The Pulitzer Prizes*, accessed September 9, 2025.

26   Eboni Boykin-Patterson, "*SNL* Boss Lorne Michaels Changes Tune on Sinéad O'Connor's Infamous Stunt," *The Daily Beast*, January 24, 2025; Alex Galbraith, "'I Admired The Bravery:' Lorne Michaels Has Come Around on Sinéad O'Connor's 'SNL' Pope Photo Stunt," *Salon*, January 24, 2025.

27   McCabe, *Why Sinéad O'Connor Matters*.

28   O'Connor, *Rememberings*, xii.

29   O'Connor, *Rememberings*, 181.

30   *Framing Britney Spears*, directed by Samantha Stark (*New York Times*, 2021).

31   Tess Barker and Babs Gray, hosts, *Toxic: The Britney Spears Story*, season 1, episode 3, "Boys," Stitcher Studios, July 13, 2021, 40 minutes.

32   Brooke Gladstone, host, *On the Media*, "Maligned Women," August 20, 2021, WNYC Studios, 60 minutes.

33   Barker and Gray, "Boys"; Jesus Jimenez, "Britney Spears Announces Engagement to Longtime Boyfriend, Sam Ashgari," *New York Times*, September 12, 2021.

34   Lauer was accused of sexual harassment in 2017 as part of the #MeToo movement and subsequently fired from NBC. See Ellen Gabler, Jim Rutenberg, Michael M. Grynbaum, and Rachel Abrams, "NBC Fires Matt Lauer, the Face of 'Today'," *New York Times*, November 29, 2017; *Framing Britney Spears*, Stark.

35   Ronan Farrow and Jia Tolentino, "Britney Spears's Conservatorship Nightmare," *New Yorker*, July 3, 2021.

36   Amanda Hess, "Watching Britney Spears, as a Girl and a Woman," *New York Times*, October 30, 2023.

37   Farrow and Tolentino, "Britney Spears's Conservatorship Nightmare."

38   Farrow and Tolentino, "Britney Spears's Conservatorship Nightmare."

39   Lynne Spears, *Through the Storm: A Real Story of Fame and Family in a Tabloid World* (Thomas Nelson, 2008).

40   Spears, *Through the Storm*, ix.

41   Spears, *Through the Storm*, x.

42   Spears, *Through the Storm*, 84.

43   Spears, *Through the Storm*, 134.

44   Spears, *Through the Storm*, 125.

45   Lindsay Ferrier, "And the Award For the Worst Celebrity Mom Goes to …" *Suburban Turmoil*, September 22, 2008.

46   Spears, *Through the Storm*, 122.

47   Farrow and Jia Tolentino, "Britney Spears's Conservatorship Nightmare."

48   Barker and Gray, "Boys." Tess Barker and Babs Grey, hosts, *Toxic: The Britney Spears Story*, season 1, episode 4, "Lonely," Stitcher Studios, July 20, 2021, 40 minutes; Julia Jacobs and Sarah Bahr, "The Britney Spears Transcript, Annotated: 'Hear What I Have To Say'," *New York Times*, June 24, 2021.

49   Jacobs and Bahr, "The Britney Spears Transcript, Annotated."

50 Barker and Gray, "Lonely"; Farrow and Tolentino, "Britney Spears's Conservatorship Nightmare"; Jacobs and Bahr, "The Britney Spears Transcript, Annotated."

51 Jan Hoffman, "Alabama Says Embryos in a Lab Are Children. What Are the Implications?" *New York Times*, February 21, 2024. See also Morgan Nichols, "Activists Call Out Legacy of Racism and Sexism in Forced Sterilization," *Project Censored*, November 9, 2021.

52 Spears, *The Woman in Me*.

53 Leah Greenblatt, "In Britney Spears's Memoir, She's Stronger Than Ever," *New York Times*, October 19, 2023.

54 Spears, *The Woman in Me*, 87.

55 Spears, *The Woman in Me*, 104–5.

56 Spears, *The Woman in Me*, 88.

57 Spears, *The Woman in Me*, 148.

58 Spears, *The Woman in Me*, 166.

59 Spears, *The Woman in Me*, 146.

60 Spears, *The Woman in Me*, 170.

61 Spears, *The Woman in Me*, 187.

62 Spears, *The Woman in Me*, 200.

63 Spears, *The Woman in Me*, 237.

64 Amber Tamblyn, "Britney Spears's Raw Anger, and Mine," *New York Times*, June 26, 2021; Amanda Hess, "Watching Britney Spears"; Andi Zeisler, "The Arc of Britney Spears Bends Towards Justice," *New York Times*, December 31, 2023.

65 Britney Spears (@britneyspears), Instagram.

66 Britney Spears (@britneyspears), Instagram.

67 Spears, *The Woman in Me*, 96.

68 Joe Coscarelli, "Britney Spears Announces 'Indefinite Work Hiatus,' Cancels Las Vegas Residency," *New York Times*, January 4, 2019.

69 Coscarelli, "Britney Spears Announces 'Indefinite Work Hiatus'."

70 *The Assistant*, directed by Kitty Green (Bleecker Street, 2019).

71 Jodi Kantor and Megan Twohey, *She Said: Breaking the Sexual Harassment Story That Helped Ignite a Movement* (Penguin Books, 2019).

72 Emily Steel and Michael S. Schmidt, "Bill O'Reilly Settled New Harassment Claim, Then Fox Renewed His Contract," *New York Times*, October 12, 2017.

73 Elizabeth Warren, *Persist* (Metropolitan Books, 2021).

74 Warren, *Persist*, 129.

75 Warren, *Persist*, 130.

76 Warren, *Persist*, 130.

77 Warren, *Persist*, 130–131.

78 Anne Helen Petersen, *Too Fat, Too Slutty, Too Loud: The Rise and Reign of the Unruly Woman* (Plume, 2017); Kantor & Twohey, *She Said*.

79 Kate Moore, "Declared Insane for Speaking Up: The Dark American History of Silencing Women Through Psychiatry," *Time*, June 22, 2021.

80 In 2024, some of the charges in New York were overturned on a technicality. See Maria Cramer, "Harvey Weinstein's New York Conviction is Overturned," *New York Times*, April 25, 2024.

81 Jodi Kantor and Megan Twohey, "Harvey Weinstein Paid Off Sexual Harassment Accusers For Decades," *New York Times*, October 5, 2017; Ronan Farrow, "From Aggressive Overtures to Sexual Assault: Harvey Weinstein's

Accusers Tell Their Stories," *New Yorker*, October 10, 2017; Laura Yuen, "How Minnesota Native Gretchen Carlson Faced Down a Giant and Propelled the #MeToo Movement," *Star Tribune*, September 19, 2023; Gabriel Sherman, "Megyn Kelly Told Murdoch Investigators That Roger Ailes Sexually Assaulted Her," *New York Magazine*, July 19, 2016.
82 Peterson, *Too Fat, Too Slutty, Too Loud*, xv.
83 Monica Lewinsky, host, *Reclaiming*, "Tarana Burke," Wondery, March 18, 2025, 60 minutes.
84 Michelle Penelope King, "Alyssa Milano on What is Next for #MeToo," *Forbes*, February 27, 2018.
85 Tarana Burke, *Unbound: My Story of Liberation and the Birth of the MeToo Movement* (Flatiron Books, 2021); Lewinsky, "Tarana Burke."
86 Lewinsky, "Tarana Burke."
87 Sarah Marshall, host, *You're Wrong About*, 2018–present.
88 Hobbes and Marshall, "Tonya Harding"; Sarah Marshall, "Remote Control: Tonya Harding, Nancy Kerrigan, and the Spectacles of Female Power and Pain," *The Believer*, January 1, 2014; Sarah Marshall, "Making an Ice Queen," *The Baffler*, December 11, 2017; Yarrow, *90s Bitch*.
89 Kim Masters, "Lorena Bobbitt: Sex, Lies, and an 8-Inch Carving Knife," *Vanity Fair*, November 1, 1993; Charles Krauthammer, "Revenge Disguised as Self-Defense," *Washington Post*, January 13, 1994; Eric Shorey, "6 of the Most Insane Things Howard Stern Said About Lorena Bobbitt," *Oxygen True Crime*, February 19, 2019.
90 David Margolick, "Lorena Bobbitt Acquitted in Mutilation of Husband," *New York Times*, January 22, 1994.
91 Phyllis Chesler, *Patriarchy: Notes of an Expert Witness* (Common Courage Press, 1994).
92 *Simone Biles Rising*, directed by Katie Walsh, television series (Netflix, 2024).
93 Yarrow, *90s Bitch*.
94 *I, Tonya*, directed by Craig Gillespie (30West, 2018).
95 julieta.la.chulita (julieta.la.chulita), TikTok.
96 *At the Heart of Gold: Inside the USA Gymnastics Scandal*, directed by Erin Lee Karr (SJ Gibson Films, 2019).
97 *Simone Biles Rising*, Walsh.

CHAPTER FOUR

WHEN WOMEN OCCUPY A SPACE THAT IS NOT THEIRS

HARASSMENT: GET USED TO IT

When six women fell to the ground after running the 800-meter track and field race in the 1928 Olympics, the event was forbidden for women through the 1960s.[1] Never mind that the women fell from *joy* at completing their race and that the journalists watching the race fabricated the falls as a *collapse*. This framing is key: To fall from joy versus to collapse from exhaustion. A slight difference in word choice can blossom into a significant change in perception. This framing foments and normalizes the understanding of where and how women belong (or not). In 1928, it also solidified the belief that women should not engage in vigorous athletic pursuits (never mind that women had been engaging in physical labor for eons and that domestic labor, especially before electricity, was highly demanding). Critics warned that physical activity and competition might disrupt the reproductive organs, causing the uterus to fall out.[2] And, as we have already seen, a woman is, conventionally, only as valuable as her ability to reproduce.

Those six women did not mark the end of women in sports in any way. But an important stage was set: Women who attempt to occupy space that is not theirs will be pushed out, sometimes quite literally. For example, by sneaking onto the course, Bobbi Gibb became the first woman to run the Boston Marathon in 1966, when women were not officially allowed to run. Race director Will Cloney rejected her application to participate and told her that women were not "physiologically capable of running 26 miles;" never mind that Gibb had run up to forty miles in training to prepare for the race.[3] She chose to run the marathon anyway. On the course, fellow runners and spectators supported and cheered for her. One year later, when Kathrine Switzer registered for the Boston Marathon, she did so as "KV Switzer," at a time when there was no question of gender on the registration form.[4] Race official Jock Stemple attempted to rip Switzer's race bib off her body *while* she was running.

Caster Semenya, a South African runner who has won two Olympic gold medals, three world championships, and more than a dozen Diamond League events, was prevented from competing in 2019 by the International Association of Athletics Federations (IAAF) because of her difference in sex development (DSD). Semenya has a vagina, but no uterus and cannot menstruate; her body produces elevated testosterone levels, so she is more muscular and has a deeper voice than most women, including women athletes. In no way can Semenya biologically create a child. In her memoir, she notes,

> Like every human being, I am many things—a proud Black woman from Limpopo, a rural province in South Africa, a daughter, a sister, a wife, and now I am a mother to two baby girls ... I feel and I hurt just like a regular person, although I am not considered by science or some people to be a regular woman.[5]

Semenya quotes Sebastian Coe, the president of the IAAF, as stating, "No line is more important, no line more worth protecting, than the difference between men and women in sports competition."[6] Left unaddressed—by Coe and others like him—is *why* this is the most important line in sports and *what* women and men are being protected from. Semenya has been banned from running because women are a protected class and her DSD is "considered a threat to the line between genders."[7] When women dare to cross boundaries into places that are not deemed traditionally feminine, what do they find?

This chapter focuses on women who challenge spaces where the question of whether they belong or not remains unsettled. The chapter addresses feminist punk rock musician and artist Kathleen Hanna, whose artistry spawned the feminist youth movement Riot Grrrl and whose music challenges the gendered norms of punk rock, and Anita Sarkeesian, Brianna Wu, and Zoë Quinn, who were digitally attacked and doxed, in what became known as Gamergate, for being involved in video game development, participation, and critique. The chapter argues that when women step into places that are not "theirs," and do so in ways that do not capitalize on mainstream sex appeal or sexual availability, they are subjected to emotional and physical threats. Equally problematic, when women step into places that *are* theirs, such as the role of presidential First Lady, they are *also* set up for emotional difficulties that arise from conflicting expectations about the performance of those roles.

TERRITORIAL RESTRICTIONS: PUNK ROCK

For a brief moment in time, mainstream America saw what it would look like for girls and young women to occupy, powerfully and with great conviction, a space that was not theirs. Largely rooted in punk music, art, and subversive appearances, such as pairing babydoll dresses with combat boots, the Riot Grrrl movement was centered on fanzines, indie rock, and cultivating forms of self-protection during a time when young women lacked codified protections. The name itself was a way to push back against the dismissive way all women were referred to as "girls." Changing the spelling to "grrrl"—evoking a growl—challenged accepted notions of femininity.

In an otherwise fluff piece on the 1990s Riot Grrrl movement, *Newsweek* observed with callous fatalism, "All girls get harassed. Most learn during adolescence to ignore it, hoping it will end."[8] While the article was mostly respectful of the anger of the teen girls and young women who, in the 1980s and 1990s, flipped the script by finding release and mutual support in the typically male domain of fanzines, punk music, politics, and fashion, it provided a superficial, non-threatening representation of the movement.

Newsweek's coverage conveyed a barely restrained awe at the political awareness of teen girls and young adult women. Overall, the piece worked to normalize the Riot Grrrl movement for *Newsweek*'s non-Riot Grrrl readers, emphasizing, for instance, how mainstream pop culture, including Madonna and *Sassy* magazine, supported it, and how the movement was, the magazine claimed, limited primarily to White, middle-class, suburban girls.

Newsweek highlighted that the politics of Riot Grrrl encouraged girls' wholesome activism (volunteering, starting school clubs) and clean living (this was not a subculture associated with drug or alcohol use). This normalization served a dual purpose: It eased the fears the *Newsweek* readership may have had about "riotous" girls, and it invoked a well-worn trope, favored by older generations whenever a younger generation questions the status quo: Like so many other things, this embrace of radical gender politics would be only a passing phase.

As part of Bikini Kill, Hanna was one of the feminist punk rockers who helped validate the Riot Grrrl movement, which included young women defying the beauty and pop culture standards of the day. A key component of the punk scene at the time, and a low-fi technology that occupied a very particular moment in history, was the zine. An abbreviation of "magazine," zines were handmade, photocopied mini-publications focused on particular topics of interest, manifestos for social change, progressive movements, and, often, tirades against capitalism and corporatized versions of popular culture. During the summer of 1991, when Hanna and her bandmates and friends were living in Washington, DC, they put together the first issue of their zine, which they named *Riot Grrrl*. They planned to produce one issue per week, using standard office paper, which was reproduced on a photocopier in the office where one of their fathers worked, folded and stapled to make small booklets, then distributed by hand. The zine was political and aggressive, acknowledging "the general lack of girl power in society as a whole, and in the punk rock underground specifically," and arguing against the Supreme Court nomination of Clarence Thomas.[9]

Hand-drawn, photocopied, stapled, and mailed, zines had a limited run of popularity until digital technological advancements began to flourish. Although Hanna and her bandmates and friends coined the term "girl power" for their zine, it was subsequently marketed and became the brand for the Spice Girls, who made significantly more money than Bikini Kill ever did. "At the time, it felt bad that I couldn't pay my rent and it seemed like the Spice Girls were making millions saying it," Hanna recalled. "It was not the feminism that I cared about."[10] Capitalizing on a new (or, more precisely, new to them) market, the major record labels softened political feminism for commercial purposes. Riot Grrrl was repackaged and repurposed as a more consumer-friendly girl power movement, exemplified by the mainstream popularity of the Spice Girls and Destiny's Child, two musical groups whose members embraced more conventional, market-friendly feminist perspectives.

Since the 1980s, Kathleen Hanna has been the lead singer of three indie punk bands, Bikini Kill, Le Tigre, and The Julie Ruin. For much of her career, Hanna has defended herself and her female colleagues, arguing that they deserve a space in punk cultures. The punk movement was understood as predominantly male; the physicality of the mosh pits at shows, not to mention the misogyny in many song lyrics, catered to adolescent boys and men, leaving female musicians and fans on the outside. Although punk music, which is inherently mistrustful of corporate culture and external authority, never claimed wide appeal, Hanna, her bandmates, and the punk subculture she helped pioneer did receive a fair amount of press. Much of it was, of course, focused on their bodies and written with shock that women could be punk musicians.[11]

One way that Hanna became more well-known, beyond punk circles, was through her connection to Kurt Cobain, the lead singer of the band Nirvana, who, after toiling for years in the underground Pacific Northwest grunge scene, was catapulted into fame in 1991, with Nirvana's smash hit, "Smells Like Teen Spirit." Hanna and Cobain were friends and, long before either of them became famous, in an otherwise forgettable moment, she wrote the phrase—smells like teen spirit—on his bedroom wall during a conversation when they were making fun of a brand of teen-focused deodorant. When Cobain wrote the song, he asked Hanna if he could borrow the phrase for its title, and she became connected to the song in perpetuity.[12] As an artist, singer, writer, and feminist activist, Hanna deserved to be known for her own work, but for years, she was most well-known as the inspiration for the title of a wildly successful, genre-shifting *song*.

The Riot Grrrl movement began before most people had access to the internet, let alone social media. Its fans and aspirants sought each other out through mixtapes, the aforementioned zines, flyers, advertisements in underground music publications, at shows, and by word of mouth. Riot Grrrl began at a time when popular psychology lamented the fragility of pre-teen and teen girls.[13] The inclusivity of Bikini Kill and their colleagues made the space for feminist punk rock more visible. Riot Grrrl shifted the gaze of the punk subculture *away* from the boys *toward* a politicized female one. The 1992 *Newsweek* article, noted above, referred to the young women of the Riot Grrrl movement as "sexy, assertive and loud."[14]

The larger feminist movement of the 1980s and 1990s was fractious, divided by many issues, including, specifically, sex and pornography, as exemplified in Chapter 2 by Paglia's reading of Madonna. In her history of the Riot Grrrl movement, writer Sara Marcus observed,

> For critiquing domestic roles, feminists were labeled anti-family; for calling out male misbehavior, they were tarred as man haters; for agitating to expand the lexicon of acceptable female appearances, they were caricatured as "someone who is masculine and who doesn't shave her legs and is doing everything she can to deny that she is feminine."[15]

Embroiled in all of this was the reality that *older* feminists were not taking into account the concerns and interests of young women or what they could bring to the movement. What young women at the time saw was a feminist movement primarily focused on debates about what other *adults* were doing. Younger women did not see themselves in this movement, and were less likely, for example, to be concerned with the labor market and workplace equity, because they were trying to survive in school and at home. What could young women do to be seen and heard? Hanna became a role model for other Riot Grrrls partly because of the zine she and her band created, but also because she exemplified young feminist activism. In fact, Hanna started Bikini Kill partly because of a conversation she had with feminist author Kathy Acker, who suggested Hanna do so as a way to be heard.[16]

Because girls and young women lacked significant access or influence in the media, they had to find innovative ways to be seen and heard. Girls and young women interested in feminist ideals and feminist politics needed to carve out their own space. The feminism of older adults left them out by focusing on issues that did not (yet) concern them, and mainstream culture wanted them to be conventionally docile and apolitical.

In 2024, Hanna released her memoir *Rebel Girl: My Life as a Feminist Punk*, which tells the intertwined stories of her life and her experiences in the feminist punk rock movement. The process of writing the book was draining, Hanna explained, requiring her to relive past struggles. At one point, she stopped writing, sought therapy, and was diagnosed with PTSD, which helped her get the treatment she needed.[17]

Born into a financially struggling family that moved back and forth between Oregon and Maryland, Hanna and her sister were raised by their abusive, alcoholic father and a mother who did what she could to protect her daughters. As a teenager, Hanna saw the 1980s female new-wave band The Go-Go's and realized that Charlotte Caffey "played lead guitar like it was a totally normal thing for a girl to do, which made it a totally normal thing for a girl to do."[18] The ability to see someone do something that had otherwise seemed an utter fantasy shifted her ambitions. When Hanna struck out on her own, she was determined to live her life as a feminist artist, including, and especially as, a musician.

At a pivotal moment in her life, her roommate was attacked and nearly raped during a robbery in their apartment, which inspired Hanna to volunteer at a domestic violence center in Olympia, Washington.[19] As part of that volunteer work, she started a discussion group where women were invited to talk about their trauma.[20] Hanna credits this work for helping her learn more about women's lives, about feminism, and about understanding and making sense of her own experiences of being raped.[21] In a seeming contradiction, she also worked as a dancer at various strip clubs. Hanna was neither shy nor ashamed about the work, which provided her with the income to pay her bills and pursue her passion for music and art. She did not see dancing as antithetical to her feminism. When Bikini Kill gained more recognition in the punk scene, this choice, and her lack of chagrin about it, brought ire from crowds who were contending with what they saw as mixed messages. She recounted that at one show, audience members screamed, "How can you call yourself a feminist when you're a stripper?" and "It's one or the other!"[22] These reactions perpetuate the notion that feminism can only be one thing: "Good" feminists would never earn their livings as sex workers.

The feminist punk scene, always pitted in opposition to its

male counterpart, faced its own challenges, including especially attempts to create safe spaces for female fans. Though the punk subculture prided itself on challenging the mainstream, in many ways it replicated the mainstream in its treatment of gender. Girls interested in punk music "found more of the same crap. Boys' efforts were lauded and girls' were unrecognized. Objectification and sexual assault went unaddressed."[23] Girls and young women had to work doubly hard to make space where they were centered, included, and not just holding boys' jackets when they dove into the mosh pit. Many female artists, including Hanna, made concerted efforts to hold space for girls and women. Hanna remembers,

> I had a bunch of addresses of women that I'd collected on our previous tour, so I sent out postcards asking them to come to our shows and bring more girls. "Draw hearts and stars on your hands," it read, "and if you see a girl with hearts or stars go ask her if she got a postcard too, strike up a conversation." The postcards worked: way more women were showing up to our shows. Between songs, I would ask if any girls had zines for sale and bring the writers on stage to show their work to the audience. A few times women took to the stage for other reasons, like if a man was fucking with them and they wanted to point him out. I was saying, "Girls to the front" at all our shows now.[24]

Marcus—who titled her book about the Riot Grrrl movement, *Girls to the Front*—tells the story of how she first learned to identify fellow fans and found her way into a Riot Grrrl discussion group. These discussion groups, which in many ways echoed the consciousness-raising conversations of the second-wave feminist movement, chipped away at the isolation of teen girls and young adult women who did not feel seen in the pop culture of the era. The conversations became havens for young women, "stuck in that aggravating period of time when girls get hit from all sides, belittled as children *and* sexualized as women. They needed safety and support; they needed one another."[25] In reaching out to girls to come to the shows, Hanna increased female attendance by creating safe spaces and foregrounding girls' experiences. "Girls to the front" was both practical—making a safe space for women in an environment that did not otherwise welcome them—as well as symbolic—centering women as key stakeholders in this subculture.[26] At shows, Hanna often addressed male violence in song lyrics and during between-song conversation; this led her to invite young women to come talk with her after the show about their own trauma, as a processing mechanism, which was affirming but also exhausting for her.[27]

Even as a woman occupying a space that was not automatically hers, Hanna, too, had to learn lessons about inclusion and support. The women who occupied punk spaces were most often White and from middle-class families, affording them both race and class privilege. One might expect the feminist punk scene to be fully inclusive—after all, as outsiders themselves, one might assume that members would recognize and respect one another's outsider statuses. However, this was not entirely the case. Hanna shared her own awakening, relating an occasion when she realized that "many BIPOC women were as disappointed in White punk feminists as I'd been by White male punks."[28] She also realized that her phrase "Girls to the front," which invited those who identified as *girls*, centralized a gender binary. Trans people and people of color interested in punk music were afforded less safety and faced greater exclusion than White, cisgender girls. This outsider status is evident within and across professions and subcultures where women are not thought to belong. If the world of feminist punk rock could be cruel, so, too (in similar and different ways), is the world of gaming.

TERRITORIAL CRUELTY: GAMING

The world of video gaming—which encompasses not only playing games but also the industry that creates them—is predominantly male territory. Women who occupy the space are in the minority. Highly sexualized female bodies play a large role in game *content*, but real women involved in game creation, development, and critique are often treated as interlopers or threats to the industry. For example, at one 2014 game jam, where groups competed in rapid-fire game creation, poor event planning led to several technical and structural problems. One major disruption occurred when multiple teams were goaded because they included female members, with comments running the gamut from accusations that those teams were at a *dis*advantage because they included women, to assertions that this was an *advantage* for the teams that had *pretty* women.[29] Between 2012 and 2014, three women—Zoë Quinn, Anita Sarkeesian, and Brianna Wu—became emblematic of all the women who were harassed or doxed online and harassed or threatened at their homes, in what became known as Gamergate, a campaign waged against these women for their criticisms of the gaming industry in which they worked.

The hashtag #gamergate was first used by actor Adam Baldwin, reposting a lengthy attack against Zoë Quinn, a developer and gamer, by her ex-boyfriend Eron Gjoni. While the initial attack was against Quinn, the hashtag expanded as a means to attack any woman in gaming, including, but not limited to, Quinn, Sarkeesian, and Wu.[30] At various points, all three women had to relocate from their homes to protect themselves and their privacy. For several years, none of them could go out in public without the protection of security services. Gamergate was a "concentrated harassment campaign" to remove women from gaming, with Quinn, Sarkeesian, and Wu at the center of its ire.[31]

Men regularly expressed anger at women involved in video gaming, often seeking to exclude them from participating as developers or gamers. Figures like Quinn, Sarkeesian, and Wu threatened male power in the industry. Quinn first became known for creating *Depression Quest,* a non-traditional role-playing game (RPG) that used gaming to navigate mental health struggles. After their breakup, Gjoni lambasted Quinn in an online essay that alleged she had sex with influential people in the industry as a means to advance her career.[32] People in chat rooms like 4Chan exploited the leak of Quinn's personal information, shared nude photos of her, and carefully calculated other crude attacks on her.[33]

Gjoni's diatribe, which expanded to a blog series he called *The Zoe Post,* laid out in angry detail a number of people Quinn slept with, while they were together and after they had broken up, as well as a litany of lies she allegedly told him.[34] This relationship and its highly publicized demise illustrated a shift in how bad breakups were managed. While bad breakups have been happening for as long as people have partnered and separated, the internet has changed how people can react to bad breakups, giving them new ways to exact public revenge, for anyone to see. Had this breakup happened before the rise of the internet, it might still have been terrible and drawn out, but it would likely have remained mostly private, known primarily by a close circle of friends and family.

Gjoni's blog post reads as the tale of a truly dysfunctional relationship gone wrong. Even *if* Quinn did all the things Gjoni alleged, his response—smearing her publicly in ways that threatened her physical and emotional security—was highly disproportionate and, because it was digital, nearly impossible to undo. Gjoni was angry, and Baldwin's commentary on the blog amplified its reach.[35] The consequences for Quinn and other women in gaming were truly horrific. At its *least* harmful (but still unbelievably tacky), Gjoni referred to Quinn with the moniker "Five Guys," using the name of the popular fast-food chain as a reference to the number of other men she slept with while they were together. At its most harmful, Quinn was publicly shamed and doxed, and had to move out of her home on multiple occasions as a result. The lack of awareness of how to manage *digital* harassment left Quinn isolated:

> I appealed for help through official channels, early and often. I spent countless hours documenting everything that was happening in reports to tech platforms, only to be shrugged off. I talked to lawyers and took out restraining orders, only to find myself beating my head against the brick wall of a legal system ill-equipped to handle the idea that anything real happens on the internet.[36]

The question of what is "real" on the internet had a direct impact on media critic Anita Sarkeesian, who ran the *Feminist Frequency* blog, which critiqued female tropes in pop culture, including, but not limited to, video games. Sarkeesian launched a Kickstarter campaign to fund the site, which garnered new attention from within the gaming community. Sarkeesian's interest in video games was born of a desire to acknowledge that gaming was a serious part of pop culture and to create a space where games can "portray women as capable, complex, and inspirational."[37] Evidently, through this misogynist lens, a capable, complex, and inspirational woman is one who will accept violence to her terrestrial and digital self. In response, men in the gaming community attacked, stalked, doxed, and threatened to bomb public events where she was speaking. An anonymous gamer built and published a game called *Beat Up Anita Sarkeesian*, where players could click on an image of her to add injuries to her face.[38] In defense of the game, the creator stated, "She claims to want equality: well here it is."[39]

In response, Sarkeesian used her blog to repost screenshots of Twitter comments about her, many of which characterized her as a bitch, whore, or cunt—all slurs that specifically degrade and insult women. Sarkeesian's blog also documented numerous Tweets that threatened her with rape and murder.[40] Digital vandals defaced Sarkeesian's Wikipedia page with slurs, pictures of sex acts, and death and rape threats, as journalist Helen Lewis documented; some of the *less* offensive comments included, "Why do you put on make-up, if everything is sexism? ... You are a hypocrite fucking slut," and "I'll donate $50 if you make me a sandwich."[41]

Even if Sarkeesian was an interloper in the gaming community, who lacked experience as a game developer, why attack her in such a visceral, gender-focused way, if not because of rampant sexism? If her critiques were so invalid, and she genuinely lacked insight into the world of gaming, why not critique her for insufficient insight? The only plausible answer is because the community was both mad at the criticism *and* that the criticism came from a woman. She was an outsider because of her gender, and for how being a woman informed her critique, not because of her knowledge. While Sarkeesian was not a gamer, and therefore might justifiably be subject to more constructive critique because of a lack of insider knowledge, the same cannot be argued about Brianna Wu.

Brianna Wu is a game developer and computer programmer who has defended women's roles in gaming, for which online trolls cruelly and repeatedly doxed her. In 2014, Wu publicly commented on the attacks against women in gaming and subsequently was attacked herself. Screenshots of the gaming site Kotaku captured information about an account called "Death to Brianna," whose user revealed Wu's home address and threatened her with death and sexual violence. Wu's personal information was also posted in the chatroom 8chan.[42] The attacks blended misogyny with racism and extended to disparaging attacks on her Asian husband. Wu received an email stating, "Women are the niggers of gender ... If you killed yourself, I wouldn't even fuck the corpse."[43] She writes, "If you are a woman working in the gaming industry, especially in a public way, you're going to experience harassment."[44] It is not a question of *maybe*, and Wu subsequently shared stories of four women who experienced extreme vitriol in gaming, citing common themes of disproportional criticism, assumption of privilege based on looks, belittling the seriousness of harassment, and assumptions that women simply do not like gaming. Maybe one reason why more women are not involved in gaming is because of the terrible treatment they receive, which ruins the love of the field. In order to do what one loves, must one endure unabashed and continuous cruelty? Maybe adopting a less-loved, but also less dangerous, hobby becomes understandably more appealing.

While most mainstream press defended the women named and harassed, those defenses were critiqued by gamers as coming from outsiders who were unfamiliar with the subculture of serious gamers.[45] For example, in his 2017 book, *Inside Gamergate*, gamer James Desborough argued that the real problem with Sarkeesian and *Feminist Frequency* was that she did not truly represent the gaming community.[46] Desborough claimed she lacked context and, therefore, credibility. Addressing the explicit digital attacks on Sarkeesian, he maintained that few media outlets that focused on gaming took her seriously because of her lack of expertise. The attacks were professional, not personal, because she knew so little about gaming. Rather than tackling the very real abuse that Sarkeesian, Quinn, or Wu faced, Desborough fed into beliefs that online attacks are not actually problematic, quoting rap artist Tyler, The Creator, who tweeted, "How The Fuck Is Cyber Bullying Real Hahahaha Nigga Just Walk Away From The Screen."[47] This perspective aligns with Quinn's observation that the law struggles to manage digital criminality; the serious impacts of cyberbullying require more than simply turning off a screen, which is, at best, a partial solution. Logically, perhaps, no one is *forced* to monitor cruel posts or bad online press about themselves. But what happens when online cruelty is intentionally carried over to one's real, terrestrial life, via doxxing and its consequences?

Desborough further claimed that Sarkeesian monetized her victimhood, ultimately profiting from the mistreatment, because it generated more attention for her concerns. He pointed to data that shows men are more likely than women to suffer harassment in the gaming world. This might well be true, but Desborough failed to clarify by whom men are harassed, whether the data acknowledge that men occupy more space in the gaming world (which would, of course, mean that their harassment numbers are higher), or whether online harassment translates to harassment offline. When "properly understood," he contended, Gamergate was simply a "community coming together to defend their hobby and art form."[48] Similarly, Desborough alleged that Quinn profited from "the power of being a victim."[49] Desborough defended Baldwin's attack on Quinn, arguing that it was a rare instance where a political conservative took a public stand against a perceived injustice. But, Baldwin's position was manipulated, Desborough contended, in ways that made it seem like a "reactionary backlash against progressivism," rather than accurately interpreted as a "libertarian backlash against authoritarianism and corruption."[50]

There is one more cruel irony to all of this: The first person credited with developing a video game in which players assume the identity of a character in a developing plotline was a woman. Elementary school teacher Mabel Addis partnered with IBM in the 1960s to build an educational game, using newly developed computer technology. She created *The Sumerian Game*, which taught the basics of economic theory to sixth graders as their characters made choices and advanced through increasingly complex financial situations.[51] However, much like the "human computers" of the 1950s, discussed in Chapter 1, Addis's original contribution to gaming remains unknown to most gamers, and ignored—if not erased—by the gaming industry, which has quickly become male-dominated.

WOMEN FRONT & CENTER
(WHO STILL DO NOT BELONG): FIRST LADIES

The 2020 election of Joe Biden as President of the United States introduced a new role in US politics, the role of Second

Gentleman. With the election of Kamala Harris as the first female Vice President, her husband, Doug Emhoff, became the first person to assume this role, raising new twists on old questions about what the spouses of newly elected presidents and vice presidents would do with their newfound prominence: Would Emhoff give up his job? How would he support Harris, his wife, as vice president, as well as the office of the presidency? The questions about Emhoff's intentions served as a reminder that the role of First Lady (and Second Lady), though well-established in the presidential retinue, nevertheless lacks a clear job description. Until the 2020 election, presidents and vice presidents had always been the male partners in heterosexual marriages, so their spouses' titles assumed conventional gender roles. Historically, White House life and the office of the First Lady centered and silenced the women in that role. Though very much at the center of attention, First Ladies seldom spoke for themselves. If and when they did so, crossing whatever amorphous line demarcated the boundaries of appropriate conduct for a First Lady, the power of patriarchy was always there to rein them in, subtly but firmly.

In a letter to Betty Ford, the First Lady from 1974 to 1977, a writer demanded, "You are constitutionally required to be perfect."[52] Although objectively false, the letter writer's expectation illustrates a deeper issue regarding the role of First Lady: There is "little consensus about what makes a First Lady 'good' or 'bad,'" however, it is clear that qualities that may have helped get her husband elected, such as "independence, forthrightness, even loyalty" can work against her once he is in office.[53]

In 1858, *Harper's Weekly* referred to Harriet Lane, niece of President James Buchanan, as "Our Lady of the White House." A bachelor, Buchanan brought Lane to accompany him at presidential events. Two years later, *Frank Leslie's Illustrated Newspaper* referred to Lane as "the first lady in the land."[54] Not until 2017, when Ivanka Trump began to fill in for her stepmother, Melania Trump, who had rejected much of the work expected of her as part of White House life, did another family member take on the role. There are so many expectations of a First Lady, yet no guidance, other than the correspondence shared between the women who have served in the role.[55] While there are metrics to help understand what makes a president successful, there are none for First Ladies.

The women who have served as First Ladies have taken on multiple roles, including raising children; serving as confidante to, and protector of, their husbands; and negotiating the relationship between East and West Wing staffs and priorities.[56] In general, those with jobs prior to becoming First Lady give up their paid professional work, hide their personal struggles (including, but not limited to, addiction, illness, infidelity, and mourning children and husbands who died in office), and live in the spotlight.[57] It is an unwritten rule that First Ladies take on a "cause," preferably something anodyne and apolitical. Laura Bush championed literacy and, after the 9/11 attacks, became an advocate for Afghan women and girls. Michelle Obama advocated for a fitness and nutrition program for children. Thus far, Jill Biden is the only First Lady to maintain her professional work, as a college professor at Northern Virginia Community College, while her husband served as President.[58] This decision was fraught with both controversy and insult. Before Joe Biden was even inaugurated, Jill Biden was criticized by essayist Joseph Epstein for referring to herself as "doctor," although she holds a terminal degree in education, and it is common practice to call professors by that title.[59] After a little more than a year in the White House, Jill Biden faced the impossible struggle between waiting too long versus not waiting long enough to begin to shape her legacy as First Lady by choosing a cause to champion.[60] Her defense for not having chosen a specific cause was that she was focused on healing a nation still in the depths of the COVID-19 pandemic and reeling from the January 6, 2021, attack on the US Capitol, which seemed unsatisfactory to many.[61] As First Lady from 2017 to 2020, and again starting in 2025, Melania Trump has been inconspicuous, making it clear that she was not interested in the role of First Lady and preferred to stay in New York City. Her cause, "Be Best," aimed to eradicate child bullying, but was generally received with skepticism, given her husband's reputation as a bully.[62] As of this writing, she has adopted no new cause, nor has she revived "Be Best."

Many First Ladies, including Edith Bolling Galt Wilson, Eleanor Roosevelt, and Nancy Reagan, were rumored to have assumed presidential duties themselves when their husbands were publicly or privately incapacitated.[63] Roosevelt maintained a rigorous travel schedule in her advocacy of women's rights, bringing home valuable information to her husband, Franklin, whose polio prevented him from traveling more frequently.[64] Wilson cared for her husband, Woodrow, and made many decisions in his name after he suffered a stroke. Reagan supported Ronald in what many, then and since, presumed to be dementia during his term in the White House. Laura Bush did not have career aspirations as a First Lady; as an introvert, she preferred to stay in the background. Nevertheless, in the immediate wake of the September 11, 2001, terrorist attacks, she delivered her husband's presidential radio address, and she took on the responsibility of talking with victims' families.[65]

Modern First Ladies, especially those who held their own jobs before marriage or prior to assuming the role, occupy a complicated position. They help their husbands get elected (often, multiple times), and then adopt the lesser role of unpaid spouse with limited flexibility.[66] First Ladies from the late twentieth century to the present also contend with rapid technological advancements that reveal more of their behind-the-scenes work; it would be incredibly difficult for First Ladies Wilson, Roosevelt, or Reagan to wield the same amount of backstage control in the current digital media environment.

Despite a lack of clarity about the role and its formal expectations, it is easy to violate the tacit rules about what makes a "perfect" First Lady. For example, Michelle Obama was the first Black First Lady, and therefore subjected to both racist and sexist attacks. In addition to finding a cause to champion, Obama suffered regular public attacks, including comments on her body, that questioned whether anything she did was a result of her role as an attorney, wife, mother, and First Lady, or because of her role as a *Black* attorney, wife, mother, and First Lady. When she commented at the start of her husband's presidential campaign that this was the first time she had been proud of her country, the backlash was swift, and pundits opined that her straightforward style needed to be softened.[67] Fox News referred to her as "Obama's baby mama" during the 2008 campaign, in a story about whether or not she was a political liability.[68]

No other First Lady pushed the boundaries—or had the boundaries pushed against her—so completely as Hillary Clinton, including, but not limited to, her campaign for single-payer health insurance, which was a fractious partisan issue and, therefore, a radical departure as a First Lady's cause. As First Lady, Hillary Clinton quickly established her own offices in the West Wing (where the President's office is located), rather than the expected space of the East Wing (where other work of the White House takes place), to the ire of her husband's staff and the fascination of the American people.[69] The gossip and rumors about Hillary Clinton were relentless, including that she physically assaulted her husband, a story all the more powerful because it challenged acceptable notions of femininity while simultaneously emasculating Bill Clinton. According to Kelsey McKinney's deep-dive into the culture of gossip, she argues that the rumors around Hillary Clinton during her time as First Lady helped crystallize a "national insecurity ... about the role of women and the kind of power they might have going into the new millennium."[70] Hillary Clinton is the only First Lady (thus far) to have embarked on a successful public service career after leaving the office of the presidency, first as a Senator of New York, then as Secretary of State in the Obama administration, and, most recently, as the Democratic presidential candidate in the 2016 election.[71] She has always had professional ambitions, many of which were thwarted, ironically, the closer she came to power.

While Hillary Clinton carried the burden of those rumors, it is entirely likely that their starting point was an otherwise offhand comment made by Bill Clinton while on the campaign trail when he promised that by electing him, the American people would get a "buy one get one free" deal with Hillary Clinton at his side.[72] Although he meant this in a positive way, it proved problematic because much of the public never warmed to the idea of an ambitious, politically proactive First Lady. It is also awkward that Bill Clinton described himself and Hillary in market terms as a reduced-price sales promotion.

First Ladies are often referred to informally by their first names, a slight that can be seen as an infantilization that plagues all women, famous or otherwise. When Barack Obama and Hillary Clinton were campaigning for the 2008 presidential nomination, his senate title was used more frequently than hers, and she was called by her first name more often.[73] While it might be argued that she had to be called "Hillary" because of the *other* Clinton who had been president, would it really have taken up so much more space and time to refer to each of them by their full names, or to rely on the commonsense of the people who would know that *Bill* Clinton was not running for another term (for which he would be constitutionally forbidden)?

To use one's first name is to presume a certain level of familiarity that most of the electorate does not have with the candidates. While it might be calculated in a way to make politicians appear more approachable, it can be done to men without being a mark against their gender, such as Bernie (Sanders) or Joe (Biden). Hillary Clinton suffered this indignity multiple times in her husband's political career. When she still went by Hillary Rodham, both her maiden name as well as her professional name in her work as a lawyer, this was deemed problematic for her husband's work as Attorney

General, and subsequently Governor, of Arkansas.[74] I wonder how *her* last name could have such significant influence on *his* success. As her husband gained public prominence, Hillary Clinton shifted her focus from policy work to join Bill's campaign. The irony, of course, is that the times when Bill Clinton *lost* elections, and therefore temporarily lacked a paid position, it was Hillary Clinton's work as a lawyer that kept the family financially afloat.[75] Hillary Clinton's unofficial job soon became to push back against "the suggestion that she was just too *much* of a certain something: too eager, too ambitious, too willing to tout her own credentials, all qualities that were expected of male politicians and male public figures."[76]

Most male politicians face at least some backlash and hatred, but these adverse reactions typically focus on their policies or ideas. As public servants who work for the people, it is expected that public officials and those seeking public office will be regularly critiqued for their policy positions and decision-making; their choices and actions affect the everyday lives of the people they represent. In the 2016 presidential election, by contrast, Hillary Clinton seemed to be the subject of hatred simply for being a woman. Many criticisms targeted her looks, her voice, and other feminine traits. As will be discussed in Chapter 6, she was not a good enough woman (even though there is no objective rubric of what that entails). Instead of critiquing her political views, her critics hated Clinton for being a woman. Social media critics deemed her unfit for the presidency but cited no justifiable reasoning other than her gender. Trump once retweeted that Clinton would not be able to satisfy America because she was unable to satisfy her husband, recalling Bill Clinton's extramarital affairs and blaming her for them.[77] In the presidential debates leading up to election day, Hillary Clinton embodied what it means to be centered and silenced: While she sat center stage, attempting to answer questions from a town hall audience, Trump paced behind her, distracting attention from the content of her answers to his own lurking physical presence.[78] Why did no moderators stop him? Was such behavior "expected" of Trump, at the expense of Clinton? Had his bullying become so normalized that his debate behavior warranted neither surprise nor rebuke?

Four years later, Vice Presidential candidate Kamala Harris challenged the gender disparity when, during her debate with the Republican Vice Presidential candidate, Mike Pence, he cut her off. Contesting Pence's interruption, Harris quickly retorted, "I'm speaking," and moved on with the content of her answer. There is no doubt that Hillary Clinton's experience in 2016 informed Harris's preparation for the debate. With the benefit of hindsight, would Harris have needed to employ such a defense if anyone had (successfully) stood up to Trump when he stalked Clinton on stage in 2016?

First Ladies are further centered and silenced by the protocol that exists for when they and their husbands leave office. Presidents may always be referred to as "president," in the present tense, while First Ladies are always referred to as "former First Ladies," in the past tense.[79] Her time in the White House may have been based on tacit expectations, but her role *after* is quite clear: Go away, quietly. Just as often, women cannot leave the office without residual attacks. Jake Tapper and Alex Thompson's dissection of the alleged cover-up of President Biden's health toward the end of his term in office lays the blame, in part, squarely on Jill Biden.[80] Trump 2.0 press secretary Karoline Leavitt tapped into this blame:

> The former first lady should certainly speak up about what she saw in regard to her husband and when she saw it and what she knew, because I think anybody looking again at the videos and photo evidence of Joe Biden with your own eyes and a little bit of common sense can see this was a clear cover up ... Jill Biden was certainly complicit in that cover up.[81]

While it might be true that Jill Biden shielded her husband's declining health from the public, how is it surprising that a wife, long-married to a public figure, chose to support her spouse? Furthermore, how can Republicans, specifically, criticize Jill Biden for allegedly doing the exact same thing that Nancy Reagan had done for her husband, Ronald Reagan? What might be more surprising, and more worthy of discussion, is how the establishment news media, including both left- and right-leaning outlets, are so swift to blame the wife rather than look internally to explore why they may have accepted stock answers, not dug deeper into questionable behavior, or followed up on difficult threads of inquiry.

WHERE WOMEN DON'T BELONG

While new career opportunities have certainly opened to women over the decades, there are still too many work environments, including the law, the military, and even certain kinds of criminal pursuits, where women's presence is deemed problematic. Women who invade spaces not deemed theirs become easy scapegoats for anything that goes wrong. Like Jill Biden blamed for hiding her husband's health problems, blaming women for taking up space that is not theirs serves as a distraction from the more difficult work of self-reflection on what it means to be so territorial.

Marcia Clark was the lead prosecutor in the 1995 O.J. Simpson trial, colloquially known as the "trial of the century," where Simpson was accused of murdering his ex-wife, Nicole Brown Simpson, and her friend, Ron Goldman. The accusations and the trial were shocking for many reasons, including Simpson's celebrity and how the case normalized a conversation on domestic violence.[82] Given the timing of the trial, when fewer women were in such spotlight leadership roles, it was novel and emotionally charged to choose a female lead prosecutor. Yes, a female prosecutor could play on the sympathies of the jury (and the public, who watched the trial in its entirety via the newly-popular Court TV cable television channel) and connect that sympathy to Brown Simpson. For this reason, a female prosecutor made sense.

At this point in history, the nation had watched an all-White, all-male Senate Judiciary Committee excoriate Anita Hill and, while opinion was still divided about the larger implications of Hill's testimony, what was clear was how easy it was to discredit a woman. The choice of a female lead prosecutor also meant that if and when anything went wrong in the trial, it could easily be blamed on her, and, as shown throughout the trial, she was easy to attack. Clark was struggling with her own legal battles, including a divorce and custody battle. She was mercilessly critiqued for her appearance, haircut, and clothing. In a proto-doxing, a nude photo of her was leaked during the trial.[83]

Who belongs in what job, even when that job is leading an illegal enterprise, is another site for centering and silencing women. Griselda Blanco, who led a massively lucrative drug cartel out of Miami in the 1980s, counters assumptions that the most powerful drug dealers are male. Her story is intriguing in part because of her wild success in the drug trade, even more so because she was a woman in a violent, male-dominated industry.

Blanco, known in the 1970s as the "Cocaine Godmother of Miami," was a Colombian drug lord, rumored to be involved in more than two hundred murders. Drug kingpin Pablo Escobar is quoted as allegedly saying, "The only man I was ever afraid of was a woman named Griselda Blanco."[84] Her success, as read through the lens of another financially successful, wildly notorious drug dealer, is connected to her adoption of masculine tropes. After creating a drug empire that brought in more than $80 million a month, she was arrested in 1985 for cocaine trafficking. Although the prosecution had enough evidence to put her away for life, a scandal in the attorney's office ruined the credibility of the main witness, who had reportedly had phone sex with the office's secretaries. This impropriety led to Blanco being sentenced to only ten years in prison. She was deported back to Colombia after her release, where she was fatally shot in 2012.

As the subject of the Netflix biopic series *Griselda*, Blanco became more widely known.[85] *Griselda* producer Eric Newman notes, "She is a true anomaly in that there has never been a woman who achieved that level of success in any drug cartel. Ever."[86] Online comments about the biopic noted how diluted the show was compared to the gruesomeness of her crimes.[87] Even the title—*Griselda*—reduces the main character to her first name, a method of infantilization.[88] As discussed in Chapter 1, there is a fear and fascination with women who engage in violence. When faced with a woman who commits violence, especially violence connected to a job not typically associated with women, the narrative often becomes muddled, and steps are taken to simplify the story and make it more palatable. Colombian actor Sofía Vergara was cast to play Blanco, and much of the press about the show focused on her looks and the changes she made to her body for the role. Vergara was labeled "unrecognizable" and critiqued as "too Latina."[89] How is this critique anything other than blatantly racist? If she is *too Latina*, what is the right amount? Prior to her dual role as the series' lead actor and executive producer, Vergara was most well known for playing stereotypical spitfire, spicy Latina characters, including her role as the much younger single-mom-turned-trophy-wife in the long-running sitcom *Modern Family*.[90] Comments on the YouTube trailer of *Griselda* included, "I love that Hollywood wasn't giving Sofía any complex roles to play so she got that executive producer title and said 'fine, I'll do it myself,' and now she's playing one of the most gangster women who ever lived. Can't wait to see it."[91] So flummoxed are we by a woman whose very non-traditional career choice also involves a great deal of violence, we resort to what we do know and what is comfortable: Commenting on her looks, body, and ethnicity.

Efforts to normalize the role of women in non-traditional spaces illustrate the hard work of trying to keep women away or minimize their roles. Although status in the military is based on blunt hierarchies, the role of *women* in the military has long been one without clarity or precision. In 1948, women were *officially* allowed in the military, though they had been serving long before then as nurses, spies, codebreakers, soldiers disguised as men, pilots, truck drivers, airplane mechanics, gunnery instructors, air traffic controllers, and naval air navigators.[92] In 1970, women were allowed to attend military academies, and in the 1990s, they began flying in combat missions and serving on Navy combat ships. Women had been studying and flying *long* before this, via "auxiliary" programs.[93] Between 1948 and 1967, women were limited to 2 percent of enlisted services and 10 percent of officer roles.[94] During Barack Obama's presidency, all combat positions, including ground forces, were opened to women.[95] By 2020, only six women had reached the rank of four-star general.[96]

There is a great deal of sex discrimination in the military, based on "stereotypic assumptions about the inferiority of women."[97] One glaring truth about women in the military is that they endure high rates of sexual assault. Between 2017 and 2019, after $200 million spent on prevention and education, there was a fifty percent *increase* in reported sexual assaults against women in uniform, while reported assaults against men remained flat.[98] While it is certainly plausible that the increase in reporting is directly linked to education and presumed greater awareness of what constitutes sexual assault, it is disturbing that the training in prevention did not do more to curb destructive behaviors or make it safer for men to come forward in reporting their own experiences. It must be noted that these are *reported* cases of sexual assault; the actual number of sexual assaults in the military is probably even larger, due to unreported cases. This disparity is illustrated in the sitcom *One Day At A Time*, where a subplot over the four-season series is how Penelope, a single mom, struggles with PTSD from her time in the military, including a sexual assault by a senior officer and mentor. She explains that she did not file a complaint because, as a woman, "Then that's all they know and that defines you."[99]

When a military service member reports a sexual assault, it is handled within the military justice system. Arguments in favor of this arrangement are grounded in the belief that military personnel have the necessary knowledge and insight to handle cases, which civilians lack.[100] As discussed earlier in this chapter, "insider knowledge" is often used as a cloak to shield certain behavior that might be deemed objectionable by someone outside the community. The insider-outsider narrative, common in the military, gaming, punk rock, and countless other areas, sets up the outsider as an uninformed adversary who cannot truly "get" the insider's knowledge or expertise. Rather than share or explain the unique qualities of what it means to be on the inside, the outsider is employed as a quick and convenient scapegoat. However, it can also be argued that by handling cases internally, the military preserves control, including its ability to cover up cases or downplay the prevalence of sexual assault as ways of protecting its image. In 2019, Senate Democrat, Jackie Speier (D-CA), called for legislation to create an independent prosecutor for military cases.[101] This conflict of interest could lead service women and men who are sexually assaulted to assume that any complaint they might register will be handled superficially.

Cruelty is the purview of patriarchy that works relentlessly to maintain its power. The logical end result of these attacks is a form of physical violence explicitly reserved for women, which is the focus of Chapter 5.

NOTES

1. John Branch, "They Called It 'Improper' to Have Women in the Olympics. But She Persisted," *New York Times*, July 10, 2024; Jere Longman, "How the Women Won," *New York Times*, June 23, 1996.
2. Longman, "How the Women Won.".
3. Roberta Gibb, "A Run of One's Own," *Running Past*, accessed July 25, 2025.
4. Kathrine Switzer, "The Girl Who Started It All," *Runner's World*, March 26, 2007.
5. Caster Semenya, *The Race to be Myself: A Memoir* (WW Norton, 2023), 3.
6. Semenya, *The Race to be Myself*, 4.
7. Semenya, *The Race to be Myself*, 4.
8. Newsweek staff, "Revolution, Girl Style," *Newsweek*, November 22, 1992.
9. Sara Marcus, *Girls to the Front: The True Story of the Riot Grrrl Revolution* (Harper Perennial, 2010), 82.
10. Fiona Sturges, "Riot Grrrl Pioneer Kathleen Hanna: 'A Lot of Men Really Get off on Watching a Woman Get Angry,'" *The Guardian*, May 13, 2024.
11. Marcus, *Girls to the Front*; Kathleen Hanna, *Rebel Girl: My Life as a Feminist Punk* (Ecco, 2024); Andi Zeisler, *We Were Feminists Once: From Riot Grrrl to Covergirl®, the Buying and Selling of a Political Movement* (Public Affairs, 2016).
12. Hanna, *Rebel Girl*; Zeisler, *We Were Feminists Once*.
13. Lyn Mikel Brown and Carol Gilligan, *Meeting at the Crossroads: Women's Psychology and Girls' Development* (Harvard University Press, 1992). Mary Pipher, *Reviving Ophelia: Saving the Selves of Adolescent Girls* (Penguin, 1994).
14. Newsweek staff, "Revolution, Girl Style."
15. Marcus, *Girls to the Front*, 50.
16. Marcus, *Girls to the Front*.
17. Sturges, "Riot Grrrl Pioneer Kathleen Hanna."
18. Hanna, *Rebel Girl*, 35.
19. Sturges, "Riot Grrrl Pioneer Kathleen Hanna."
20. Marcus, *Girls to the Front*.
21. Hanna, *Rebel Girl*; Sturges, "Riot Grrrl Pioneer Kathleen Hanna."
22. Hanna, *Rebel Girl*, 191.
23. Marcus, *Girls to the Front*, 92.
24. Hanna, *Rebel Girl*, 169.
25. Marcus, *Girls to the Front*, 90.
26. Sturges, "Riot Grrrl Pioneer Kathleen Hanna."
27. Hanna, *Rebel Girl*; Marcus, *Girls to the Front*; Sturges, "Riot Grrrl Pioneer Kathleen Hanna."
28. Hanna, *Rebel Girl*, 187.
29. Nathan Grayson, "The Indie Game Reality TV Show That Went to Hell," *Kotaku*, March 31, 2014.
30. W.A Stanley, "Gamergate Doesn't Pay: The Cautionary Tale of Adam Baldwin," *Medium*, May 21, 2017.
31. Sarah Marshall, host, *You're Wrong About*, "Phones Are Good, Actually, With Taylor Lorenz," June 25, 2024, 60 minutes.
32. Eron Gjoni, "Why Does This Exist?" *The ZoePost*, accessed August 4, 2025; Chris Tognotti, "Zoë Quinn Talks About Being Harassed Online," *Bustle*, September 29, 2014.

33 Zoë Quinn, *Crash Override: How Gamergate [Nearly] Destroyed My Life and How We Can Win the Fight Against Online Hate* (PublicAffairs, 2017).
34 Gjoni, "Why Does This Exist?"
35 She vehemently denies the allegations in her memoir and much of the mainstream press written about her support her.
36 Quinn, *Crash Override*, 19–20.
37 Simon Parkin, "Gamergate: A Scandal Erupts in the Video-Game Community," *New Yorker*, October 17, 2014.
38 *Eulogy for: Beat Up Anita Sarkeesian,* Newgrounds, July 5, 2012.
39 Sarah O'Meara, "Internet Trolls up Their Harassment Game with 'Beat up Anita Sarkeesian,'" *The Huffington Post,* June 7, 2012.
40 *Feminist Frequency*, September 4, 2014.
41 Helen Lewis, "Dear the Internet, This Is Why You Can't Have Anything Nice," *New Statesman,* June 12, 2012.
42 Stephen Totilo, "Another Woman in Gaming Flees Home Following Death Threats," *Kotaku*, October 12, 2014.
43 Brianna Wu, "No Skin Thick Enough: The Daily Harassment of Women in the Game Industry," *Polygon,* July 22, 2014.
44 Wu, "No Skin Thick Enough."
45 Stanley, "Gamergate Doesn't Pay"; Marshall, "Phones Are Good, Actually"; O'Meara, "Internet Trolls Up Their Harassment Game"; Lewis, "Dear the Internet."
46 James Desborough, *Inside Gamergate: A Social History of the Gamer Revolt* (Postmortem Studios, 2017).
47 Desborough, *Inside Gamergate*, 52.
48 Desborough, *Inside Gamergate*, 68.
49 Desborough, *Inside Gamergate*, 74.
50 Desborough, *Inside Gamergate*, 87.
51 Anna Diamond, "Overlooked No More: Mabel Addis, Who Pioneered Storytelling in Video Gaming," *New York Times*, August 27, 2024.
52 Kate Andersen Brower, *First Women: The Grace and Power of America's Modern First Ladies* (Harper, 2016).
53 Katie Rogers, *American Woman: The Transformation of the Modern First Lady from Hillary Clinton to Jill Biden* (Crown Books, 2024), xvii.
54 Anderson Brower, *First Women*.
55 Rogers, *American Woman*; Andersen Brower, *First Women*.
56 Andersen Brower, *First Women*; Rogers, *American Woman*.
57 Rogers, *American Woman*.
58 Rogers, *American Woman*.
59 Rogers, *American Woman;* Joseph Epstein, "Is There a Doctor in the White House? Not If You Need an M.D," *Wall Street Journal*, December 11, 2020.
60 Rogers, *American Woman*.
61 Rogers, *American Woman*.
62 Katy Waldman, "The Childlike Strangeness of Melania Trump's 'Be Best' Campaign," *New Yorker*, May 8, 2018.
63 Andersen Brower, *First Women*.
64 Rogers, *American Woman*.
65 Andersen Brower, *First Women*.
66 Andersen Brower, *First Women*.

67 Michael Cooper, "Comments Bring Wives Into Fray in Wisconsin," *New York Times*, February 20, 2008; Rogers, *American Woman*.

68 Rogers, *American Woman*; CBS/AP, "Fox News Calls Michelle Obama 'Baby Mama'," CBS News, June 13, 2008.

69 Andersen Brower, *First Women*; Rogers, *American Woman*.

70 Kelsey McKinney, *You Didn't Hear This From Me: (Mostly) True Notes on Gossip* (Grand Central Publishing, 2025).

71 Andersen Brewer, *First Women*.

72 Andersen Brower, *First Women*, 20; Rogers, *American Woman*.

73 Rogers, *American Woman*.

74 Rogers, *American Woman*.

75 Rogers, *American Woman*.

76 Rogers, *American Woman*, 29.

77 Jasmine Taylor-Coleman, "The Dark Depths of Hatred for Hillary Clinton," BBC News, October 12, 2016.

78 Sarah L. Kaufman, "Why Was Trump Lurking Behind Clinton? How Body Language Dominated the Debate," *Washington Post*, October 10, 2016.

79 Andersen Brower, *First Women*.

80 Jake Tapper and Alex Thompson, *Original Sin: President Biden's Decline, Its Cover-Up, and His Disastrous Choice to Run Again* (Penguin Press, 2025).

81 Diana Stancy, "Jill Biden Should Have to Answer for 'Cover Up' of Former President's Decline, White House Says," Fox News, May 29, 2025.

82 Michael Hobbes and Sarah Marshall, hosts, *You're Wrong About*, "Marcia Clark," November 14, 2019, and September 30, 2020, 60 minutes.

83 Gina Tron, "The Unbelievable Sexism Prosecutor Marcia Clark Faced During the OJ Simpson Trial," *Oxygen*, December 29, 2017.

84 Sam Warner and Rebecca Cook, "Narcos Boss Explains Why Netflix's Griselda is Separate From the Original Show," *Digital Spy*, January 18, 2024.

85 *Griselda*, produced by Eric Newman et al., television series (Latin World Entertainment, 2024)

86 Warner and Cook, "Narcos Boss Explains."

87 Kalia Richardson, "The True Story of Griselda Blanco, Deadly 'Cocaine Godmother' of Miami," *Rolling Stone*, February 10, 2024.

88 In contrast, *Narcos*, the title of the TV show focused on drug lord Pablo Escobar and his Medellín drug cartel, focuses on his *job* rather than his *first name*. See *Narcos*, created by Chris Brancato, Carlo Bernard, and Doug Miro (Netflix, 2015–2018).

89 Isabel Khalili, "This Former Sitcom Star Made History for Her Recent Dramatic Turn," CBR, August, 3, 2024.

90 Nina Metz, "Latinas on TV, from 'Modern Family' to 'Superstore,'" *Detroit News*, November 6, 2018; *Modern Family*, created by Christopher Lloyd and Steven Levitan (ABC, 2009–2020).

91 "Griselda | Official Trailer | Netflix," posted November 30, 2023, by Netflix, YouTube, 02:32.

92 Lori Robinson and Michael E O'Hanlon, "Women Warriors: The Ongoing Story of Integrating and Diversifying The American Armed Forces," Brookings Institution, May 2020; The Feminist Majority Foundation, "Women and the Military," accessed August 4, 2025.

93 Air Force Historical Support Division, "Women's Airforce Service Pilots (WASP), Air Force Historical Support Division, accessed August 4, 2025.
94 Feminist Majority, "Women and the Military."
95 Robinson and O'Hanlon, "Women Warriors."
96 Robinson and O'Hanlon, "Women Warriors."
97 Feminist Majority, "Women and the Military."
98 Dave Philipps, "'This is Unacceptable.' Military Reports a Surge of Sexual Assaults in the Ranks," *New York Times*, May 2, 2019.
99 *One Day at a Time*, developed by Gloria Calderón Kellett and Mike Royce, television series, (Act III Productions, 2017–2020).
100 Philipps, "'This is Unacceptable'."
101 Philipps, "'This is Unacceptable'."

CHAPTER 5

WHEN WOMEN ARE PHYSICALLY HARMED FOR BEING WOMEN

VIOLENCE AGAINST WOMEN

The 1994 Violence Against Women Act (VAWA), first enacted by President Clinton, codified certain acts of violence committed against women and provided women with improved legal protections.[1] Provisions within VAWA established federal rape shield laws, funding for community-based violence prevention programs, and services like rape crisis centers and hotlines.

Reauthorizations of VAWA over the years have expanded it to include LGBTQ+ concerns, provisions specific to Indigenous women's tribal sovereignty, and a more comprehensive definition of gender.[2] Without legal protections, women occupy a particularly dangerous place; women who have defied established legal norms prior to the development of any particular protections have been harmed in myriad ways, as previous chapters in this book have documented. At the heart of the struggle to address violence against women has been "the necessity of making women credible and audible."[3] Violent actions against women were largely constructed as isolated incidents by bad people in bad circumstances, rather than as systemic or chronic. VAWA "creates and supports comprehensive, cost-effective responses to domestic violence, sexual assault, dating violence, and stalking."[4] When President Biden reauthorized VAWA in 2022, more protections were included for economic justice, greater access to support and resources for people of all genders, and increased autonomy for Indigenous tribes to hold non-Indigenous perpetrators accountable.[5] Notably, the first Trump administration largely ignored VAWA, letting it linger with no changes, and it is safe to assume it will be ignored or excised in his second term.[6]

Violence against women *for being women* is largely represented by the media and narrated by law enforcement as individual acts and ignored as anything chronic. In her essay "The Longest War," Rebecca Solnit notes that "we have an abundance of rape and violence in this country and on this Earth, though it's almost never treated as a civil rights or human rights issue, or a crisis, or even a pattern."[7] Violence against women *is* systemic and is increasing, as documented by multiple human rights organizations.[8] In cases of violence against women, particularly sexual assault, both the burden of prevention and of proof is placed on the woman as victim and survivor.[9] That is, women should expect to be treated violently, and it is up to them to prevent violent acts. When women defend themselves against violence, narrow parameters restrict how and when they are expected or allowed to respond. Writing in the *New York Times*, Rachel Louise Snyder relates multiple tales of women who, after enduring years of serial violence, made self-defense survival choices, and, despite copious evidence justifying those choices, were punished for their actions, nonetheless.[10]

In the United States, violence against women *as women* is intimately connected to slavery. As cultural critic Angela Davis has written about enslaved women,

> ... they were victims of sexual abuse and other barbarous mistreatment that could only be inflicted on women. Expediency governed the slaveholders' posture toward female slaves: when it was profitable to exploit them as if they were men, they were regarded, in effect, as genderless, but when they could be exploited, punished and repressed in ways

suited only for women, they were locked into their exclusionary female roles.[11]

Women are taught to rationalize the violence committed against them. In her memoir, discussed in Chapter 4, Riot Grrrl pioneer Kathleen Hanna confessed, "I keep trying to make my rapes funny, but I have to stop doing that because they aren't. I want them to be stories because stories are made up words, and words can't hurt me. But the things I'm writing about aren't stories, they're my blood."[12] The women of Gamergate, also discussed in Chapter 4, were all threatened with bodily harm *specifically* because they were women in an industry broadly understood to be the province of men.

This chapter focuses on violence enacted upon women *because* they are women. While violence against anyone is problematic, some people are not only *more* frequently harmed by violent acts but also *less* supported in the justice-seeking process. Indigenous women across the globe and, for the purposes of this project, in the United States and Canada, face a disproportionate amount of violence. Missing and murdered Indigenous women and girls (MMIWG) is an epidemic that both law enforcement and the media have either addressed inadequately or ignored altogether. One consequence of this is an extension of tacit permission to target women with continued violence in both real and fictional narratives of abuse. Unless and until the media are willing to challenge the very premise of unfair and inadequate laws, the media's treatment of women will always be unfair and incomplete.

MISSING AND MURDERED INDIGENOUS WOMEN AND GIRLS

In her foreword to Canadian journalist Jessica McDiarmid's *Highway Of Tears*, Mary Teegee (White Wolf) writes, "Because I am an Indigenous woman, I am six times more likely to be murdered than my non-Indigenous sisters. I am considered a high risk just by virtue of being Indigenous and female."[13] Even a cursory glance at statistics of violence committed against Indigenous people, and Indigenous women in particular, reveals a terrible reality. The rate of violent crime against First Nations and Indigenous women is higher than all other populations, including non-Indigenous women, and, on average, four out of five offenders are male.[14] On reservations, murder rates of women are ten times the national average.[15]

Indigenous communities are often burdened with researching crime in their communities because local law enforcement will not. The laws relevant to investigating these crimes are unclear. For example, the issue of what law enforcement agencies have jurisdiction over tribal lands, reservations, and non-protected land is byzantine at best. Tribal law enforcement officials may or may not be authorized to pursue criminals who are not part of a reservation, depending on where the crime took place. Yet, it might be wholly unclear where, exactly, the crime occurred when a body shows up in a different location. The *crime* may have been committed in one location; its *discovery* may take place in an entirely different location, resulting in ambiguities of jurisdiction that thwart investigations and, ultimately, attempts at justice. Even worse, local law enforcement often fail to investigate the cases of missing Indigenous women and girls because crimes against them are often dismissed as a result of their own poor choices.[16]

Three laws in particular chipped away at the autonomy of Indigenous people, which constructed one part of the foundation for systemic mistreatment. In the Major Crimes Act of 1885, the United States assumed jurisdiction and undermined tribal authority, wherein tribes were not allowed to self-govern. The Indian Civil Rights Act of 1968 stipulated that tribal courts were only permitted to impose minor consequences. Finally, *Oliphant* v. *Suquamish Indian Tribe* of 1978, determined that Indian nations did not have the authority to punish non-Indian perpetrators when crimes occurred on tribal lands.[17] These laws constructed a racist and profoundly convoluted system that allowed Indigenous people to be forgotten or ignored.

Following these laws, there were three ways Indigenous women in particular were targeted. First, between roughly 1818 and 1950, after the majority of Indigenous families and communities had been forcibly relocated to presumably less-desirous geographic locations, various Christian organizations opened Native American residential schools, to which social workers took children from their families, willingly or otherwise.[18] Families were often told their children would receive a solid education, but in reality, they were more often trained for menial labor in servile positions.[19] Children were forced to have their hair cut, to adopt Western names, and to speak English (even if they had no prior knowledge of the language), and were not allowed to participate in any of their own cultural rituals; they were often beaten and assaulted.[20] Children were taken to schools far from their homes and often in extremely remote areas; their families often lacked the financial means to visit or to bring their children home, if they even knew where they were.[21]

By the early twentieth century, approximately 80 percent of Indigenous children had been removed from their homes.[22] Indigenous children often rejected the efforts of the social workers, nuns, and priests by running away from school (often to the detriment of their own health and just as often resulting in death). Whispers of the theft of children meant that families often hid their children during social services visits.[23]

The second effort at eradication, undertaken in the mid-twentieth century, hinged on a wave of Indigenous adoptions, in which children too young to have started school were taken from their homes and adopted by White, Christian families.[24] In many of these cases, children were never told they were Indigenous, and many grew up isolated and disconnected from their adoptive parents. Just as often, while they knew they were adopted (in part because they looked so different from their families), they did not know that they had been kidnapped. Simultaneously, their birth families did not know where they had been taken or how to find them.

The final attempt at eradication, in the 1960s and 1970s, targeted Indigenous women and girls who were forcibly, unknowingly, and without consent, sterilized, a part of the long line of the sexist, racist, and classist eugenics practices employed as a way to control poor and minority populations. Doctors affiliated with government-run health clinics worked to convince Indigenous women and girls that their traditional medicines had the potential to harm them and could lead to greater infant mortality.[25] When Indigenous women sought care (reproductive or otherwise), they were often told they needed a particular procedure, which was generally not well-explained to them. The women were not clearly informed on what the procedure was, that they were free to decline it, or that it would prevent them from having children in the future.[26] These women and girls may have only found out they had been sterilized when they sought further medical care to explore why they could not conceive.[27]

These attempts at eradication, false assimilation, and forced sterilization fomented a belief that Indigenous populations were expendable. This was all part of the legacy built by White settlers who saw Indigenous bodies as less than human, or, at best, marginal members of their settler-colonial culture. The enduring legacies of this cruel history include a remarkable ignorance among non-Indigenous people of the harms perpetrated on Indigenous populations, including the erasure of genocide, and an indelible belief, held overtly by some and tacitly by many more, that all Indigenous people, and Indigenous women and girls in particular, are disposable.

McDiarmid's *Highway of Tears* details the extraordinary number of missing and murdered Indigenous women and girls along the remote section of Highway 16 that runs through Northwest British Columbia.[28] In telling the stories of missing and murdered Indigenous women and girls, McDiarmid traces the family history of each girl she profiles, illustrating the generations of trauma that shaped their lives, including the histories of elder family members who were kidnapped and forced to attend residential schools, which operated to sever connections to their family, community, and culture. McDiarmid also addresses how media coverage—or, more accurately, the *absence* of media coverage—compounds the ongoing trauma. Many of the Canadian First Nations families she profiles felt that the Royal Canadian Mounted Police (RCMP) ignored cases, or blamed the victims and their families for being poor and unable to provide a "proper" (read: White, Christian) environment for their girls. The missing and murdered girls detailed by McDiarmid included girls who were responsible or irresponsible, reliable or unreliable, bold or timid, employed or unemployed, students or dropouts, in relationships or single. In other words, they were, in these ways, like any cross-section of rural youth from economically struggling communities. What distinguished these girls from their rural counterparts was that they were Indigenous and lived near the remote section of Route 16, along which many of them regularly hitchhiked—a common practice in the absence of local public transportation.

Mona Gable's *Searching for Savanna* details the murder of one young Indigenous woman in North Dakota, Savanna LaFontaine-Greywind, as a way to grasp the scope of murdered and missing Indigenous women and girls across the United States.[29] LaFontaine-Greywind was 22 years old and nearly nine months pregnant at the time of her murder, in which her baby was stolen from her via an amateur C-section. She and her boyfriend had been set to move in together, and were excited to become parents. Even though LaFontaine-Greywind had never run away from home or expressed any genuine displeasure with her life, police investigating her death presumed she left town on her own. LaFontaine-Greywind's body was found, bound in garbage bags, floating in a river. Police only superficially questioned her neighbors, despite the fact that two of them—Brooke Crews and William Hoehn, a White couple, who were eventually identified as LaFontaine-Greywind's assailants—had extensive criminal records. Crews had children of her own who had been removed from her custody by social services, and she was seeking a fresh opportunity at parenting. As a White woman, living with a White partner, she was not initially considered a suspect, despite the couple's proximity to the crime and their prior convictions.

Both McDiarmid and Gable use their stories to paint a larger picture of the brutal environment for Indigenous women and girls. Crimes against Indigenous people, and Indigenous women in particular, often go under-reported by police. In 2016, in the United States, there were more than 5,712 missing Indigenous women and girls, while the Department of Justice only logged 116 cases.[30] The US federal government does not collect statistics on missing or murdered Indigenous women and girls, and there is no federal agency where tribal members can document crimes specific to Indigenous people.[31] Most likely, any numbers reported are undercounts because of the lack of tracking.[32] Seventy-one percent of Indigenous people live in urban areas, but there is no specific research on their experiences of violence.[33]

In Canada, the RCMP put the numbers at about 1,200, with 1,000 of those assumed to be murders; however, the number is probably much higher because of how records are kept.[34] Police forces fail to act on or even report on missing First Nations women and girls. "Just another native" is how women feel they are treated by non-Indigenous law enforcement officials.[35] Often, Indigenous women and girls are blamed for their kidnappings and killings, "the result of the victim's wrongdoing rather than as what they truly are: an ongoing social failure."[36] Indigenous people are affected negatively by "the factors that make a person more likely to get in trouble: poverty, involvement with the child welfare system, abuse, addiction and homelessness. But there is something else at play in the equation: racism."[37]

Violence against Indigenous people is particularly severe for children and young people, who are disproportionately represented in the criminal justice system. Nearly half the children under the age of fifteen living in care in Canada are Indigenous, even though they are only seven percent of the population.[38] In British Columbia, Indigenous children account for less than ten percent of the population, but more than half of them live in care. Approximately twenty percent of Indigenous children in Canada have connections with social services, compared to "one in thirty non-Indigenous kids."[39]

McDiarmid tells a gruesome tale of a young Indigenous sex worker, regularly beaten and robbed by a particularly brutal client. This young woman never reported her abuse because this particular client was a provincial judge. Over several years and largely by a whisper campaign, it became known that the judge regularly solicited Indigenous teen girls, then beat them and stole back his money; when they appeared in his court on other crimes, they had no hope for justice. While this one particular individual was ultimately convicted for his crimes, this does not undo the harm he caused or the fact that his crimes were ignored for so long, to the detriment of so many young women. McDiarmid writes, "People did not trust the police; it was a near-daily occurrence for First Nations people to accuse the police of racism, brutality, apathy."[40] The system of policing is set up to fail Indigenous and First Nations people; the RCMP "are unequipped, untrained and incompetent when it comes to dealing with people different from themselves."[41] McDiarmid quotes retired Vancouver police detective Lorimer Shenher,

> You'll see heaven and earth moved because you'll see the White, straight, middle-class nuclear family, and they will tell you that those RCMP officers were like the best people they've ever dealt with and just were tireless in their investigation and worked so hard and did such a great job. They don't apply the same

standards to other people.[42]

As discussed in Chapter 1, there is evidence that prior to colonization, Indigenous women were highly revered and their safety within tribes was paramount.[43] While the murder of *any* person is disturbing and reveals the cracks in a society that lead some of its members to resort to deadly violence, the targeting of Indigenous women is particularly cruel. Before colonization, domestic violence "was not common nor was it tolerated"[44] in Indigenous communities. McDiarmid notes,

> In most Indigenous societies, men and women played complementary roles that were seen as equally valuable. Indigenous women were independent and powerful, with control over their property, sexuality, marital choices and resources. They were leaders in their communities, responsible for major decisions. They were revered and respected as the givers of life.[45]

Early colonizers documented their observations of Indigenous women, which may have made them a particular target for violence. It may have been quite clear to the colonizers that to subjugate and eradicate the populations of Indigenous people across the land, a focus on the women would be most effective. Within Lakota history, for example, women were considered sacred and deserving of protection in large part because "for nine months we carry the spirit world within our bodies before a new spirit is born into this earthly life."[46] The prevailing view of women is reflected in an oft-quoted Cheyenne proverb, "A nation is not conquered until the hearts of its women are on the ground. Then it is done, no matter how brave its warriors or strong its weapons."[47] To destroy Indigenous women by violence and murder, then, is to enact yet another chapter in a generations-long genocide. Through colonization, the culture of Indigenous communities shifted from one of safety to one of violence. McDiarmid argues, "Colonial legislation and policy deliberately set out to dismantle the long-held power of Indigenous women."[48]

Media Coverage of Missing and Murdered Indigenous Women and Girls

Local and national presses often do not cover the stories of missing or murdered Indigenous women. When they do, the violence against them is often framed as a result of the women's and girls' poor choices, such as hitchhiking, drug or alcohol abuse, or choosing to remain in unhealthy or abusive relationships. What media rarely examine is that many of these Indigenous women and girls hitchhike because there are limited alternative travel options, abuse drugs or alcohol as a coping mechanism responding to multi-generational trauma, and stay in unhealthy relationships because they may experience even greater insecurity by leaving them. The lack of connection *across* disappearances and murders frame these stories as individual tragedies rather than a tragic epidemic, fueled by systemic inequalities. For example, four months after one First Nations girl went missing in British Columbia, and eleven days after another did, there were stories in local papers, but little to no additional or subsequent coverage of their disappearances.[49] At the time of one girl's disappearance, a story about the potential development of a second hockey arena in the community got front-page coverage instead.[50] The RCMP did acknowledge a pattern of murders along Route 16, but only after a White girl went missing.[51] The White girl who went missing was *also* hitchhiking at night, but her case was framed differently by the RCMP and in the media.

Often, families of missing and murdered women and girls make use of whatever media they can. Social media, especially the content created by individuals and communities looking for information about their loved ones, becomes a way for families to seek information and support, especially when they are largely on their own.[52] Fully aware that the

White-dominant media establishment and non-Indigenous law enforcement do not tell their stories or treat their trauma with the attention needed to make change, Indigenous communities form their own defense networks and take their care and well-being into their own hands. In a refusal to be centered and silenced, Indigenous women create media campaigns, including, but not limited to, social media networks, podcasts, public art, and activist work, to tell their stories, ideally to find their loved ones, and hopefully to stem the tide of violence. For example, when Savanna LaFontaine-Greywind went missing, her family tapped into Facebook pages that shared information about other missing girls. When the local and national presses would not tell their stories, Indigenous groups gathered together online and in person to help each other out; for some families, this was the first time they realized they were not alone in their struggle.[53]

Capitalizing on a podcast-infused fascination with true crime, multiple stories of missing and murdered Indigenous women and girls have reached a new and eager audience. Season 1 of the podcast *Missing Justice* traces the 2020 murder of Christy Woodenthigh, who was run over outside of her home.[54] Journalist Connie Walker seeks justice for Indigenous people, weaving the connections between her ancestors' memories of abuse suffered at residential schools and the search for missing Indigenous women and children, across multiple investigative podcasts, including *Stolen* and *Missing & Murdered*.[55] Walker tells the stories of Alberta Williams, Jermain Charlo, and Cleo Semaganis, who were all last seen in public places, then never again; their disappearances were largely ignored by people outside their immediate community, and law enforcement assumed that each had run away. Beyond true-crime and murder stories, there are several podcasts about Indigenous concerns, including the generational trauma associated with residential schools, forced adoptions, and forced sterilizations.[56]

Multiple public art and social justice campaigns also address the lived realities of Indigenous and First Nations people. Artist Jay Soule (who works under the name CHIPPEWAR) creates propaganda-style posters to expose the hypocrisy of laws against First Nations people and to promote the work of Indigenous women and girls fighting back.[57] Red Dress Day (May 5) is an annual campaign marked by hanging empty red dresses to visually symbolize the thousands of women and girls who go missing each year.[58] Artists Against Racism curated and promoted a billboard campaign across twelve cities in Canada to raise awareness of missing women and girls.[59] Documentaries such as *Missing from Fire Trail Road* and *Sugarcane* tell the stories of missing and murdered women and girls and the direct connection to the horrors of residential schools and laws designed to eradicate Indigenous populations.[60] These documentaries, streaming on popular platforms and, in the case of *Sugarcane*, distributed by the well-resourced National Geographic, have the chance to reach a wider audience, thereby informing a larger public of the plight of Indigenous people and Indigenous women and girls specifically.

In addition to podcasts, campaigns, art installations, and documentaries designed to both raise awareness and talk back to a law enforcement that does not take Indigenous concerns seriously, fictional pop culture texts have taken on Indigenous stories, including, but not limited to, stories of missing and murdered Indigenous women and girls. As will be discussed later in this chapter, fictional representations of violence can often inform and educate audiences about real-world violence. The fourth season of the anthology show *True Detective*, for example, focused on a group of Indigenous Alaskan women seeking vengeance against a murdered female tribal member.[61] In the TV drama *1883*, a season-long storyline focused on a young Indigenous woman suffering abuse in a residential school and her choice to run away in an attempt to find her family.[62] The streaming sitcom *North of North*, which focuses on the interpersonal and professional relationships within an Inuit community in the Arctic Circle, is effortlessly inclusive and non-pathologizing.[63] The show works to emphasize the joy, connection, and love found within the community, thereby avoiding the reduction of the characters to stressed and struggling *because* they are Indigenous. Several episodes of *Reservation Dogs* focus on different characters' experiences in both nineteenth- and twentieth-century residential schools.[64] What is particularly special about *Reservation Dogs* is that the *entire* production, including the series' producers, writers, directors, cast, music, clothing, and art, is Indigenous. The only non-Indigenous people on the show are those playing non-Indigenous characters.

This attention to Indigenous people, especially to Indigenous women, can work to stem the tide of violence by increasing awareness of, and attention to, Indigenous concerns for those outside Indigenous communities. When Indigenous stories are not relegated to obscure or hard-to-find outlets, and when non-Indigenous people have the opportunity to stumble across stories on Indigenous people's lives via major entertainment options, there exists a greater chance to learn, to better understand, and, possibly, to fight for and on behalf of Indigenous people's inherent value.

PERMISSION TO ATTACK WOMEN

When she was elected as a city commissioner in Hallandale Beach, Florida, in 2018, Sabrina Javellana, then 21 years old, accepted that her progressive values would raise the ire of her political opponents in her Republican-dominant state. She grew accustomed to the vitriol directed at her on social media until one day, an anonymous commenter pointed her to nude pictures of herself posted online. Javellana had *not* taken any nude selfies, though the image of her face *was* adapted from a selfie she had taken. She was the victim of a deepfake, an image or video convincingly manipulated by AI. Javellana grew nervous about being photographed at press events and began to wear more conservative clothing, even though she knew doing so gave her little control over anyone who might want to post altered images of her. Javellana sought to educate herself about how she could legally push back against the perpetrators. She learned, through direct experience, that the law lags notoriously behind digital advancements. Javellana partnered with Senator Lauren Book (D-FL)—who had a similar experience—and testified in favor of a bill that would criminalize deepfakes. She was rebuffed by Senator Ileana Garcia (R-FL), who acknowledged that deepfakes were a terrible problem, but admonished social media users, like Javellana, for posting so many images of themselves online, increasing vulnerability to digital manipulation.[65]

This victim-blaming squares with the neoliberal emphasis on hyper-individuality. The Florida law does not acknowledge how the tech industry facilitates the public use of deepfakes, but instead focuses on the policing of individual users who manipulate images. One consequence of this legal emphasis is reduced protection for individuals whose images have been manipulated. In 2022, when the bill championed by Javellana and Book eventually passed, a slew of new digitally-altered lewd images of each of them appeared online, and Javellana and her mother were both doxed. Even after the law went into effect, *more* images of her appeared.[66]

Generative AI has made the process of manipulating images extremely easy.[67] What happened to Javellana exemplifies one current trend in the development of "nudify" sites that use generative AI to digitally "undress" pictures of fully-clothed bodies, which users of the sites can then post online.[68] The now-defunct DeepNude app had nearly forty million users in 2021, and boasted that "not a woman in the world, regardless of race or nationality, is safe from being 'nudified.'"[69] Overwhelmingly, deepfake images and videos target women and girls and, curiously, the codes to "undress" digital images of women do not work on men.[70] "Nudify" apps empower users to publicly humiliate people they hold grudges against (or strangers, who may be randomly targeted), while the law provides little recourse for those whose images have been doctored.[71] Current laws against non-consensual pornography and child pornography do not cover AI-generated images and, as currently written, proposed bills punish individual content creators rather than those who develop the apps. Therefore, individuals who get caught will be punished, but not those who profit from the development and distribution of these technologies.[72]

The development and popularity of "nudify" apps expose the misogyny and sexism of a brotopia tech industry in which most developers are male.[73] It also speaks to the lack of protection for those whose images have been falsified. At a point in the not-so-distant digital past, young women were warned not to take or share nude pics of themselves, even if the recipient promised not to share them.[74] The threat of sharing was ever-present and, in relationships gone sour, revenge porn was a ready weapon, as Zoë Quinn, the game developer profiled in Chapter 4, experienced when her ex-boyfriend and his defenders targeted her. The threat *then* was that the pictures could be widely shared; the threat *now* is exponentially more severe: *Any* pic, even where the female subject is fully clothed, may be manipulated to disastrous ends. Deepfake nude images and videos put women in an even more precarious bind in which even innocent images can be manipulated to make them appear naked. While it is good that there are laws to hold those creating and distributing the images accountable, those who are profiting the most have little incentive to stop building the technologies, because "nudify" apps are popular and, therefore, profitable for developers, and there is no legal recourse to prevent them from doing so.

Even existing laws provide only partial protections to the targets of unwanted deepfakes. Following up on violations is cumbersome and expensive. The victim of the deepfake must file a claim for *each* picture and is largely responsible for doing this on their own. In large part, because deepfakes significantly alter so much of a woman's image, victims often cannot sue for copyright infringement.[75] These stealthy, subtle attacks against women function as a type of symbolic violence, where women's bodies are remotely violated. Although they do not involve actual physical attacks, they illustrate how harming women is, by default, condoned in the absence of laws to prevent such violence and, more importantly, shared cultural values that judge the harming of women (or, more generally, any sentient being) as patently unacceptable.

As noted earlier in this chapter, there was a time in history when Indigenous women's bodies were staunchly revered and protected. To see women's bodies (or, more generally, *any* bodies) as less than sacred must be taught; it can, therefore, be untaught. Discussion of how women's bodies have been policed shows that permission to harm women is *part of* the development and maintenance of the law and the cultural values that uphold it. When news media do not interrogate or challenge those laws in their coverage and when entertainment media do not tell stories that highlight or shift the narrative, the process of silencing women is normalized and reinforced. Without holding media institutions accountable, it is easy for a negative narrative to dominate the conversation. Kathleen Hanna remembers the letters section of *NME*, a popular British music magazine, including one that read, "I am fucking horrified that crock of shit Riot Grrrl acts have the audacity to say they are discriminated against. The only reason they're fucking famous is because they are shitty women."[76] While it is problematic that this letter was written in the first place (if you don't like feminist punk rock, then don't listen to it), what is even more problematic is that the editors at *NME* thought it was publication-worthy.

Permission to Harm Young, Single, Pregnant Women

When young women found themselves pregnant in the times before *Roe* (and, in several states, today as well), they had few safe options other than carrying their babies to term and giving them up for adoption. There were no laws protecting single women, and the presumption was that a young woman who got pregnant before marriage had only herself to blame. In Ann Fessler's oral history of women who gave up babies for adoption, about 7 percent of the women "became pregnant as a result of rape—not by the violent sex criminals who have become the staple of television dramas, but by *nice* young men."[77] At the time, there was no language for distinguishing what we know today as date rape or acquaintance rape, much less laws against it. The lack of discussion and the lack of legal prohibitions made women doubly vulnerable, not only to rape by perpetrators with whom they had social relationships but also to an enforced silence when the assaultant was a husband, boyfriend, date, coworker, or neighbor.

At the same time, contraception was unavailable or inaccessible to single women. Pharmacies kept condoms behind the counter, "and in some towns just asking to purchase one might result in a phone call from the pharmacist to the boy's parents."[78] It was not until 1965's *Griswold* v. *Connecticut* that *married* couples had the legal right to receive information and services to prevent pregnancy, under the belief that this was a legal right to privacy within a marriage.[79] And it wasn't until Title IX of the Educational Amendments Act of 1972 that schools were prevented from expelling young women for being pregnant.[80]

Permission to Harm Trans People

Denial of one's identity and the development of laws to eradicate particular identities are other ways to silence women and girls. Trans girls and young women are often harmed for being trans.[81] Trans people are four times more likely than cisgender people to be victims of violent crime.[82] As of this writing, twenty-three states, including Tennessee, Oklahoma, Florida, and Texas, ban gender-affirming treatment for minors, despite the American Medical Association's research-based evidence that gender affirming care is beneficial for young people.[83]

Since 2019, American lawmakers have proposed nearly one thousand anti-trans bills, of which (as of this writing), 113 have become law.[84] The ACLU and other progressive legal organizations push back against these bills, many of which have been found unconstitutional, but even when a law is overturned or rejected, many trans girls and women are harmed in the process. Anti-trans laws focus on school curricula, library catalogs, so-called "bathroom bills," and athletics.[85] Teachers are often prevented from using a student's preferred pronouns or name, and when students push back against bathroom rules, they may be instructed to use the nurse's bathroom.[86] The Alliance Defending Freedom (ADF), a right-wing Christian-based legal organization focused on overturning any and all socially progressive laws, centered its anti-trans work on school locker rooms and bathrooms, "portraying transgender girls as a menace to others."[87]

Trans people were the focus of deep ire during the 2024 presidential election, including in advertisements, orchestrated by Republican organizations, deriding their existence.[88] Since taking office in 2025, Trump 2.0 has accelerated anti-trans rhetoric via executive orders.[89] Trans youth are centered through very public pronouncements about their supposed confusion, lack of legitimacy, and non-human status. After the 2024 death of a gender nonbinary student, Oklahoma State Superintendent Ryan Walters doubled down on his defense of his state's anti-trans laws, insisting, "There's not multiple genders. There's two. That's how God created us."[90] Kristen Waggoner, the Chief Executive and general counsel for the ADF, does not believe in transgender identity, only that "there are people uncomfortable in their bodies."[91] Concerted efforts by Republican politicians and conservative Christian organizations worked to silence trans youth. For many trans youth (and trans people, more broadly), it is safest to be in private, out of the public eye. As they become more invisible to the larger society, the message sent is that they no longer exist. Similar to pregnant young women pre-*Roe* who were hidden for the duration of their pregnancies, trans youth are to be kept a secret. "Bathroom bills" and other laws of this kind attempt to erase the very presence of trans people by regulating their bodies. If a young trans person cannot use a bathroom that matches their gender identity in their school, maybe that trans person stays home from school. If that trans person stays home long enough, and if enough trans people stay home, then trans identities slowly but surely become erased. How will trans youths' teachers or classmates know that anything is wrong when there is no longer a body in front of them, asking to be seen and to be acknowledged? Forced invisibility does not make these bodies *actually* disappear, but it does send them into a type of hiding where they can be publicly ignored and forgotten. Because the law will not keep them safe, their self-silencing becomes their only outlet for self-protection. In this way, the media can center certain bodies as problematic without actually doing the work of silencing them because these bodies may choose to self-silence as a form of protection.

Permission to Harm Women of Color

As the chapter's discussion of missing and murdered Indigenous women and girls makes clear, women of color face particularly dangerous intersections of physical and symbolic violence. When women of color are physically attacked, their stories often get less attention than the stories of White women or men of color.[92] And when news media do tell these women's stories, they often center on the women's complicity or how they should have behaved differently to prevent any negative outcome. These stories are typically treated as individual, isolated incidents rather than instances of a more systemic pattern of harm to the most vulnerable groups in our society. Through the legacy of racism connected to slavery, women of color are expected to be fully deferential in order to be accepted in society.

When police kill Black women, the narratives articulated in police and news reports often highlight what might be deemed the negative or aggressive behavior of the victim.[93] In 2015, Sandra Bland, a 28-year-old Black woman living in Texas, was arrested during a routine traffic stop. Bland was pulled over for a lane change violation, and, after she allegedly refused to comply with an officer's demands, was arrested and taken to jail. Controversy ensued. Was her arrest necessary? Would *any* White person, even one acting hostile—as Bland allegedly was—be arrested and brought to jail for a *lane change* violation? Bland was found dead in her cell, by an apparent suicide, but was there another explanation for her death? Protests and social media movements sought justice for Bland, while others criticized her and blamed her for what had happened, noting, for example, how her drug use contributed to the problem and that if "she had just obeyed the officer," none of it would have happened.[94] A CNN profile of Bland runs seven paragraphs deep before even mentioning her death; the first six paragraphs discuss her social media posts expressing her frustration with racism and police brutality.[95] In this way, CNN normalizes the actions of law enforcement, and Bland's death is framed as a terrible tragedy.

Was it a terrible tragedy? Yes. But was it an *isolated* tragedy? Or part of a larger, chronic pattern where Black women's bodies are seen as expendable and police action as excusable? In 2020, Breonna Taylor, a 26-year-old Black medical worker in Louisville, Kentucky, was shot and killed by police in her home. Police officers forced their way into the apartment Taylor shared with her boyfriend, Kenneth Walker. When Taylor and Walker heard officers opening the front door, presumably believing it was an intruder, Walker fired his gun, inadvertently shooting a police officer in the leg. The police fired back, resulting in Taylor's death. Her killing was either seen as a murder by police, one in a long line that treated Black people as expendable, or an "incident," a tragic accident by the police handling of the case.[96] The cruel and brutal irony is that the police *had the wrong apartment* and were looking for an entirely different person; they used warrantless, forced-entry rules to their advantage, and, in retrospect, the presence and use of a gun by Walker as their defense. Ultimately, felony charges against the two officers who wrote the bad warrant that led to the forced entry were dropped, and *Walker* was found legally responsible for Taylor's death. According to US District Judge Charles Simpson, Walker's "conduct became the proximate, or legal, cause of Taylor's death," because he interrupted the police "when he decided to open fire."[97] This rationalization of the error is part of a long line of excusing police officers for decisions that go wrong, rather than questioning their actions as part of a pattern of systemic violence.

When police make fatal choices, the justifications provided to explain and rationalize their behavior typically attribute blame to the person they injured or killed. In July 2024, Sonya Massey, a resident of Springfield, Illinois, phoned the police after suspecting an intruder in her home. When police arrived at Massey's apartment, they surveilled the area around her building and found no prowler. When Massey, who had been boiling water on her stove, moved the pot to the sink, one of the two police officers on the scene, Officer Sean Grayson, demanded she put the kettle down. They reportedly exchanged words, which Grayson took to be threatening. When Massey dropped the kettle, Grayson shot her three times, including a fatal round to her head.[98] The officer's defense was that he feared for his safety. He also rejected his partner's request for emergency medical care for Massey. Massey suffered from mental health struggles and, days before, her mother had phoned the police saying her daughter was having a breakdown and needed support, but not from combative police.[99]

This treatment of women becomes even more pronounced when the women are private citizens and the men are famous. A famous, even notorious, man may garner more press attention, and their behavior is contextualized and rationalized in a way that downplays or dilutes their violent behavior.

Singer-songwriter Prince, whose career spanned genres and who is remembered as embodying genius-level talent, was also known for his temper, which involved attacking women. Allegedly, Prince believed that people, especially women, needed to behave in particular ways, a rigid expectation that did not necessarily translate to his own behavior.

In the mid-1980s, Prince was involved with a woman named Jill Jones; one night, when he began kissing her friend, Jones reacted and slapped Prince. Prince responded by punching Jones repeatedly, and when she considered pressing charges, Prince's manager told her that it would ruin his career.[100] There was little to no discussion on how his violence might ruin *her life* or *her career*. In the profile of Prince that details this story, this description of his violent behavior comes *after* a paragraph where his sister contextualizes the violence of their childhood. The profile of Prince, which draws from footage from a lengthy documentary a public audience may never see because the executors of his estate are fighting it, creates space for Prince's conflicted roles to be embraced. The filmmaker Ezra Edelman "manages to present a deeply flawed person while still granting him his greatness—and his dignity."[101] This generosity is not often extended to women, who, at least in the public treatment of them, are not granted complexity of character.

This rapid escalation to gendered violence was evidently typical for Prince, with similar incidents involving other, more celebrated women. Sinéad O'Connor became globally famous, in part, because of her song "Nothing Compares 2 U," which Prince wrote. Despite the connection, the two did not know each other until after the song exploded on the music scene. Then, Prince invited O'Connor for a visit. In her memoir, she describes him reprimanding her for swearing in public, berating his staff for their lack of attention to his needs, and further scolding O'Connor for not wanting to share a meal with him. According to O'Connor, Prince pivoted and proposed a pillow fight—odd in and of itself for two adults who barely knew each other—and then proceeded to hit her with a pillow stuffed with something hard.[102] In part because of her experiences with domestic violence, O'Connor recognized Prince's mood swings and did what she could to escape his home as quickly as possible. Prince demanded that she not leave and chased her in his car when she did. While violence against any person is problematic, there is a certain hubris when a famous man enacts violence against a famous woman. As a celebrity, O'Connor occupied a powerful, if messy, public platform; there was a chance that she could have immediately gone public about Prince's mistreatment of her. In her detailed discussion of Prince's treatment of her—which took place over the course of an entire night, finally ending near sunrise—O'Connor weaves in observations, phrases, and sentences on her familiarity with domestic violence, including the decision to stay quiet. Upon reaching safety, O'Connor told her manager; she indicates that there may have been some legal proceedings, for which she wanted no part, writing, "I dunno anything more about it. I don't care either. I never wanted to see that devil again."[103] Patriarchy, once again, made space for a man to behave badly, with minimal consequence.

Another story, one that continues to develop as this text is written, demonstrates how extreme the narratives about violence against women—especially violence against women of color perpetrated by famous men of color—can become. In fall 2024, rap artist and music producer Sean "Diddy" Combs was arrested on multiple counts of violence against women, including rape, abuse, racketeering, and sex trafficking, as well as arson, bribery, kidnapping, and obstruction of justice. A video from 2016, showing Combs beating his then-girlfriend, Cassie Ventura, was made public.[104] As more about Combs's decidedly scandalous past became known and the story gained traction in the media, the women abused by Combs were reduced to accessories or props to bolster various conspiracy theories.[105]

As is often the case when stories of abuse are published and reach a wide audience, survivors are reminded of their own experiences; this was the case for journalist Danyel Smith, who, upon the publication of the charges against Combs, spoke out about her own experiences. In 1997, Smith was the editor-in-chief of *Vibe* magazine, which chronicled Black music and culture. After the murder of rapper Biggie Smalls, *Vibe* planned to feature Combs on the cover in homage to his friend and collaborator. As per protocol, Smith did not show Combs the cover mock-ups, which made him angry. He threatened her, said he would see her "dead in the trunk of a car," stalked her at the *Vibe* offices, and ultimately beat her.[106] Smith says that she knew the rumors of Combs's serial abuse of women, but was in a bind because her job, which often involved public events, meant she would be photographed with artists. Whether she wanted to or not, she needed to smile for the camera, no matter how noxious the behavior of those with whom she was photographed. Her assessment echoed the concerns expressed by the judge in the case, who documented at the pretrial hearing that some of Combs's alleged victims were particularly susceptible to abuse because of the power differential.[107] Smith blocked out her own attack for years, suppressing its severity and arranging for her staff to shuttle her between offices to avoid subsequent contact with Combs. Smith did not report Combs to law enforcement or her supervisors because "to report sexual misconduct—whether it was to attorneys or law enforcement or even your supervisor—often meant losing your job."[108] For a woman to succeed in any area of the industry meant she had to conform and give up some level of personal autonomy; for Black women, the stakes are even higher. As demonstrated by Anita Hill's testimony against Clarence Thomas, discussed in Chapter 2, a Black woman speaking out against a Black man may be seen as a betrayal of the larger professional and personal gains made by the Black community. Furthermore, a Black woman speaking out against a White man, particularly a White man with a great deal of power, is often ignored. Tarana Burke, founder of the MeToo movement, notes that *White* actors who spoke out against film producer Harvey Weinstein were believed, while *Black* women who spoke out against him were ignored or dismissed.[109] Further, Burke illustrates that Black women who "had been screaming at the top of our lungs for ten years" about the serial abuse at the hands of musical artist R. Kelly were summarily ignored until the virality of MeToo enabled the amplification of a group called Mute R. Kelly.[110]

Initially, Combs's arrest and the consequent disclosure of his misconduct offered a glimmer of hope for activists who see the music industry as having largely escaped the MeToo movement.[111] Throughout the trial, the press treatment of Combs's alleged victims was squarely on their side; daily updates in the *New York Times* painted a scathing image of Combs as a boss, boyfriend, and abuser.[112] However, the judgment in the trial was minimally damning of Combs's behavior. He was acquitted of the severest charges—sex trafficking and racketeering—and convicted of lesser charges, including transportation to engage in prostitution.[113] Evidently, the video of Combs kicking and punching a woman in a hotel hallway was insufficient to convince the courts of his violence or cruelty. The verdict in the Combs case illustrates that the public does not yet have a nuanced understanding of sex trafficking or coercion, that we still expect it to look like being kidnapped, whisked off the street.[114] For women of color, in particular, the lesser verdict was a double blow: A reminder that women, in general, are not believed and that women of color are not believed, their claims are not taken seriously, and their traumas are downplayed.[115]

Overall, these different stories illustrate that, across a variety of contexts, there is still broad permission to attack women. Any woman is susceptible to attack, physical, symbolic, or otherwise, and women who are attacked are either dismissed as incredible or blamed for their own vulnerability.

IT ENDS WITH US: WHAT FICTIONAL VIOLENCE CAN TEACH US ABOUT REAL VIOLENCE

Summer 2024 saw the release of the film *It Ends With Us*, based on the 2016 book of the same name by Colleen Hoover, about a young woman who escapes a violent childhood only to find herself married to a violent man.[116] The film, which grossed over $100 million within two weeks of release, was seen as yet another testament to the power of the female audience.[117]

The story's main character, Lily Bloom, opens a flower shop and meets Ryle Kincaid, a handsome and ambitious neurosurgeon in residence. The two embark on a powerful love affair, and their lives become quickly and deeply entwined. Meanwhile, Bloom runs into a boy she once loved, Atlas Corrigan, whose parents had kicked him out as a teenager, forcing him to squat in an abandoned house behind her childhood home. When Bloom pursues her relationship with Kincaid, which quickly turns violent, she spends time thinking about Corrigan and the role he played in her teenage life as her protector from her father's violence.

Those who counsel women working to escape domestic violence report that the book and the film oversimplify the reality of domestic violence. While the *arc* of the violence may feel realistic, the *quantity* of acts (a childhood of chronic violence, followed by one relationship with three discrete instances of violence) feels oversimplified. While most women need an average of seven attempts to leave their abuser, Lily Bloom leaves on her first attempt, with zero retaliation.[118] Bloom's departure is swift and effective; she faces no stalking, harassment, or increased violence, and there is no custody battle over their newborn child.[119] In the book, there appears to be no concern that Kincaid will ever lose his temper with their child, and Bloom maintains a close relationship with him and his family.

What the film and the book get right is how abusive relationships can often start off promising, before kindness shifts to violence.[120] Viewers of the film and readers of the book may see themselves in the characters, which may have an impact on their understanding of domestic abuse. In the book, readers have access to Bloom's thoughts, including her memories of her childhood experiences with violence. Upon release of the film, in August 2024, the No More Foundation, which focuses on building awareness about domestic abuse, saw an 800 percent increase in website visits and a 525 percent increase in resource downloads, compared to the prior month.[121]

There are three central problems with both the film and the book *It Ends With Us*, two texts that simultaneously center and silence women. For one, the book is a story of domestic abuse couched in a *romance* story, and while the violence is *bad*, the narrative is simplistic. Hoover presents the domestic abuse as incidental and out of Kincaid's control. His temper and violence against Bloom—which shows up nowhere else in his life—are directly connected to a singular childhood trauma: He and his older brother were playing with a gun that they did not realize was real, and Kincaid accidentally shot the gun and killed his brother. On the three occasions that he is violent towards Bloom, he does so in a blackout rage, rather than in any calculated manner. While the violence is terrible, there is also a built-in excuse: Had he not experienced this one terrible moment in childhood, he would be a different man.

Second, what goes unexamined in both the film and the book is that Corrigan is *also* violent. In one instance, he beats up Kincaid under *suspicion* that he had been violent to Bloom. Corrigan and Bloom's friendship ended abruptly when Corrigan left for the Marines (as an escape from homelessness); they had no contact for about seven years, and yet, because of an internal bond between the two, he knows the shape of Bloom's life and her dangerous circumstances before she does. His violence is represented as righteous and good, in the service of protecting Bloom. Corrigan is coded as the hero, Bloom's savior, and the man she should choose.

Third, and maybe most important, the content of the book and the film and their larger message about breaking the cycle of domestic abuse were overshadowed by the offscreen drama of the film's stars, the marketing plan, the accusations of harassment and retaliation on set, and the smear campaign against Blake Lively. The film's co-star and director, Justin Baldoni, who plays Ryle Kincaid, did not pose with his fellow castmates or participate in interviews at premiere events, with rumors that this was a marketing tactic to bring attention to abuse and avoid romanticizing the relationship between the characters.[122] Baldoni focused most of his press discussing domestic abuse and highlighting ways that women, in particular, could learn from the film.[123] Lively, who plays Bloom, her husband Ryan Reynolds, other cast members, and Hoover all unfollowed Baldoni on social media.[124] Lively used the film premiere after-party to promote her cocktail brand, and the press junkets to announce and promote her new hair care line and talk about the clothing worn by her character, specifically floral outfits that matched her work as a florist.[125] Hoover and her publisher, Atria Books, planned an *It Ends With Us* coloring book before conceding that it was a tone-deaf choice.[126] At this point, the women most closely associated with the film, Lively and Hoover, were seen as tacky and self-serving. In contrast, viewers saw Baldoni as thoughtful and attentive to domestic violence. Months later, news broke about Lively having sued the film studio, the film's producer, the public relations firm, and Baldoni for sexual harassment on set, claiming that physical boundaries had been violated, inappropriate sexual comments were made, that no safeguards had been put in place, and there was retaliation during the promotion of the film.[127]

The accused immediately fired back, denying all claims.[128] What got the most attention was a leaked portion of a text from the Joneswork PR firm, republished without context, that read, "You know we can bury anyone," referencing the ability to tarnish and, ultimately, silence Lively.[129] Chances are good audiences will never know the full truth of what happened on set, and, it is likely that "truth," in this instance, is not one-sided. Drawing from countless other stories of powerful men who do not believe their behavior is problematic, Baldoni and producer Jamey Heath may quite genuinely believe their behavior was acceptable in part because of their unearned privilege as powerful men. One might also argue that a PR firm's job is to fiercely protect their client. Joneswork could plausibly argue that the actors were doing their jobs with the passion required. Even though a judge threw out Baldoni's defamation lawsuit, Lively's reputation was still damaged, and she was yoked with age-old tropes used against outspoken women, including "bossy, flippant and difficult."[130]

While the film and the book undoubtedly bring much-needed attention to domestic abuse, what does it mean that the story is rooted in a romance-gone-wrong, that the legacy press decentralized the topic of violence to instead focus on cosmetics, clothing, and cast disputes, and that the accusations of sexual harassment were not surprising? Overall, both the book and the film are superficial treatments of relationships and domestic violence, with characters who are two-dimensional at best.[131]

Women who speak out against mistreatment may draw attention to their cause, *and* they also face the serious risk of being relentlessly attacked in the process. What is clear is that, no matter the story, women are easily scapegoated, easily blamed, and quickly sidelined in a pop culture that thrives on celebrity gossip and a political environment where a man convicted of sexual assault is re-elected to the nation's most powerful, prestigious office.[132] Sadly, we are a society comfortable with, and mired in, the mistreatment of women, *even when the topic is the mistreatment of women.*

Much can be learned about the world from fiction, and fictional depictions of reality, yet the reality is that many of our fictional stories are rooted in truth. The truth, in this case, is that actual violence against women is all too real, systemic, and dangerous. One way to dampen that harsh reality is to create and promote simplistic stories with easy solutions, and blanket them in love stories with an emphasis on flowers and friendship. This is one way that women become their own worst enemies and work against their best interests, inadvertently adopting the tools of patriarchy in actions that harm other women, which is the focus of the next chapter.

NOTES

1. "Violence Against Women Act," National Network to End Domestic Violence (NNEDV), accessed August 4, 2025.
2. "Violence Against Women"; Jacqueline Agtuca, "Beloved Women: Life Givers, Caretakers, Teachers of Future Generations," in *Sharing Our Stories of Survival: Native Women Surviving Violence*, ed. Sarah Deer, Bonnie Clairmont, Carrie A. Martell, and Maureen L. White Eagle (Altamira Press, 2007), 3–27.
3. Rebecca Solnit, *Men Explain Things to Me* (Haymarket Books, 2014), 6.
4. "Violence Against Women Act,"
5. "Violence Against Women Act,"; Agtuca, "Beloved Women."
6. Mona Gable, *Searching for Savanna: The Murder of One Native American Woman and the Violence Against Many* (Atria Books, 2023).
7. Solnit, *Men Explain Things to Me*, 21.
8. Arden Kurhayez, "Femicide Census Connects UK Killings with Global Wave of Violence Against Women, *Project Censored*, November 9, 2021.
9. Solnit, *Men Explain Things to Me*.
10. Rachel Louise Snyder, "Who Gets to Kill in Self-Defense?" *New York Times*, September 4, 2024.
11. Angela Davis, *Women, Race and Class* (Vintage Press, 1981), 6.
12. Kathleen Hanna, *Rebel Girl: My Life as a Feminist Punk* (Ecco, 2024), 1.
13. Mary (White Wolf) Teegee-Gray, "Foreword." In *Highway of Tears*, author Jessica McDiarmid (Atria, 2019), xi.
14. Agtuca, "Beloved Women"; Jessica McDiarmid, *Highway of Tears* (Atria, 2019). Ybanez, Victoria, "Domestic Violence: An Introduction to the Social and Legal Issues for Native Women," in *Sharing Our Stories of Survival: Native Women Surviving Violence,* ed. Sarah Deer, Bonnie Clairmont, Carrie A Martell, and Maureen L. White Eagle (Altamira Press, 2008); *Missing from Fire Trail Road*, directed by Sabrina Van Tassel (Canal+, 2024).
15. Gable, *Searching for Savanna*.
16. Jessica McDiarmid, *Highway of Tears*; Laura Stewart, "Missing and Murdered Indigenous Women and Girls: A Crisis Hiding in Plain Sight," *Cultural Survival*, June 1, 2023.
17. Agtuca, "Beloved Women"; Gable, *Searching for Savanna*.
18. Brenda J. Child, *Boarding School Seasons: American Indian Families, 1900–1940* (University of Nebraska Press, 2000); McDiarmid, *Highway of Tears*.
19. Child, *Boarding School Seasons*.
20. Child, *Boarding School Seasons*.
21. Child, *Boarding School Seasons*.
22. Casey Cep, "On Native Grounds," *New Yorker*, May 6, 2024, 28–39.
23. Child, *Boarding School Seasons*.
24. McDiarmid, *Highway of Tears*.
25. Kylie Rice, "A Brief History on the Forced Sterilization of Indigenous Peoples in the US," The Indigenous Foundation, accessed August 4, 2025.
26. Agtuca, "Beloved Women."
27. Agtuca, "Beloved Women."
28. McDiarmid, *Highway of Tears*.
29. Gable, *Searching for Savanna*.
30. Annita Lucchesi and Abigail Echo-Hawk, "Missing and Murdered Indigenous Women and Girls," Urban Health Institute, 2019.

31 Gable, *Searching for Savanna*.
32 Gable, *Searching for Savanna*.
33 Lucchesi & Echo-Hawk, "Missing and Murdered Indigenous Women and Girls."
34 McDiarmid, *Highway of Tears*.
35 McDiarmid, *Highway of Tears*, 5.
36 McDiarmid, *Highway of Tears*, 6.
37 McDiarmid, *Highway of Tears*, 65.
38 McDiarmid, *Highway of Tears*.
39 McDiarmid, *Highway of Tears*, 59.
40 McDiarmid, *Highway of Tears*, 107.
41 McDiarmid, *Highway of Tears*, 109.
42 McDiarmid, *Highway of Tears*, 123.
43 Agtuca, "Beloved Women."
44 Ybanez, "Domestic Violence," 50.
45 McDiarmid, *Highway of Tears*, 146.
46 LaPointe, "Sexual Violence," 32
47 McDiarmid, *Highway of Tears*, 146.
48 McDiarmid, *Highway of Tears*, 146.
49 Jeramy Dominguez, Katrina Tend, and James Byers, "Missing and Murdered Indigenous Women and Girls," *Project Censored*, December 1, 2020; McDiarmid, *Highway of Tears*.
50 McDiarmid, *Highway of Tears*.
51 McDiarmid, *Highway of Tears*, 134.
52 Gable, *Searching for Savanna*; see the hashtag #missingandmurderedindigenousrelatives, Facebook and Instagram groups such as Families of Sisters in Spirit, Federation of Sovereign Indigenous Nations, and No More Stolen Sisters, who share stories, provide support, and advocate for justice for Indigenous peoples and their families.
53 Gable, *Searching for Savanna*.
54 Cara Korte and Bo Erickson, hosts, *Missing Justice*, CBS News, 2022, 34 minutes.
55 Connie Walker, host, *Stolen*, Spotify, 2021–present, 50–60 minutes; Connie Walker, host, *Missing & Murdered*, CBC, 2016–2018, 30–60 minutes.
56 Nick Estes and Jen Marley, hosts, *The Red Nation Podcast*, 2019–2024, 20–90 minutes; Cara Korte and Bo Erickson, hosts, *Missing Justice*, CBS News, 2022, 34 minutes; Walker, *Stolen*.
57 Jay Soule, "Built on Genocide," accessed August 4, 2025.
58 Robin George, "What is Red Dress Day? How Missing and Murdered Indigenous Women, Girls, and Two-Spirit People are Honoured on May 5," *Globe and Mail*, May 4, 2025, updated May 5, 2025.
59 Ka'nhehsí:io Deer, "National Billboard Campaign Honours Missing and Murdered Indigenous Women," CBC, June 19, 2019.
60 *Missing from Fire Trail Road*, directed by Sabrina Van Tassel (Canal+, 2024); *Sugarcane*, directed by Julian Brave NoiseCat and Emily Kassie (Impact Partners, 2024).
61 *True Detective: Night Country*, showrun by Issa López (HBO, January 14–February 18, 2024).
62 *1883: A Yellowstone Origin Story*, created by Taylor Sheridan (101 Studios, December 19, 2021–February 27, 2022).

63 *North of North*, created by Stacey Aglok MacDonald and Alethea Arnaquq-Baril, television series (Northwood Entertainment and Red Marrow Media, 2025–present).

64 *Reservation Dogs*, produced by Sterling Harjo, Taika Waititi, and Garrett Basch (Waititi Productions, August 9, 2021–September 27, 2023).

65 Coralie Kraft, "Trolls Used Her Face to Make Fake Porn. There Was Nothing She Could Do," *New York Times*, July 31, 2024.

66 Kraft, "Trolls Used Her Face."

67 Nicholas Kristof, "The Online Degradation of Women and Girls That We Meet with a Shrug," *New York Times*, March 23, 2024.

68 Jesselynn Cook, "A Powerful New Deepfake Tool Had Digitally Undressed Thousands of Women," *Huffington Post*, August 10, 2021.

69 Cook, "A Powerful New Deepfake Tool."

70 Cook, "A Powerful New Deepfake Tool"; Kristof, "The Online Degradation Of Women."

71 Natasha Singer, "Spurred by Teen Girls, States Move to Ban Deepfake Nudes," *New York Times*, April 22, 2024.

72 Kraft, "Trolls Used Her Face"; Singer, "Spurred by Teen Girls."

73 France Winddance Twine, *Geek Girls: Inequality and Opportunity in Silicon Valley* (NYU Press, 2022); Emily Chang, *Brotopia: Breaking Up the Boys' Club of Silicon Valley* (Portfolio, 2018).

74 Carolyn Twersky and Leah Campano, "What You Should Know Before Sending Nudes," *Seventeen*, April 6, 2023.

75 Kraft, "Trolls Used Her Face."

76 Hanna, *Rebel Girl*, 190.

77 Ann Fessler, *The Girls Who Went Away: The Hidden History of Women Who Surrendered Children for Adoption in the Decades before Roe v Wade* (Penguin Books, 2006), 33.

78 Fessler, *The Girls Who Went Away*, 42.

79 Griswold *v* Connecticut (1965), Oyez, accessed August 4, 2025.

80 "Sex Discrimination," U.S. Department of Justice Civil Rights Division, accessed August 4, 2025.

81 All trans people are at greater risk for violence against their person; for the purposes of this text, I am focusing on trans girls and women.

82 Emily Witt, "A Trans Teen in an Anti-Trans State," *New Yorker*, October 9, 2023.

83 Edgar Sandoval, "Autopsy Shows Nex Benedict Died By Suicide," *New York Times*, March 13, 2024; Witt, "Passages"; "AMA To States: Stop Interfering In Health Care of Transgender Children," American Medical Association, April 26, 2021.

84 Witt, "Passages"; Anti-Trans Bill Tracker, The Legislation Tracker, accessed August 4, 2025.

85 Witt, "Passages"; J. David Goodman and Edgar Sandoval, "After Nonbinary Students' Death, Schools Chief Defends Restrictive Gender Policies," *New York Times*, February 23, 2024; Sandoval, "Autopsy Shows Nex Benedict Died By Suicide."

86 Witt, "Passages."

87 David Kirkpatrick, "The Next Targets for the Group That Overturned Roe," *New Yorker*, October 2, 2023.

88 Erin Keller, "Trump's Transgender Ad About 'Misplaced Priorities,' Campaign Director Says," *Newsweek*, November 11, 2024.

89 Madison Pauly and Henry Carnell, "'Dystopian:' Trump Issues New Order to Stamp Out Trans Youth Healthcare," *Mother Jones*, January 28, 2025; Danielle Kurtzleben, "Trump Signs Order That Seeks to Ban Transgender Athletes from Women's Sports," *NPR*, February 5, 2025.

90 Goodman and Sandoval, "After Nonbinary Students' Death."

91 Kirkpatrick, "The Group That Overturned Roe."

92 Zakeycia Briggs and Melissa Harden, "Underreporting of Missing and Victimized Black Women and Girls," *Project Censored*, December 1, 2020.

93 Alec Karakatsanis, *Copaganda: How Police and the Media Manipulate Our News* (The New Press, 2025).

94 Matt Taibbi, "Sandra Bland was Murdered," *Rolling Stone*, July 24, 2015.

95 Ray Sanchez, "Who Was Sandra Bland?" *CNN*, July 23, 2015.

96 Richard A. Oppel, Jr., Derrick Bryson Taylor, and Nicholas Bogel-Burroughs, "What to Know About Breonna Taylor's Death," *New York Times*, December 13, 2023.

97 CBS/AP, "Judge Rules Breonna Taylor's Boyfriend Caused Her Death, Throws Out Major Charges Against Ex-Louisville Officers," *CBS News*, August 26, 2024.

98 Alexandra E. Petri, "Deputy Fatally Shot Woman over Pot of Hot Water, Records Show," *New York Times*, July 17, 2024.

99 Amanda Holpuch, "In a 911 Call, Sonya Massey's Mother Asked That Police Not Hurt Her," *New York Times*, August 1, 2024.

100 Sasha Weiss, "The Prince We Never Knew," *New York Times*, September 8, 2024.

101 Weiss, "The Prince We Never Knew."

102 Sinéad O'Connor, *Rememberings* (Houghton-Mifflin-Harcourt Publishers, 2021).

103 O'Connor, *Rememberings*, 162.

104 Julia Jacobs and Ben Sisario, "Sean Combs's Likely New Home: A Brooklyn Jail," *New York Times*, September 18, 2024; Ben Sisario and Julia Jacobs, "Drugs, Sex, Baby Oil: The 'Freak-Offs' at the Core of Sean Combs's Trouble," *New York Times*, September 22, 2024; Ben Sisario and Julia Jacobs, "Sean Combs's Trial: What to Know," *New York Times*, May 21, 2025; Danyel Smith, "I Knew Diddy For Years. What I Now Remember Haunts Me," *New York Times*, July 12, 2024, updated July 17, 2024.

105 Aaratrika Ball, "Diddy Conspiracy Theory Suggests Jay-Z and Beyoncé Are Involved in Aaliyah's Death," *SportsSkeeda*, October 4, 2024; Craig Jenkins, "The Diddy Discourse Has Lost the Plot," *Vulture*, October 7, 2024.

106 Smith, "I Knew Diddy For Years."

107 Jacobs and Sisario, "Sean Combs's Likely New Home."

108 Smith, "I Knew Diddy For Years."

109 Monica Lewinsky, host, *Reclaiming*, "Tarana Burke," Wondery, March 18, 2025, 60 minutes.

110 Monica Lewinsky, "Tarana Burke."

111 Ben Sisario, "Sean Combs's Arrest Has the Music World Asking: Is Our #MeToo Here?" *New York Times*, September 23, 2024.

112 Ben Sisario and Julia Jacobs, "Sean Combs's Trial"; Julia Jacobs, Ben Sisario, Benjamin Weiser, and Thomas Fuller, "Sean Combs Trial Begins with

Explicit Accounts of Sex and Violence," *New York Times*, May 12, 2025; Joe Coscarelli, "Cassie's Trip from Star to Star Witness May Spell Trouble for Sean Combs," *New York Times,* May 13, 2025.
113 Julia Jacobs and Ben Sisario, "Sean Combs's Winning Defense: He's Abusive, but He's Not a Racketeer," *New York Times*, July 3, 2025.
114 Nadra Nittle, "'We Are Not Believed:' For Black Women, the 'Diddy' Verdict is a Reminder of Justice Denied," *The 19th*, July 3, 2025.
115 Nittle, "'We Are Not Believed'."
116 *It Ends with Us*, directed by Justin Baldoni (Sony Pictures, 2024). Colleen Hoover, *It Ends with Us* (Atria Books, 2016).
117 Rebecca Rubin, "'It Ends with Us' Crosses $100 Million at Domestic Box Office After 11 Days," *Variety*, August 20, 2024.
118 Annie Aguiar, "What 'It Ends With Us' Gets Wrong (and Right) About Domestic Abuse," *New York Times*, August 21, 2024.
119 Aguiar, "What 'It Ends With Us' Gets Wrong."
120 Aguiar, "What 'It Ends With Us' Gets Wrong."
121 Aguiar, "What 'It Ends With Us' Gets Wrong."
122 Shivani Gonzalez, "'It Ends With Us': The Press Tour Drama, Explained," *New York Times*, August 16, 2024.
123 Entertainment Tonight, "Justin Baldoni Made 'It Ends With Us' For The Lily Blooms," TikTok, 2024, 0:41.
124 Gonzalez, "'It Ends With Us': The Press Tour."
125 Lillian Gissen, "Disturbing It Ends with Us Detail Sparks Fury Among Fans as Blake Lively and Justin Baldoni Drama Continues," *Daily Mail UK*, August 16, 2024; Blake Brown Beauty, accessed August 4, 2025; Kate Erbland, "'It Ends with Us' Is a Movie About Domestic Violence, so Why Are Blake Lively and Colleen Hoover Acting like It Isn't?" *IndieWire*, August 16, 2024.
126 Erbland, "*It Ends With Us* Is A Movie About Domestic Violence."
127 Manatt, Phelps, and Phillips, LLP, "Complaint for Damages," 2024. Megan Twohey, Mike McIntire, and Julie Tate, "'We Can Bury Anyone:' Inside a Hollywood Smear Machine," *New York Times*, December 21, 2024.
128 Bryan Freedman, "Read the Statement," *New York Times*, December 21, 2024.
129 Twohey, McIntire, and Tate, "'We Can Bury Anyone."
130 Kat Tenbarge, "Blake Lively vs. The 'Misogyny Slop Ecosystem,'" *New York Times*, July 7, 2025.
131 Admittedly a petty complaint: While the characters are in their early-to-mid-twenties, the actors playing them are all in their forties.
132 Shealeigh Voitl, "From #MeToo to Misdirection," *Project Censored*, January 23, 2025.

CHAPTER SIX

WHEN WOMEN HARM OTHER WOMEN

UNEXPECTED BEHAVIOR

Powerful men caught in sex scandals are not surprising. Powerful men caught in sex scandals with minors, while disturbing, are also not surprising. *Women* caught in sex scandals are more surprising. Women caught *coordinating* and *facilitating* sex scandals that involve minors are both surprising and horrific. Women's involvement in the sexual exploitation of children is something that might cause a double-take when reading a headline or invite a re-examination of what we typically assume about intersections of power: How can women be complicit in harming other women and girls?

In 2021, a federal jury convicted British socialite Ghislaine Maxwell on multiple charges of sex trafficking. For years, Maxwell had been the partner, friend, and business associate of convicted sex trafficker Jeffrey Epstein, who died in prison before his sentencing trial.[1] Maxwell and Epstein were romantically involved for several years. When the romantic relationship ended, they remained friends, and she continued to manage his financial and social affairs, including, according to court documents and testimony, trafficking female minors to fulfill Epstein's sexual proclivities. Maxwell, the daughter of British media mogul Robert Maxwell, had long travelled in high-profile circles, an environment that Epstein was not from, but sought out.[2] Through Maxwell, Epstein was able to reach a social echelon for which he was not primed, and via Maxwell, he was able to secure the bodies of young women for his own gain.

Maxwell came to be seen as a scapegoat, and, despite being convicted, maintained her innocence.[3] Neither her trial nor Epstein's trial clarified her motivations in aiding and abetting Epstein, nor how she rationalized her involvement. Because Epstein's death preempted his sentencing, many people saw the court's treatment of Maxwell as punishment for both her conduct and Epstein's criminal acts. Maxwell's defense team argued that she had not been involved in the trafficking or abuse and that the women who came forward against Epstein were doing so for their own financial gain.[4] By this point in your reading, it should not be surprising to see that women were blamed for being caught in Epstein's orbit. What is perhaps more astonishing is that, according to a court of law, a powerful woman facilitated this connection.

The normalization of patriarchy is most obviously illustrated in men harming women; less obvious, but equally hurtful, is when women adopt the tools of patriarchy and are complicit in harming other women. At a 2016 rally for Hillary Clinton's presidential bid, former Secretary of State Madeleine Albright exclaimed, "There's a special place in hell for women who don't help each other."[5] In an op-ed penned after the statement—which went viral and was (mis)interpreted as meaning that, no matter what, women should support other women *because* they are women—Albright clarified that this was a phrase she had been using for twenty-five years, especially when she was just one of a few women in high-level diplomatic positions. The statement reflected her belief that "in a society where women often feel pressured to tear one another down, our saving grace lies in our willingness to lift one another up."[6]

Feminist scholar Phyllis Chesler tells the story of her thoughts on the divisions within feminist movements and her attempts to better understand women's mistreatment of other women.[7] When she first began discussing this idea with friends and colleagues, they repeatedly advised her not to pursue the issue, because it would be too detrimental to the movement. The assumption that women will automatically be kind to, and supportive of, other women, she learned, was a naïve belief, one that many women depended on and made excuses for, even when it was conspicuously absent. Women are oppressed by patriarchy *and* have "internalized the prevailing misogynist ideology which we uphold both in order to service and in order to improve our own individual positions vis-à-vis all other women."[8]

This chapter focuses on how women can bring down other women via patriarchal means in efforts to gain power. While it is upsetting, it cannot be surprising that women—long used to being ogled, having their appearances, their behaviors, indeed, their very existence, assessed, often critically, by men—internalize this type of approach and, in turn, inflict this mistreatment against other women. This chapter focuses on Linda Tripp and Maureen Dowd, who, separately and by duplicitous means, made the affair between Monica Lewinsky and Bill Clinton public and extended the narrative of Lewinsky's responsibility. Tripp, a coworker of Lewinsky's, recorded their conversations and shared them with FBI investigators. With her *New York Times* platform, Dowd made space for the popular press to pillory Lewinsky on a seemingly endless loop. Dowd's op-eds effectively destroyed Lewinsky's public reputation after details of the affair with President Bill Clinton surfaced. Dowd skewered Lewinsky week after week, while paying scant attention to Clinton. For this, Dowd was awarded the 1999 Pulitzer Prize for Distinguished Commentary for her "fresh and insightful columns" about the affair.[9]

Tripp's and Dowd's treatment of Lewinsky demonstrates that women do not live outside of patriarchy and can adopt its tropes for their own gain. Connected to the longstanding ideological narrative that, as caretakers and nurturers, women are therefore less competitive, is the acknowledgement that individual women do have power over other women and, ideally, women will use that power ethically.[10]

However, women are not immune to patriarchy and will collaborate in it as well.[11]

A TRIANGLE OF HURT:
LINDA TRIPP, MAUREEN DOWD,
AND MONICA LEWINSKY

Monica Lewinsky's affair with President Bill Clinton was tabloid fodder that disproportionately harmed her. The majority of the nation favored Clinton's policies and was willing to overlook his less-than-upstanding personal behavior. Because Clinton was "just being himself by having an affair with a White House intern," the blame for the scandal was put squarely on Lewinsky's shoulders.[12] While Clinton had a reputation as a womanizer, whether by consent or coercion, he was *also* known as a man who protected women's rights. He nominated Ruth Bader Ginsburg to the Supreme Court, publicly supported women's reproductive autonomy, and signed into law the Violence Against Women Act (VAWA), discussed in Chapter 5. He was always allowed to be a complicated, even contradictory figure. In contrast, the women in his sphere, including his wife, Hillary Clinton, and any number of the women with whom he was involved in extramarital affairs, were not afforded this luxury.

The public first heard rumors of the affair in 1997, when it had already been underway for about two years. The 1998 release of the 445-page Starr Report, excerpts of which were published in major newspapers, exposed the affair in unforgiving detail. A particular cruelty of the Starr Report is that it was never intended to focus on Lewinsky or any of Clinton's other alleged affairs. Lewinsky was, in many ways, a victim of Special Counsel Kenneth Starr's spite for both Bill and Hillary Clinton. Starr initially set out to investigate a potentially nefarious real estate deal gone bad, known by its shorthand, Whitewater. Starr and his team exhausted every possible resource but could not find any untoward connections in the real estate exchange. Because of comments made on the record about *other* actions of Clinton's, specifically his extramarital affairs and alleged sexual assault, Starr was able to expand the scope of his search. Ultimately, Clinton was exonerated of any wrongdoing in the Whitewater real estate deal, but publicly shamed for his extramarital affairs, especially with Monica Lewinsky.

What the Starr Report ultimately revealed was that, between 1995 and 1997, Clinton and Lewinsky shared late-night phone calls and met in person about 20 times.[13] Much of what the public learned focused on oral sex in the Oval Office and the notorious semen-stained blue dress that Lewinsky saved. Clinton's self-defense was that, based on the definition of "sexual relations" (provided for him in *another* accusation of sexual assault), he was not guilty because *he* did not perform sex acts with or on Lewinsky.[14]

In his memoir, *My Life*, Clinton shared the legal definition of sexual relations as the "most intimate contact beyond kissing by the person being asked the question, if it was done for gratification or arousal."[15] This definition was how Clinton justified his infamous claim, "I did not have sexual relations with that woman."[16] He did not initiate actions that could be described as "intimate contact beyond kissing" because Lewinsky had been the one to perform oral sex on him on multiple occasions, and because the one time she was penetrated, it was by a cigar, not by any digit attached to his body. Based on this self-serving logic, Lewinsky was the one who behaved badly. The majority of the coverage of Lewinsky's role in the affair applied age-old sexist stereotypes to Lewinsky's body, sexual proclivities, and poor judgment. She was deemed "slutty, dumb, entitled, and fat" and was blamed for the affair because she (allegedly) liked sex.[17]

One year after the affair between Lewinsky and Clinton became public, Andrew Morton published her biography, *Monica's Story*.[18] For more than a decade, this was the only outlet for audiences to learn Lewinsky's side of the story, while *countless* newspaper columns, websites, and late-night talk show monologues were devoted to mocking her.[19] Morton is vague about his research, thanking Lewinsky, her family, and friends for speaking with him; one is left to assume that all his data comes from conversations with Lewinsky's inner circle. Morton distilled the chaotic affair as "the tale of how an immature and emotionally vulnerable young woman came to Washington and fell for the world's most powerful man, himself a flawed individual riddled with doubt and desire."[20] Throughout *Monica's Story*, Morton regularly connects Lewinsky's lack of intellect (she's repeatedly described as bright, but not smart), her weight fluctuations, her emotional neediness, and her poor choices in boys and men as contributing factors for why she began an affair with Clinton. Recalling her high school boyfriends, Morton writes, "Monica's romantic spirit, her search for security and love, for emotional nourishment, led her to a series of inconclusive relationships."[21] Who has "conclusive" relationships in high school? And, perhaps more to the point, what *is* a "conclusive" relationship? Despite Morton's gentle derision, *Monica's Story* was, for a time, the most sympathetic treatment Lewinsky received in the popular press. Indeed, Lewinsky only agreed to the biography because the payout for participation helped cover her exorbitant legal fees, totalling close to $1 million.[22]

What must be made clear is that while "affair" is the word used to describe the roughly two years of interactions between Lewinsky and Clinton, it might not be the most appropriate or even accurate term. Lewinsky and Clinton met publicly at several White House events and less frequently in private, with a total of about twenty meetings; there were also several phone calls, all of which Clinton initiated. While Lewinsky made her presence known at the White House and acknowledged being in close communication with Betty Currie, Clinton's private secretary, in order to better know the President's schedule, all interactions between the two were initiated by Clinton. Morton notes, "Monica strongly repudiates the notion that somehow she was stalking the President, arguing that they were in a genuine relationship, but the communication was, by the very nature of his position, an entirely one-way traffic."[23]

In Morton's biography, Lewinsky tells multiple stories of staying home, waiting by the phone for either the President or Currie to phone to say that he was available to see her. Many of their encounters took place in the President's bathroom, a room within the private study of the Oval Office (one where they were less likely to be interrupted).[24] In many ways, Clinton was a typically crappy boyfriend. Over the course of their affair, Morton reported, "He would tell her that it was over, and then shortly afterwards would call her or even see her."[25] An admitted romantic, Lewinsky believed these reignitions of contact would lead to a real relationship once Clinton left office.

Born in July 1973, Lewinsky grew up in Southern California with her parents and brother. She grew up wealthy, but maybe emotionally neglected and never in the inner circle of wealth, exemplified by her lack of an invitation to the birthday party of classmate Tori Spelling, daughter of television producer Aaron Spelling.[26] Lewinsky self-described as largely directionless after high school, completing two years at a community college before transferring to a small liberal arts college in Oregon. Interwoven into her last years of high school, community college, and departure from California was an affair with Andy Bleiler, a married man several years Lewinsky's senior. He had been a theater teacher in her high school, married to an older woman with children, for whom Lewinsky babysat. When the Bleiler family also moved from California to Oregon, Lewinsky and Andy reignited their affair. Once this affair was revealed, it was taken as evidence that Lewinsky could *never* make healthy choices about the men with whom she was involved. After graduating from college, and unsure of her next steps, Lewinsky secured a White House internship via a friend of her mother's, although Lewinsky later explained that she was not all that interested in politics *or* the president.[27]

Lewinsky started working at the White House at age

twenty-two. Her first six-week internship led to a second one, which led to an entry-level position in the Office of Legal Affairs at the Pentagon. The particular timing of Lewinsky's start, at the outset of a government shutdown when paid employees were sent home, and interns were given greater responsibilities—including admittance to the West Wing of the White House—provided access to the president that would have otherwise been unlikely.

Lewinsky's familiar nature and belief in romance colored her relationship with Clinton as well as how it was perceived by those who either suspected or knew about the affair. She was seen as overly friendly, overly familiar, too flirty, too quick to make jokes, and insufficiently serious.[28] *Newsweek* reported that her body type departed from tacit assumptions about female White House interns, who tended to be "willowy and well-bred," as if her physicality was itself news.[29]

There are multiple ways to view the relationship between Bill Clinton and Monica Lewinsky. As a man with significant power, he abused that power for his own sexual pleasure; as a young, impressionable woman, she got caught up in the thrill of being power-adjacent, of the clandestine meetings, and the (however unlikely) promise of something *more*. In her own words, they had a deep connection and enjoyed talking with and confiding in each other.[30] In his memoir, which spans more than a thousand pages, Clinton devotes little time to Lewinsky and, when he does, his recollections are indirect and couched in the massive global good he did. The chapter that covers 1998 begins,

> I had no idea it would be the strangest year of my presidency, full of personal humiliation and disgrace, policy struggles at home and triumphs abroad, and, against all odds, a stunning demonstration of the common sense and fundamental decency

of the American people.[31]

Following his oblique reference to "personal humiliation and disgrace"—a characterization of the relationship that takes no responsibility for his role in the affair—Clinton thanks the American people for looking past the public exposure of his affair with Lewinsky, which seems to be an equally oblique reference to his subsequent impeachment by the House of Representatives. When he actually describes his relationship with Lewinsky, his description is detached and understated:

> During the government shutdown in late 1995, when very few people were allowed to come to work in the White House and those who were there were working late, I'd had an inappropriate encounter with Monica Lewinsky and would do so again on other occasions between November and April, when she left the White House for the Pentagon. For the next ten months, I didn't see her, although we talked on the phone from time to time.[32]

This bland description—an "encounter" that was "inappropriate"—is markedly different from Lewinsky's description of their physical encounters, their lengthy and emotionally vulnerable in-person conversations, and their phone sex.[33] Clinton continues, "What I had done with Monica Lewinsky was immoral and foolish. I was deeply ashamed of it and I didn't want it to come out."[34] Regarding his testimony, he writes,

> I admitted that "on certain occasions in 1996 and once in 1997" I engaged in wrongful conduct that included inappropriate intimate contact with Monica Lewinsky; that the conduct, while morally wrong, did not constitute "sexual relations" as I

understood the definition of the term.[35]

The account in his memoir then moves quickly on to the tentative peace deal he brokered in the Middle East. Clinton rationalizes this particular affair as a personal weakness, which he claimed to have realized and dealt with in therapy: "I also came to understand that when I was exhausted, angry, or feeling isolated and alone, I was more vulnerable to making selfish and self-destructive personal mistakes about which I would later be ashamed."[36]

Lewinsky got caught up in Starr's investigation through a complex web of her own. Her overly friendly behavior around the President raised red flags for some White House staff. Multiple people, including Linda Tripp, identified Lewinsky as someone who might have inside knowledge of the President's activities, based on their suspicions about her relationship with him. In 1996, she was transferred to the Pentagon, far from the West Wing of the White House. When Lewinsky was called to give a deposition in the case of Paula Jones, a woman who had accused Clinton of sexual assault, Lewinsky was in the midst of her affair with the president and deeply loyal to him. Lewinsky testified that she had not witnessed the president engage in any inappropriate sexual behavior and that she, herself, was not having any sort of sexual relationship with him. This lie was ultimately the wedge used to garner her confession.[37] When Starr published his report, it included precise and unsparing details of Lewinsky and Clinton's sexual encounters—yet what seemed to hurt Lewinsky the most, at the time, was how the Starr investigation had forced her into a position in which she had to betray her man.[38]

As the private affair became a public scandal, Lewinsky was caught between two women, Linda Tripp and Maureen Dowd, who secured their legacies by damning her, while effectively exonerating Clinton. Although by her own account, Tripp despised the Clintons, she focused her vitriol on Lewinsky. An unknown woman prior to the affair's public disclosure, Tripp became notorious for her subterfuge, including recording their (presumed) private conversations, goading Lewinsky into discussing the affair, and notifying the FBI of her insider knowledge that Lewinsky had lied in a deposition. *New York Times* columnist and opinion writer Maureen Dowd was already a public figure, known for her weekly columns that critiqued pop culture and politics. Her series of essays for the *New York Times* on Monica Lewinsky illustrated how cruel women can be to other women. Both Tripp and Dowd drew from the neoliberal ethos of individual advancement, each boosting their own public profile by drawing attention to another woman's (perceived) bad behavior. In pointing out the misgivings and bad behavior of others, both women were able, if only briefly, to shift the public's attention from their own bad behavior and make space for relentless media criticism and mockery of Lewinsky.

The Triangle, Side One: Linda Tripp

Linda Tripp, a White House and Pentagon employee, was so involved in the Clinton-Lewinsky scandal that many argue she instigated its exposure. She began her work in the White House during the George W. Bush administration in 1994, stayed through Clinton's term, and was eventually transferred to the Pentagon's public affairs office, in part because of her open disdain for the Clintons. At the Pentagon, she met Lewinsky and became her mentor and friend. Accounts of the character of their relationship vary, depending on who tells the story and when. Was it a genuine friendship that soured because of poor choices? Or was it a friendship in name only, orchestrated by Tripp to bring down a powerful man? When Lewinsky confided in Tripp about her affair with President Clinton, Tripp began recording their conversations, even though doing so was illegal in Maryland, where Tripp lived. Tripp's illicit recordings provided her with ammunition against the Clintons and the only incontrovertible evidence of the affair. Although she characterized herself as a "whistleblower" who acted "out of patriotic duty," much of the public saw Tripp as a hypocrite and a bad friend.[39]

Described as "unlovely" and "nosy, shrewd, principled, conniving, cynical, and moralistic," Linda Tripp used her knowledge of the affair to stake her own claim against the Clintons.[40] A lifelong Republican, Tripp was aghast at the Clinton White House, seeing it as overly casual and undisciplined.[41] During the course of the affair, Lewinsky first confided in a few close friends, her mother, and her aunt. Over time, she included Tripp in her confidence, and Tripp was able to manipulate Lewinsky's trust. While others with knowledge of the affair encouraged Lewinsky to end it, Morton wrote that Tripp encouraged Lewinsky to continue, so that, he claimed, Tripp could write a "tell-all" book that would destroy the Clintons.

Probably the most famous aspect of the affair can be summed up as "the blue dress." Lewinsky wore a blue dress to one of her meetings with Clinton. As recounted in excruciating detail in the Starr Report, the blue dress was the indefatigable evidence that shifted the rumors of the affair from "he said, she said" to provable. Based on a DNA test, the semen stain on Lewinsky's dress was undeniably Clinton's. Multiple stories have been told about why Lewinsky saved the dress in its stained state, rather than having it cleaned. According to Morton, she saved the dress because she had gained weight and it no longer fit; she tossed it in the back of her closet, perhaps to be worn again if she later lost weight.[42] According to Tripp, Lewinsky saved the dress as a "souvenir of her love for the big guy," and Tripp "quickly made sure" she did not have the dress cleaned: "I said, 'I would tell my own daughter to save that dress for your own ultimate protection.'"[43]

Fiercely denying anyone's claims (including Morton's) that she was motivated by the financial or political benefits of a tell-all book, Tripp wrote her analysis of the Clinton White House, including her relationship with Monica Lewinsky, after self-proclaimed soul-searching. Before she gained Lewinsky's confidence and learned about the affair, Tripp had been approached by a literary agent, Lucianne Goldberg, about writing a book on her experiences working in the White House. At the time, however, there was no "hook" for the story, which Goldberg knew would be necessary.[44] Simultaneously, Tripp was in conversation with Michael Isikoff, then of *Newsweek*, who was looking for insider information about the Clintons.[45] Tripp claimed she ultimately chose to write her book as a way to explain to her grandchildren what really happened. *A Basket of Deplorables*, written with crime writer Dennis Carstens (whose self-published courtroom mysteries Tripp enjoyed), was self-published in 2020, not long after she died, following a brief, difficult battle with cancer.[46] From the book's outset, Tripp set herself apart from the "liberal elite," noting, "as is true in most of academia, publishing houses tend to be a part of the liberal establishment. I was the enemy."[47] Much of the book justifies her behavior as patriotic and protective (of herself and Lewinsky). Tripp warns readers,

> Don't be fooled by the images you have seen of her, or you may remember her as the beautiful young woman gracing the pages of *Vanity Fair*, the well-coiffed woman in photos snapped by the paparazzi, or even the poised adult on TV. These are the images of the Monica Lewinsky the world met in 1998. This Monica was created by the Clinton-friendly media to portray her as a consenting adult, to provide cover for Bill Clinton as a sexual predator.[48]

Tripp's account appears to imply that, even while Clinton and his administration were complicit in nearly unredeemable damage to Lewinsky, they were also somehow in control of cultivating her public image in the affair's aftermath.

Linda Tripp's narrative of her relationship with Lewinsky is couched in pity, for Lewinsky and for herself. She portrays

Lewinsky as selfish and immature:

> She was a likeable young woman, pleasant, affable, even sweet and kind. In fact, over time, I grew quite fond of her. She was also the center of her own universe, believed she controlled events even as they swirled around her, totally out of control.[49]

Tripp painted Lewinsky as an emotional tornado, a toxic part of her life that made her world shrink. Because she was consumed with gathering evidence, Tripp claims to have sacrificed time that she would have otherwise devoted to her children or other social connections. She painted herself as a patriot and a victim of both the Clintons and Lewinsky.

In late 1997, Tripp started recording her phone calls and, in some instances, her in-person meetings with Lewinsky. She had listened to Lewinsky's "sordid tale" before the 1996 election, but took no steps to record the conversations right away.[50] The triangle of Tripp's own concerns regarding the Clintons and Lewinsky, combined with Isikoff's search for information and Goldberg's book deal proposal, convinced Tripp that recording was justified and necessary. When she did start recording them, she maneuvered the conversations to get Lewinsky to talk about events from the previous year. In her memoir, she acknowledged that, from 1997 onwards, "virtually everything I said to Monica was either a lie or at least not the total truth."[51] Tripp rationalized her actions as more painful for herself than harmful to Lewinsky, "For someone who had spent a lifetime laboring under an oath of office, who took the words 'duty,' 'honor,' and 'country' so seriously, this was not easy."[52] Tripp claimed it was Goldberg "who suggested I start to surreptitiously tape record my conversations with Monica."[53] Tripp started recording about a year and a half into her friendship with Lewinsky as a way to get "all the abuse on the record." Rather than seeing the recording as a violation of Lewinsky's trust, Tripp lamented that, if she had started recording earlier, "the horror of it all as it occurred in real time, the result likely would have been very different."[54] Tripp repeatedly defended her actions:

> My motivation had nothing to do with Bill's politics ... It was about a sick, reckless, corrupt president who indulged his predatory needs ... of course, I took a massive beating for the lies and the manipulation. Fair enough. It was not nice, but it was necessary ... I naively believed that exposing his sexual abuse was not the bad thing; the behavior itself was.[55]

In January 1998, Tripp met with members of the Independent Counsel and told them she had "tape recordings of phone calls from a woman who'd had an affair with the president," who had lied about the affair in a deposition in the Paula Jones case and was trying to coerce her into lying.[56] Tripp built a narrative that Clinton aides were securing a new job for Lewinsky to buy her silence.

While Tripp acknowledged that recording Lewinsky was illegal, she justified her action as a form of protection. She saw Lewinsky as obsessed with Clinton, which, Tripp remembered, prevented Lewinsky from recognizing that her "'abusive' friend—me—had saved her from a sexual predator."[57] While there is no doubt that, as a charismatic male occupying the most powerful role in the world, Clinton willfully abused his influence, what Tripp did might well be equally predatory. She established a young woman's confidence and then manipulated it to disastrous ends. Lewinsky was collateral damage in Tripp's effort to discredit the Clintons. Reflecting on her choices, Tripp stated,

> Given the same set of circumstances today, I would do it all again—not to betray a young girl, but to save a young girl and at the same time, to expose a dangerous predator once and for all ... Suffice it to say that the dangerous predator became one of the

> more popular presidents of all time. I went on to
> be roundly hated. And that's how things work in
> Clintonland.[58]

What Tripp does not seem able to see is that *both* she and Clinton are villains in this story. Both took advantage of an immature, emotionally vulnerable young woman with little to no power. Tripp may have disrespected, and been disrespected by, the Clinton White House, but, in her efforts to bring down the Clintons—efforts that ultimately failed—she betrayed Lewinsky's trust and destroyed her professional and personal life.

Tripp's memoir concludes with the confrontational meeting between the FBI and Lewinsky, which Tripp helped bring about. According to Dennis Carstens's epilogue, this was as far as Tripp got in writing *A Basket of Deplorables* before she died. There is no way to corroborate this: Was it Carsten's decision to end the narrative at the moment just before Tripp may have needed to take greater responsibility for her actions? Or is it truly as simple and tragic as Tripp stopped writing in the face of her fatal cancer diagnosis?

The Triangle, Side Two: Maureen Dowd

After the affair was made public via the Starr Report, Maureen Dowd took up the charge of pillorying Lewinsky. Dowd, who has written for the *New York Times* since 1983, was only the second woman to work as a White House correspondent.[59] In 1995, she began work as a columnist on the *Times's* op-ed page, in part because her reporting and writing were deemed too casual and colloquial for the standards of front-page reporting. Her columns became well known for their incisive, biting critiques of powerful men.

In 1998, Dowd wrote a series of ten columns on the Clinton-Lewinsky affair that were influential in framing how the public saw Lewinsky. Dowd's early columns on the affair seemed supportive of Lewinsky, predicting, for example, that

Lewinsky would be made expendable, and noting, "once you decide it's o.k. to sacrifice individual women for the greater good, you set a dangerous precedent."[60] In later columns, Dowd herself did exactly that, sacrificing Lewinsky in the cruelest, most unoriginal way, by condemning Lewinsky's body, her intelligence, and her sexual proclivities. Dowd referred to Lewinsky as "the girl who was too tubby to be in the high school 'in crowd'," who arrived in Washington, DC, "like a heat-seeking missile to seduce the President," as if her only goal upon getting her job was to have an extra-marital affair.[61]

In one satirical column, Dowd imagined Lewinsky's diary, replete with what she fancied as Lewinsky's "stream of consciousness ramblings," written "in a girlish scrawl, with loopy letters, little hearts and breathless punctuation."[62] Dowd punctuates her (imagined Lewinsky) writing with multiple question marks, exclamation points, and frowny faces. She concludes with Lewinsky's fears about her fate, "I do feel like an orphan in the storm. No, a pawn in a chess game. No, a candle in the wind. Will I ever get another date?? Who will want to marry me now??? Who will help me get a big job in New York even though I can't type and have no experience except delivering pizza and mail to the President??"[63] What was this column, if not exactly the sort of "sacrifice" Dowd had previously bemoaned? Dowd's columns faulted Lewinsky for poor management of the affair and for being too obvious and emotionally needy, ultimately painting Lewinsky as solely responsible for the affair and for it going awry. Dowd was not the only one to blame for sacrificing Lewinsky; the Pulitzer committee awarded her the Pulitzer Prize for Commentary on "the impact of President Clinton's affair with Monica Lewinsky."[64] Except that Dowd *did not* write about the "impact" of the affair; instead, she created a damning, salacious, indelible image of Lewinsky.

While Lewinsky was unknown prior to the affair, Dowd was a nationally known columnist at the most prestigious newspaper in the country. She could have used that influential platform to shape the developing media narrative about the affair in ways that did not tear Lewinsky apart or portray her as solely responsible for it. Was embarking on the affair a good choice for Clinton *or* Lewinsky? No. One can imagine the ways Dowd could have used her platform (especially at a time when the Thomas hearings were recent history) to dissect the structures of patriarchy. She did, after all, have a reputation for skewering those in power. Dowd's acidic critiques of powerful men had always been more impactful because a woman wrote them. But Dowd also regularly uses her column to attack women *as* women.

Dowd has regularly attacked Hillary Clinton, particularly during her 2016 presidential bid, when she criticized Clinton for not being sufficiently feminine. "The most famous woman on the planet," Dowd wrote, "can't figure out how to campaign as a woman."[65] Dowd painted Hillary Clinton in a negative light; in 72 percent of her *New York Times* columns, she used gendered criticism to mock Clinton, according to a 2015 analysis by Media Matters.[66]

Curiously, Dowd herself admits to being thin-skinned when she herself is criticized.[67] For example, when Lewinsky confronted her at a restaurant and demanded to know why she was writing "such scathing articles about her," Dowd "'wimped out' and said she didn't know."[68] When she takes women, such as Monica Lewinsky and Hillary Clinton, to task, her columns focus more on her subjects' gender (and perceived shortcomings connected to gender) rather than on their professional conduct. While she has a way with words, constructing crisp sentences, timely zingers, and quippy retorts, when the substance of her arguments is dissected, it is revealed that there is not much there.

The Triangle, Side Three: The Press Coverage of Monica Lewinsky

It wasn't until decades later, as the MeToo movement overtook social media, that Dowd's portrayal of Lewinsky as a reckless, manipulative 20-year-old and a "crazy bimbo" was subject to questioning and revision.[69] Curiously, Dowd has defended the MeToo movement, writing,

> It took far too long, but something finally snapped with women. Why had we allowed ourselves to think of abusive behavior as the norm for so long? Maybe it was all this pent-up anger that has given the cascading accusations such a feral edge.[70]

Nevertheless, the columns Dowd wrote about the Clinton-Lewinsky affair make her complicit in having helped to cover up one of the most glaring instances of sexual misconduct by a powerful male from the pre-MeToo era. In the intervening years, Dowd refused to take any responsibility for potentially harming Lewinsky.[71]

Lewinsky bore the brunt of the publicity of the affair for decades before her story was revisited. "To come of age in the early 1990s was to be fed one idea, over and over again, by nearly every prevalent form of mass media: Monica Lewinsky was a punchline," journalist Emma Specter wrote for *Vogue* in 2021.[72] The pop culture narrative of Lewinsky is problematic and contradictory. While she was blamed at the time of the affair for being fat, she was also mocked when she tried to slim down. Though their stock rose by 32 percent when they first signed Lewinsky in 1999, weight loss food producer Jenny Craig dropped her as a spokesperson in 2000 because she did not lose enough weight.[73] Lewinsky launched a line of handbags, appeared in documentaries, left the United States, gave a TED talk, and developed a line of anti-bullying emojis.[74] For years, Lewinsky was reduced to her looks, her weight, and her sexual acts.[75] The public comments on the retrospective video, "The Scandal That Changed How the Media Covers Politics," produced by CNN in 2019, are revealing. "Poor Monica ... She will always be remembered for being the presidential side piece," one commenter wrote. "What I found very interesting," noted another, "is how 50%

of men wanted him held accountable for his own behavior whereas 50% women thought it to be a right wing conspiracy. Really tells you how women defend men with bad behavior."[76]

Over the years, and especially in the wake of MeToo, Lewinsky's story has been revisited; pop culture narratives have begrudgingly recognized that being mean to Lewinsky gave Clinton a pass. Journalist Amanda Hess observed that "many Americans have come to realize that Lewinsky got a raw deal," yet neither Tripp nor Dowd sees how the roles they played may have fueled that fire.[77] According to feminist scholar Phyllis Chesler, women are more likely to forgive and be sympathetic towards men than other women, even if men hurt them more often.[78] For Lewinsky, this narrative may have shifted. The television series *Impeachment: American Crime Story*, a biopic about the relationship between Lewinsky and Tripp, focuses on the fallout of the affair, where Monica Lewinsky and Linda Tripp are centered, and Lewinsky is presented favorably as a young woman caught in a series of dilemmas that she cannot escape.[79] Unfortunately, *so much* of the series focuses on the women's bodies, which are represented as departing from conventional feminine ideals. Journalist Emma Specter described the *Impeachment* series as "off the mark and not quite in the spirit of Lewinsky's reinvention."[80] Most recently, as of this writing, Lewinsky is taking command of her own narrative, and highlighting the stories of other people pilloried in the press, via her podcast *Reclaiming with Monica Lewinsky*.[81]

PATRIARCHY MAKES IT EASY FOR WOMEN TO HARM OTHER WOMEN

While it feels logical to believe that the destructiveness of patriarchy is exclusively foisted by men, women do not live outside of patriarchy. In fact, they are influenced by patriarchy, and they can consciously or unconsciously adopt its tropes in ways that lead them to harm other women, whether inadvertently or intentionally. Women who harm other women perpetuate a neoliberal ethos of individual advancement. Individualistic competition, focused on "winning," dilutes feminism, leaving women "bereft of unity, momentum, and power as we compete against each other" to achieve success within male-dominated and male-organized spaces, as Charlotte Shane, author of "No Wave Feminism," has observed.[82]

While we may cringe at women harming other women, it is exponentially more awful when we see mothers harm their own daughters, especially when financial gain is the motive. Kris Jenner, mother of Kardashian siblings Kim, Kourtney, Khloe, and Rob Kardashian, and Kylie and Kendall Jenner, was a largely unknown wealthy wife and mother, once married to Robert Kardashian, who was made famous as part of O.J. Simpson's legal team. Jenner propelled her family to fame through her daughter, Kim; in 2007, she allegedly sold a sex tape of her daughter and then-boyfriend Ray J.[83] Capitalizing on the tape, the Kardashians soon became famous for being famous, which they parlayed into various business ventures, including clothing, cosmetics, retail, reality TV, endorsements, and social justice projects.[84] While Jenner sold her daughter's sex tape well before social media and influencer culture were something that private individuals could capitalize on, it set the stage for a particular type of platform for mothers to exploit their daughters.

Women without significant social or cultural power also employ the tools of patriarchy in ways that harm other women and girls. In the world of social media, some of the most prominent influencers harming young women are mothers of daughters. While there are undoubtedly fathers involved in their children's social media profiles as well as sons managed by mothers and fathers, the dominant narrative is that of girls and young women whose social media presences are managed by their mothers. In an investigative profile of mothers who promote their daughters via social media, journalists Jennifer Valentino-DeVries and Michael

Keller reported that

> what starts as a parent's effort to jump-start a child's modeling career, or win favors from clothing brands, can quickly descend into a dark underworld dominated by adult men, many of whom openly admit on other platforms to being sexually attracted to children.[85]

Online groomers seek out and manipulate parents, particularly mothers, encouraging them to post more provocative images of their daughters, sometimes by offering money. The mothers who spoke with Valentino-DeVries and Keller defended their initial, positive reactions to the increased attention as cool and exciting, based on the belief that their daughters' increased popularity would lead to more formal opportunities as an influencer and greater financial remuneration.[86] By the time many of these mother managers figured out they were being manipulated, they had already sold pictures of their daughters.

While as a society we are largely uncomfortable with women committing acts of violence, "violence" is usually thought of as physical.[87] Is it possible to consider selling a young girl's image—and subsequently selling the clothes she wore in that picture to her unknown followers—as a form of symbolic violence? When asked about their culpability in this market, many mothers expressed a certain helplessness. Having initially felt compelled to help promote their daughters, they came to feel deceived when they realized that the attention from some of their daughters' more fervent followers was evidently sexual. When the current iteration of social media influencers fades, will these mothers look back with regret and remorse at how they treated their daughters?

Powerful women may become powerful, in part, because they use the tools of patriarchy to best other women. Gloria Allred is a fierce feminist lawyer, fighting on behalf of survivors of sexual harassment and assault. And yet, Allred constructs women as victims, rather than survivors, and works to expand definitions of victimhood.[88] She is criticized for ostensibly holding court via press releases and press conferences. She is known to be an "ambulance chaser," someone more interested in "money and media attention than her clients."[89] While Allred has spent a great deal of time in court arguing on behalf of and for women, she primarily focuses on "a blend of high-profile legal advocacy and public relations."[90] She is a powerful legal voice that has centered the conversation of sexual assault while simultaneously silencing women via settlements and non-disclosure agreements (NDAs).

Allred is a champion of NDAs, arguing, "No one has ever forced anyone to sign an NDA ... Nobody is holding a gun to their head."[91] Although this may be literally true—no actual gun is held to a woman's head—it does not follow that women are not coerced by less blunt, more subtle means. For Allred, public announcements of charges followed by NDAs or private settlements are key tactics of "creative lawyering." There is no courtroom hearing, but by highlighting the perspectives of the victims she represents, Allred threatens legal defendants with high-visibility public embarrassment.[92]

Critics of Allred see her as a "media hound who has undermined her reputation by pushing victim-feminism well past the point of caricature."[93] Allred's version of feminism is so theatrical, others contend, that "even when she represents a woman bringing grave charges ... the whole thing ends up looking like a bit of a farce."[94] The conundrum, as another skeptic put it, is that "few have done more to advocate on behalf of sexual-harassment victims. And few have done more to make harassment seem laughable."[95]

Sheryl Sandberg, the former Chief Operating Officer (COO) of Facebook (before it was subsumed by Meta), is one of the nation's most prominent female executives. She became well-known outside of corporate America via her book *Lean In*, which encouraged women to speak up more at work, to ask more directly and declaratively for what they wanted and needed in the workplace, and to take up more space.[96] Sandberg believes that women are their own barriers to success:

> We hold ourselves back in ways both big and small, by lacking self-confidence, by not raising our hands, and by pulling back when we should be leaning in. We internalize the negative messages we get throughout our lives—the messages that say it's wrong to be outspoken, aggressive, and more powerful than men.[97]

For Sandberg, the solution is simple: To gain power, one must overcome one's own barriers and speak up. Sandberg's focus on women's individual agency is easy for her to argue because she already has power. She was a top executive at Google before moving to Facebook and lives an economically secure life with assured access to the very best health and child care.[98] She also appears to assume that women *want* to be powerful in the mold that endorses the outspokenness and aggression associated with hyper-individuality. She is White, well-educated, and married to a man, which makes her appear less threatening. As COO of Facebook, she was older than CEO and founder Mark Zuckerberg, so she also presented as the wise mother/nurturer, another relatively familiar, safe role for "model" feminine behavior. Charlotte Shane questioned the value of this:

> If patriarchy's worst offense were keeping women out of the workplace, then sure, women like Sheryl Sandberg would be triumphs of the cause. But the notion that women shouldn't work outside the home was always unique to the white upper and middle classes. Poorer women never had the option to stay at home, and Black women in the United States have virtually always been expected to work, if not in the fields then in white homes as "domes-

tic" servants. The far more noxious effects of patriarchy, like rendering women incapable of exercising autonomy over their reproduction or paying them lower wages for their work, can and do endure even with more women "on top."[99]

This is sadly evidenced by the re-election of Donald Trump and his connection to Project 2025, which promises federal bans on abortion and a re-assertion of even more retrogressive, restrictive gender roles, among other horrors.[100] Women willing to work within the patriarchy's rules, whether consciously or unwittingly, will always be held up and lauded as evidence of change or progress. Yet, for as long as we live within patriarchy's barriers, the preponderance of men in power will maintain systemic control, to the detriment of all women.

In 2024, when Representative Marjorie Taylor Greene (R-GA) disagreed with Representative Jasmine Crockett (D-TX), instead of concentrating on the substance of their disagreement, Taylor Greene said, "I think your false eyelashes are messing up what you're reading."[101] Representative Alexandria Ocasio-Cortez (D-NY) quickly snapped, "How dare you attack the physical appearance of another person!"[102] Greene's attack on Crockett's physical appearance exploited the intersection of gender and race. It is not new to attack women—and, especially, women of color—for their appearances, but the legacy of weaponizing appearance was given a greater platform during and after the first Trump administration.

The final chapter lays out a plan of action, based on insights from critical media literacy education, to explore more thoroughly how women and girls are centered and silenced. I provide activities and questions for analysis and action steps to recognize and counter the silencing of women in pop culture. These actions can be undertaken in classrooms, as part of formal education, or informally in living rooms, conversation groups, and consciousness-raising sessions—in other words, wherever people want to identify problems with how women and girls are represented and, on that basis, push back against patriarchy in the many forms it takes.

NOTES

1. Jaclyn Diaz, "Negligence, Staff Failures Led to Jeffrey Epstein's Suicide, a DOJ Report Says," NPR, June 27, 2023.
2. Ben Schreckinger and Daniel Lippman, "Meet the Woman Who Ties Jeffrey Epstein to Trump and the Clintons," Politico, July 21, 2019.
3. Clare Hymes, "Jury Finds Ghislaine Maxwell Guilty on Charges Tied to Jeffrey Epstein's Sex Trafficking Run," CBS News, December 30, 2021; Schreckinger and Lippman, "Meet the Woman"; Luc Cohen, "Ghislaine Maxwell Convicted of Recruiting Teenage Girls for Epstein Sex Abuse," Reuters, December 30, 2021.
4. Cohen, "Ghislaine Maxwell Convicted."
5. Madeleine Albright, "My Undiplomatic Moment," New York Times, February 12, 2016.
6. Albright, "My Undiplomatic Moment."
7. Phyllis Chesler, *Woman's Inhumanity To Woman* (Chicago Review Press, 2009).
8. Chesler, *Woman's Inhumanity To Woman*, 2.
9. "Maureen Dowd of the New York Times," The Pulitzer Prizes, accessed September 10, 2025.
10. Chesler, *Woman's Inhumanity To Woman*.
11. Chesler, *Woman's Inhumanity To Woman*.
12. Allison Yarrow, *90s Bitch: Media, Culture, and the Failed Promise of Gender Equality* (Harper Perennial, 2018), 45.
13. Kenneth W. Starr, "Communication From Kenneth W. Starr, Independent Counsel," 1998; Michael Hobbes and Sarah Marshall, hosts, *You're Wrong About*, "Monica Lewinsky," June 2, 2018, 60 minutes; Andrew Morton, *Monica's Story* (St. Martin's Press, 1999); Yarrow, *90s Bitch*.
14. Hobbes and Marshall, "Monica Lewinsky"; Leon Neyfakh, host, *Slow Burn: The Clinton Impeachment*, "Alone, Together," season 2, episode 4, Slate, August 29, 2018, 50–60 minutes.
15. William Clinton, *My Life* (Alfred A. Knopf, 2004), 773.
16. James Bennet, "The President Under Fire: The Overview; Clinton Emphatically Denies an Affair with Ex-Intern: Lawyers Say He Is Distracted by Events," New York Times, January 27, 1998.
17. Yarrow, *90s Bitch*, 73.
18. Morton, *Monica's Story*; Lewinsky agreed to participate in the biography in part to pay for her legal bills, which were well over $1 million in total. See Elna Baker, special host, *Reclaiming*, Wondery, February 18, 2025, 60 minutes.
19. Michael Isikoff and Evan Thomas, "Clinton and the Intern," Newsweek, February 2, 1998; Caroline Pate, "Proof That Slut-Shaming Seriously Hurts," Bustle, May 6, 2014.
20. Morton, *Monica's Story*, 12.
21. Morton, *Monica's Story*, 30.
22. Baker, "Monica Lewinsky."
23. Morton, *Monica's Story*, 88.
24. Morton, *Monica's Story*.
25. Morton, *Monica's Story*, 103.
26. Isikoff and Thomas, "Clinton and the Intern"; Morton, *Monica's Story*.
27. Morton, *Monica's Story*.
28. Morton, *Monica's Story*.

29 Isikoff and Thomas, "Clinton and the Intern."
30 Morton, *Monica's Story*.
31 Clinton, *My Life*, 771.
32 Clinton, *My Life*, 773.
33 Morton, *Monica's Story*.
34 Clinton, *My Life*, 774.
35 Clinton, *My Life*, 801.
36 Clinton, *My Life*, 811.
37 Morton, *Monica's Story*.
38 Morton, *Monica's Story*.
39 Emma Dibdin, "What to Know About Linda Tripp, a Key Player in the Clinton-Lewinsky Scandal," *Elle*, September 7, 2021.
40 Morton, *Monica's Story*, 92; Isikoff and Thomas, "Clinton and the Intern."
41 Morton, *Monica's Story*; Linda Tripp, with Dennis Carstens, *A Basket of Deplorables: What I Saw Inside the Clinton White House* (Post Hill Press, 2020).
42 Morton, *Monica's Story*.
43 Tripp, *A Basket of Deplorables*, 179.
44 Isikoff and Thomas, "Clinton and the Intern."
45 Isikoff and Thomas, "Clinton and the Intern."
46 Tripp, *A Basket of Deplorables*.
47 Tripp, *A Basket of Deplorables*, viii.
48 Tripp, *A Basket of Deplorables*, 121.
49 Tripp, *A Basket of Deplorables*, 121.
50 Tripp, *A Basket of Deplorables*, 155.
51 Tripp, *A Basket of Deplorables*, 176.
52 Tripp, *A Basket of Deplorables*, 176.
53 Tripp, *A Basket of Deplorables*, 178.
54 Tripp, *A Basket of Deplorables*, 179.
55 Tripp, *A Basket of Deplorables*, 180.
56 Tripp, *A Basket of Deplorables*, 195.
57 Tripp, *A Basket of Deplorables*, 122.
58 Tripp, *A Basket of Deplorables*, 127.
59 Peter McDermott, "Echo Profile: A Necessary Woman," *Irish Times*, February 22–28, 2006.
60 Maureen Dowd, "The Slander Strategy," *New York Times*, January 28, 1998.
61 Maureen Dowd, "President Irresistible," *New York Times*, February 18, 1998.
62 Maureen Dowd, "Monica's Frowny Face," *New York Times*, May 31, 1998.
63 Dowd, "Monica's Frowny Face."
64 "Maureen Dowd of the New York Times," The Pulitzer Prizes, accessed September 10, 2025.
65 Maureen Dowd, "Granny Get Your Gun," *New York Times*, April 18, 2015.
66 Alexandrea Boguhn, "Maureen Dowd's Advice for Hillary Clinton is Full of Sexist Tropes," Media Matters, April 19, 2015.
67 Howard Kurtz, "Sex & the Single Stiletto," *Washington Post*, November 5, 2005.
68 Kurtz, "Sex & the Single Stiletto."
69 Amanda Hess, "'Ditsy, Predatory White House Intern'," *Slate*, May 7, 2014.
70 Maureen Dowd, "Roadkill on Capitol Hill," *New York Times*, December 9, 2017.
71 Maxwell Tani, "Maureen Dowd: The Only Thing I Wish I Could Take Back Is a Negative Column I Wrote About Seinfeld," *Insider*, September 14, 2016.

72 Emma Specter, "The Decades-Long Shaming of Monica Lewinsky Wasn't Just Sexist – It Was Fatphobic Too," *Vogue*, September 8, 2021.
73 Constance L. Hays, "Monica Lewinsky Meets Jenny Craig, and a Spokeswoman Is Born," *New York Times*, December 28, 1999; Yarrow, *90s Bitch*.
74 Yarrow, *90s Bitch*.
75 Pate, "Proof That Slut-Shaming Seriously Hurts."
76 "The Scandal That Changed How the Media Covers Politics," posted February 26, 2019, by CNN, YouTube, 17:50.
77 Amanda Hess, "'Ditsy, Predatory White House Intern'," *Slate*, May 7, 2014.
78 Chesler, *Woman's Inhumanity to Woman*.
79 *Impeachment: American Crime Story*, produced by Chip Vucelich, Eric Kovtun, Lou Eyrcih, Eryn Mekash Krueger, Beanie Feldstein, and Monica Lewinsky (FX Productions, 2021).
80 Specter, "The Decades-Long Shaming."
81 Lewinsky, *Reclaiming*.
82 Charlotte Shane, "No Wave Feminism," in *Can We All Be Feminists?* ed. June Eric-Udorie (Penguin Books, 2018), 9.
83 Emma Nolan, "Fact Check: Did Ray J, Kim Kardashian, Kris Jenner Make Sex Tape 'Deal'?" *Newsweek*, May 5, 2022.
84 Sophie Dodd and Zoey Lyttle, "A Comprehensive Guide to all of the Kardashian-Jenner Siblings' Business Ventures," *People*, September 28, 2023.
85 Jennifer Valentino-DeVries and Michael H. Keller, "A Marketplace of Girl Influencers Managed by Moms and Stalked by Men," *New York Times*, February 22, 2024.
86 Jennifer Valentino-DeVries and Michael H. Keller, "The Men Who Use Instagram to Groom Child Influencers," *New York Times*, December 30, 2024.
87 Elizabeth Flock, *The Furies: Women, Vengeance, and Justice* (Harper Collins, 2023); Anna Motz, *If Love Could Kill: Myths and Truths of Women Who Commit Violence* (Knopf, 2024).
88 Michelle Goldberg, "Funny Business," *Tablet Magazine*, November 29, 2011; Jia Tolentino, "Gloria Allred's Crusade," *New Yorker*, September 25, 2017.
89 Tolentino, "Gloria Allred's Crusade."
90 Tolentino, "Gloria Allred's Crusade."
91 Jodi Kantor and Megan Twohey, *She Said: Breaking the Sexual Harassment Story That Helped Ignite a Movement* (Penguin Books, 2019), 77.
92 Tolentino, "Gloria Allred's Crusade."
93 Goldberg, "Funny Business."
94 Goldberg, "Funny Business."
95 Goldberg, "Funny Business."
96 Sheryl Sandberg, *Lean In: Women, Work, and the Will to Lead* (Knopf, 2013).
97 Sandberg, *Lean In*, 8.
98 *Wall Street Journal* staff, "Sheryl Sandberg's 14-Year Career at Facebook: Growth and Controversy," *Wall Street Journal*, June 2, 2022.
99 Shane, "No Wave Feminism," 7.
100 "The 'Mandate for Leadership' Series," Mandate for Leadership, accessed August 4, 2025.
101 Vanessa Friedman, "The Ugly Effect of Physical Insults," *New York Times*, May 17, 2024.
102 Friedman, "The Ugly Effect of Physical Insults."

CONCLUSION

WHAT CAN BE DONE?

ROE, *DOBBS*, AND WHAT'S NEXT

The legal restriction of access to safe abortions is an act of symbolic violence against women. As of 2022, women in the United States are constitutionally less than fully autonomous humans. Indeed, in the years since the *Dobbs* decision, fully sentient female bodies have fewer legal rights than either fetuses or embryos.[1] This legal protection was a huge moral victory for anti-abortion activists because it expanded the definition of "conception" beyond the uterus and granted "personhood" to fetuses and embryos who cannot act independently.[2] Legal restrictions on abortion are not only about women opting to end their pregnancies; instead, the right to abortion is ultimately about women maintaining control of their own bodies.[3] On June 24, 2022, when the Supreme Court issued its decision in *Dobbs v. Jackson Women's Health Organization*, every one of the nation's otherwise fully-functioning women lost independent control over their own bodies.[4] The five Justices, one female and four male, who authored the Court's majority opinion—Samuel Alito, Amy Coney Barrett, Neil Gorsuch, Brett Kavanaugh, and Clarence Thomas—ignored decades of established legal precedent and public opinion to do so.

In the years since the overturning of *Roe*, women are not electing to have fewer abortions; instead, they are accessing them in new ways. Muscle memory not engaged since 1973 was reinvigorated, including whisper networks, protests, clandestine support, and ballot initiatives in obvious and surprising places.[5] Within one year of the *Dobbs* decision, the number of *legal* abortions increased by about 2 percent, and by 2024, legal abortions increased by another 1 percent.[6] The largest increases documented were in states that bordered those that had criminalized abortion after the *Dobbs* decision. In 2023, for example, more than fourteen thousand women travelled from Texas to New Mexico, sixteen thousand journeyed from Southern states to Illinois, and about twelve thousand traveled from South Carolina and Georgia to North Carolina for legal abortions.[7] Researchers documented an increase in telemedicine for abortion pills, increased need for financial support for women forced to travel out of their home states for abortions, and increased publicity about ways to secure safe abortions.[8] Since *Dobbs*, twenty states and Washington, DC, have passed or strengthened laws that protect women seeking abortions and those providing abortions.

Those in favor of women's bodily autonomy, including the right to an abortion, saw the time between the 2022 *Dobbs* decision and the 2024 presidential election as an opportunity to reshape the nation's political landscape. Vice President Kamala Harris was the first vice president to visit an abortion clinic. She spoke about abortion by name, in defiance of a tacit embargo on the word established or reinforced by the silence of every prior vice president.[9] Upon announcement of the *Dobbs* decision, Harris issued a public response that questioned the Court's assertion that, in Justice Alito's words, the right to abortion is "not deeply rooted in the Nation's history and traditions." Harris warned,

> They offer that as a foundation for the decision they rendered today. In holding that it is not deeply rooted in our history, today's decision, on that theory, then, calls into question other rights that we thought were settled. Such as the right to use birth

control. The right to same sex marriage. The right to interracial marriage.[10]

Harris's statement established a small, but significant distinction between herself and President Joe Biden. While Biden defended women's reproductive autonomy, he never said the word "abortion" while in office.[11] While he centered women's reproductive health, when it came to using the politically fraught word, he was silent; Harris used the word "abortion," giving a clear voice to the sentiments and concerns of countless women.

One group in particular is largely responsible for bringing down *Roe*: The Alliance for Defending Freedom (ADF). ADF is a legal defense fund for conservative Christian causes that has capitalized on the conservative, rightward shift of Trump court appointees.[12] The ADF and their supporters believe the decades of liberal policies that have expanded personal rights have restricted the right of conservatives to be shielded from that which upsets them on moral grounds, such as transgender persons, marriage equality, or reproductive autonomy. ADF began to adopt "rights talk" as a means to counter these and other perceived threats to their exclusive conception of "freedom." According to Kristen Waggoner, the ADF's chief executive and general counsel, the expansion of personal rights has led to a "new kind of police state":

> one in which dissenters who believe that marriage can involve only a man and a woman are forced to salute the rainbow flag flying outside every town hall, in which teachers are required to indoctrinate children into the belief that gender is not binary, and in which shelters for battered women must make room for trans females.[13]

According to Waggoner, conservative Christians "are now the besieged minority in need of protection."[14] As hard as I have worked to find a variety of perspectives to contextualize and provide evidence for the examples I think are vital to, and exemplify the thesis of, this narrative, I cannot find *any* evidence *anywhere* that *anyone* has been forced to salute a rainbow flag, any teachers forced to teach a gender-expansive curriculum, or any shelters forced to give space to trans women instead of abused women. I do believe, however, that rainbow flags can be a source of connection and community for people under legal attack, that a gender-expansive curriculum can support young people with a sense of belonging, and that trans women who seek space in shelters have also probably been abused. What Waggoner and her colleagues have done is weaponize the very real fears people have that, with these civil rights expansions, the foundations on which they have relied are starting to fragment. Capitalizing on people's political fears of change and difference is a particular type of unconscionable cruelty, from which Waggoner and her colleagues have profited immensely.

What the *Roe* and *Dobbs* decisions both reveal is that it is constitutionally, legally, and socially acceptable to put women and girls at the center of the conversation while simultaneously manipulating them in duplicitous ways. Thus far, this text has laid out a series of overlapping problems that women and girls have faced for generations. What can be done to effect change so that, perhaps, we can move on to new and different conversations? If we could stop fighting over gender and all its intersections, and stop trying to compartmentalize women and girls into smaller and less threatening roles, then maybe we can all work together on new projects that respect the complexities of our planet.

WHY AREN'T WOMEN ALLOWED TO BE COMPLICATED?

As discussed in Chapters 5 and 6, while in office, President Bill Clinton had an affair with an intern, Monica Lewinsky, *and* also signed into law the Violence Against Women Act (VAWA), which codified particular types of violence enacted specifically against women and provided protections for the women who suffered from those violent acts. We live in a world where men are allowed to be complicated, allowed to be, for example, both abusers of their power for their own personal gain as well as wielders of their power for the well-being and protection of others. Media portrayals and lived experiences of women seldom permit them similar degrees of freedom.

For the most part, the media construct women as one thing at a time. A woman is *either* the perfect victim and therefore can fight back publicly against sexual assault charges, *or* her past is too varied, her story too muddled, and so the legitimacy of her claims is to be doubted. If she is violent in a particular situation, she cannot be reasonable or rational in any other situation. If she is sexually available with one person, her saying "no" in another situation is not credible.

In being centered and silenced, media establish women as one-dimensional beings. Why are women, and the stories told about them, not allowed to be complicated, multidimensional, and even contradictory? When pop culture pays attention to women and women's issues connected to them, the narratives, more often than not, follow singular, linear paths. If that simple, straightforward path is muddled or complicated in any way, the plot unravels and, for those paying close enough attention, the firm but typically taken-for-granted boundaries of the tidy compartments that confine women become clear. Media representations of real women as well as fictionalized stories about them often relate just one aspect of what are, for every woman, larger, more complex stories. Media then present and codify that reduction as *the* story—until, perhaps, sufficient time has passed to allow re-assessments, as we have seen, in Chapter 3 in the cases of Sinéad O'Connor and Britney Spears.

As has been shown throughout the text, women *are* complicated. There is no valid reason why the stories told about them cannot *also* be complicated. If the composition of the corporate media are so sexist that they can only envision a singular through-line for women's stories, that is a clear place for engaged audiences to push back. If media corporations are so convinced that audiences cannot comprehend or make sense of a multidimensional narrative or character, then that, too, is a place for audiences to push back. As this book seeks to make clear, how women and girls are constructed, represented, and discussed in popular culture matters.

In the limited biopic series *Mrs. America,* which tells the story of Phyllis Schlafly's work against the ratification of the Equal Rights Amendment (ERA), feminist congresswoman Bella Abzug runs into some of Schlafly's support staff at an event, women proudly self-described as homemakers and housewives with no jobs outside the home.[15] When Abzug questions their role in opposing the ERA, she points out that they *do* have jobs: Campaigning to oppose the passage of the amendment. The historical accuracy of the conversation is less important than the larger complication it highlights: Women's work is typically understood as either/or. Either she works outside the home or she does not. As discussed in Chapter 2, tradwives *do* have jobs. They are in the business of advertising and marketing a certain type of home life, and often their own branded products. Tradwives who use social media may represent themselves as *not* working, but they work very hard to hawk their wares and promote their brands, and quite often are the breadwinners of their families.

Women who "behave badly" in ways that contradict or threaten expected gender roles are often punished for doing so. Women con artists, such as Anna Sorokin, who passed herself off as an heiress when in fact she had no money at all, and Rosie Ruiz, who may or may not have run the Boston Marathon in 1980, do not appear to have much in common; but when looked at closely, they both suffer from similar one-dimensional treatments. As examined in Chapter 3, Sorokin, with her plans to build luxurious art clubs in cities around the globe, convinced banks and financiers to lend her money that underwrote her lavish lifestyle, rather than the construction of any of those clubs.[16] Ruiz won the Boston

Marathon with a time believed unattainable by a woman at a point in history when women's athletic abilities were still doubted.[17] What is most likely is that Ruiz hopped onto the course at the last mile in an effort to claim victory. Both women, when caught, refused to accept the accusations and expressed zero regret. And curiously, even though Ruiz was quickly assumed to have falsified her participation in the race, *after* her con, more women started running.[18] Yes, she probably lied. And also yes, she inspired women to do something they previously thought impossible, partly due to restrictions imposed on them, and partly due to limiting self-beliefs, no doubt reinforced by those external restrictions.

Psychology professor Christine Blasey Ford, who brought charges of sexual assault against Supreme Court nominee Brett Kavanaugh, was thrust into the public eye and labeled a "new feminist icon," as discussed in Chapter 2.[19] Her testimony certainly complicated the official narrative supporting Kavanaugh's nomination. But even as she courageously confronted Kavanaugh and raised public awareness about sexual assault, Blasey Ford enjoyed music playlists that featured, in her words, "all male musicians, some even a bit misogynistic. I worried that people would eventually find out I was not the advocate for women's rights they'd made me out to be and I'd get raked over the coals."[20]

Bikini Kill lead singer Kathleen Hanna, profiled in Chapter 4, has been credited with founding the 1980s–1990s Riot Grrrl movement, a multifaceted, many-layered feminist subculture loosely organized around music, politics, and social justice. The Riot Grrrl movement never was singular in focus or defined by rigid boundaries, which means that, to this day, Hanna is continuously asked what the movement *means*, a question that suggests girl cultures may be hard for outsiders to understand and, in order *to* understand them, they must be distilled to a digestible meaning.[21]

Activist lawyer Gloria Allred has taken on many high-profile sexual assault cases, making the conversation of sexual assault part of the public sphere. But she is accused of doing so for her own publicity and her own gain, as discussed in Chapter 6.[22] While her tactics may be rightfully seen as self-serving, they can also be used for good. Allred attended and spoke at the trial of Brooke Crews and William Hoehn, convicted of murdering Indigenous woman Savanna LaFontaine-Greywind for the purpose of stealing her unborn baby, as discussed in Chapter 5. Allred brought much-needed national attention to the plight of missing and murdered Indigenous women and girls, a story largely ignored by the establishment press.[23]

When Monica Lewinsky was *the* topic of conversation after the fallout from her affair with Bill Clinton, as discussed in Chapter 6, most media outlets and many people who ostensibly identified as feminists treated her terribly for a number of years. Media downplayed the power differential between her and President Clinton for decades in favor of conversations about Lewinsky's sexual prowess and body size. In 1998, one month after the affair was made public, in a private room at high-end New York City restaurant Le Bernardin, ten women met over cocktails to talk about "the only topic anyone talked about all week."[24] The women at the table included authors, designers, editors, and restaurateurs, who collectively agreed that sexual affairs had probably been happening in the White House for ages, and the problem with this one in particular was that Lewinsky had been indiscreet in many ways, from not insisting her man use a condom to misunderstanding the risks he was willing to take. In these women's dinner conversation, Clinton was allowed to be a complex individual with multiple, conflicting needs and desires; Lewinsky was simply an unattractive, unintelligent, pitiful girl who could not understand her man, much less the complexity of conducting an affair in the White House. As of 2025, Lewinsky revisits the public and press treatment of her, as well as of other people who have been misunderstood and misconstrued, in pop culture in her podcast *Reclaiming*.[25]

Zoë Quinn, profiled in Chapter 4, was abused both online and in the physical world for her participation in the gaming industry, sparked by a bad breakup with a boyfriend who used a newly-personal internet to tell his side of their story.[26] When read closely, it is clear they had a volatile relationship, including multiple alleged instances of infidelity on her part. Assuming this is true and that Quinn and her boyfriend were in agreement about being in a monogamous relationship, then, by any reasonable standard, she behaved badly in their relationship. The reaction to her bad behavior, however, was extraordinarily disproportionate. His ten-thousand-word manifesto against her went viral, sparking the hashtag #Gamergate, which opened the floodgates to vicious attacks on women, both digitally and in real life, all because they did not "fit" the chauvinist model of gaming as an industry and community where women were second-class citizens.

To a lesser extent, this can be seen in comedian, actor, and former talk show host Ellen DeGeneres, whose daytime show *Ellen* was cancelled in 2022 after revelations that she fostered a toxic work environment.[27] While I am in no way defending *any* toxic work environment, the disconnect between DeGeneres's public persona and the revelations about her conduct on set and behind the scenes is, arguably, surprising because she is female. Would we be shocked that a publicly popular male boss was also toxic and mistreated his staff? Probably not. In fact, at this point, we have seen so many prominent men brought down by their own hubris that it is barely surprising. DeGeneres may have been a cruel boss whose backstage personality did not square with her friendly talk show demeanor. This inconsistency begs (at least) two questions: Why do audiences continue to confuse the art with the artist? And why do women have to behave in a singular manner? DeGeneres acknowledged that she was an "immature boss, a poor fit for the job," but also that female bosses are "expected to act differently than male ones are."[28] Women who do *anything* outside expected gender roles are treated with, at best, curiosity and, at worst, cruelty.

For years, "feminism" was the public province of White women, which served to silence many other complex and complicated beings, as if their stories not only did not matter but also did not exist. When White women shared the oppression of women of color, they did so in a way that indicated they had *discovered* oppression.[29] The popular narrative of mid-twentieth-century feminism, for example, centered primarily on White, well-educated women who had the time, space, and economic security to make change in their lives. Women of color, poor women, women who did not have time for consciousness-raising conversations, queer women, and so many others were more often than not left out of this conversation. As bell hooks argued, "Feminism in the United States has never emerged from the women who are most victimized by sexist oppression."[30] In the mid-twentieth century and at other times in history and today, marginalized women pushed back against oppression, but the stories of their fight are told less often, if at all. Specifically critiquing Betty Friedan's *The Feminine Mystique,* hooks notes that it was written as if other, non-White, non-privileged women did not exist, with no attention to who would care for children or maintain the home once White women were freed from their pressures.[31]

While the feminist movement of the mid-twentieth century has rightly been critiqued for being focused on middle-class, White, well-educated women's concerns, this too begs at least two questions: Why are women—and women's issues—not allowed to be complicated? And why can women not be understood beyond a singular, tidy narrative?

Maybe one reason women and girls cannot be understood as complex and complicated beings is that we have not taken enough time or made enough effort to analyze and take action on the stories told about women every day in pop culture across a variety of media. Critical media literacy can help with this through its attention to analysis and action.

WHAT CAN BE DONE? CRITICAL MEDIA LITERACY

Change begins with understanding. Critical media literacy

encourages us to examine the stories told in the media beyond their surface-level representations. Critical media literacy focuses on power, including how media ownership, production, and distribution shape the answers to fundamental questions about specific media messages: How did these particular stories get told? Who gets to tell the story? All media are constructed, and those constructions serve a purpose.[32] The vast majority of mainstream media in the United States are approved, produced, and distributed by private, for-profit corporations whose primary priority is profit. The stories that have been told are repeated over time because, at least in financial terms, they have been deemed successful. If we are entertained and informed by these stories, that is an additional benefit; however, it cannot be underestimated that the number one goal *is profit*.

Critical media literacy also invites us to explore what *is not* there; the *absence* of data is itself data. Whose stories are missing? Why might they be missing? As discussed in Chapter 5, why did a new hockey arena get front-page coverage in a small-town newspaper while a missing girl was ignored by that very newspaper for days on end? Once we understand that media companies profit from audiences and the labor we undertake to watch, read, listen to, and share these stories, we can begin to ask for—to demand—something different. For the purposes of this text, we can begin to ask for stories of multi-dimensional women and girls told in more complex ways. Critical media literacy invites us to think conceptually and to engage in a process of continuous critical inquiry, asking questions about the production, content, and distribution of entertainment and information across a variety of technologies.[33] To think conceptually is expansive, enabling us to see our stories and the technologies used to tell them, not as isolated bits but as situated within broader social, political, and technological contexts.[34] Thinking critically invites us to see our media stories as mutually beneficial (or harmful) relationships. Audiences accept or reject the intended messages of certain stories, perpetuating or recasting those messages, depending on whether and how they retell (or, on social media, share) those stories.

Once we have that understanding, we can work to make a change. We can say "no" to unfair or limiting stories of women and girls by simply ignoring them (and therefore not contributing to further views, clicks, or likes of them, online), and we can actively push back by demanding change from media producers. Media producers profit off our attention; if we shift that attention, we may be able to shift their power.

CRITICAL MEDIA LITERACY ACTIVITIES

I. ANALYSIS

ANALYSIS	QUESTIONS
Review and audit one's own media habits	What TV shows, movies, music, influencers, and authors do you watch, read, follow, and listen to the most? What can you do to expand (or contract) your media consumption?
Different media consumption	Watch a movie, TV show, follow an influencer, or listen to a podcast on a topic you are not interested in or actively disagree with. How does the "other side" construct and talk about women and girls (if at all)? What do you learn from their perspective?
Popular press review of public women from partisan media	Compare headlines from opposing news media. What adjectives are used to describe the woman profiled or discussed? What images are used?

I. ANALYSIS (CONTINUED)

ANALYSIS	QUESTIONS
Review science media	Review the language of scientific studies as explained through pop culture. Where is the story published? Who is the author of the story? What is their background? When/how are women named/included? If women are not named or included, why?
Review (and disrupt) the algorithm of social media	Click on a few posts in any social media feed that focuses on women and girls. Over time, do more of these types of stories appear in your feed? As you track changes in your feed based on these choices, do you also notice changes in how women and girls are discussed in this broader scope of posts?

ANALYSIS	QUESTIONS
Look at news headlines and photos	Examine the headlines and photographs of women covered in the news. What words are used to describe their actions? Are they positive/negative terms? Are there active/passive verbs associated with women's actions? Are women's appearance, age, race, sexuality, and ability discussed in ways that are pertinent or extraneous to the content of the story? What story is told by any accompanying photos?
Analyze biopics	When are women named/labeled? When are men? Are there easily-accessible biopics of non-White, non-hetero, non-cis women? Who are the writers, directors, producers, and distributors?

I. ANALYSIS (CONTINUED)

ANALYSIS	QUESTIONS
Explore gender in pop culture → Choose the top ten movie or TV show recommendations from any streaming site	Determine the writer, producer, director, studio, and leading cast members for each. How many characters are women? Men? What is the basic plot of the movie/TV show? If possible, conduct this search once a month to observe how the recommendations evolve over the course of a year and see if there are any significant changes over time. (For example, are there more movies/TV series with women during women's history month? Or maybe around the holidays?) Choose one movie/TV show to watch and analyze how women are represented and how their stories are told.

ANALYSIS	QUESTIONS
Choose any social media story focused on women or girls and review the comments	How many comments are there? What is the language use/word choice in the comments? What products are named, and is that naming a paid sponsorship? If so, how might you re-view this post as an advertisement (versus a spontaneous post)?

II. ACTION

ACTION	TASKS
Letter writing campaign: Hollywood	Based on any analysis from above, write a letter critiquing (or praising) the treatment of women and girls in a particular media product. Ask for less (or more) content of that nature.
Letter writing campaign: School boards, city councils, local news (paper, TV, radio, etc.)	What have you learned from your analysis? Should this learning be part of school curricula and/or community discussion?
Explore your own community	How does your community tell the stories of women and girls? What stories does your local news cover? Are there laws in your local area focused on women and girls? If so, what do they say? What might be missing or in need of change/adaptation?

ACTION	TASKS
Build social connection and social capital	Start a group/club and/or host discussions focused on the representation of gender in the media. Despite its moniker, "social media," so much of what we do in the digital space leaves us isolated. Get together in person to share concerning and complex media examples; talk about what you're seeing and how you understand it.
Families: Talk to each other	Talk with the people in your life about their media consumption. What are they engaging with that might be concerning or amazing? How are they understanding gender in their media choices? What can be gained from cross-generational conversations?

WHAT'S NEXT

The time is now for all people to work together to support women and girls by organizing against the patriarchy and the media institutions that help uphold it.

This is not a call to exclude or excoriate individual men, and this work need not be politically divisive. Men and boys are also harmed by patriarchy, albeit in different ways, especially if they do not live up to impossible expectations of masculinity. The rise of the "manosphere" and the proud defense of toxic masculinity illustrate that manhood itself is under threat.[35] What if, by dissecting the rigid structures of patriarchy, we can free women and girls *and* our brothers, sons, fathers, boyfriends, and husbands? Men who recognize patriarchy's damaging consequences can also employ their influence to help change our media's stunted narratives about women and girls. Our society is conditioned to see boys and men in nearly as limiting ways as we are conditioned to see girls and women. For example, what are action figures, such as GI Joe or superheroes, if not cleverly re-named and re-packaged dolls for boys? *Play* is not gendered; all children engage in some form of play. However, toy manufacturers and media narratives have bifurcated play along gender lines. What would our world look like if toys were both gender-neutral and gender-inclusive?

Throughout this text are examples of men and women behaving terribly in ways that target and harm women and girls. Despite some obvious outliers, bad behavior and poor treatment of women and girls cuts across political party lines; it is not a partisan left/right, Democrat/Republican, blue/red issue. Yes, it is horrific that a sexual predator has been elected not once but twice to be president; this sentence works for both Bill Clinton (a Democrat) and Trump (a Republican). Yes, it is terrible that a female candidate for president was mocked repeatedly via gender stereotypes; this sentence is true for Hillary Clinton (a Democrat), Kamala Harris (another Democrat), and Nikki Haley (a Republican). Yes, it is cruel that aging White men questioned the veracity of a young, Black woman's claims of sexual assault, but senators on both sides of the aisle, including Orrin Hatch and Alan Simpson (both Republicans), and Patrick Leahy and Arlen Specter (both Democrats), have done just that.

We may like to believe that "our" party behaves better, but when we look more closely, poor treatment of women is not the sole province of one political party or another. Those in charge of media coverage of the 2024 election did their best to emphasize the left/right, Democrat/Republican, blue/red divisions in the American populace, which, although grounded in some partial reality, are not the whole, exclusive truth of our political differences. A fascinating future study will explore the similarities and commonalities of poor treatment that cut across and run through political positions that are otherwise in opposition.

Women, especially women with relative power, need to recognize the absence of power in other women and work to make a change. In *Down Girl*, Kate Manne examines the logic of misogyny, which harms all women, and "harms the most vulnerable women disproportionately," especially non-White, trans, and other marginalized women.[36] As June Eric-Udorie, the editor of *Can We All Be Feminists?*, asks of White women,

> Organize with us, but let us be the authority on our own experiences and in our activism. Don't speak for us—we can speak for ourselves. And if we can't, because it's too dangerous or the consequences might be too much to bear, then use your privilege to raise our voices and our struggles. Show up and show out for us.[37]

The work is not easy, but it must be done. As trans justice activist Naiymah Sanchez stresses, "We must exert the extra effort to honor Black, brown, and trans women whose contributions have historically been excluded from mainstream conversations and celebrations."[38]

We should not accept that women will occupy one space, good or bad, but instead look more closely at the nuances of what roles powerful women play and learn to ask, all the time, about whose stories are told, whose stories are left out, who tells those stories, and what can be done to construct more complex, inclusive narratives about a variety of bodies. For example, while lawyer Gloria Allred is deeply complicated, Jia Tolentino points out,

> The world has changed since Allred first started practicing. She has anticipated, and helped create, a variety of cultural shifts: the advent of unapologetic, mainstream, professionalized feminism; a valuation of victimhood; a broad embrace of personal branding; a tabloid energy that consumes even the White House; a society in which ordinary women have begun to feel confident accusing powerful men who abuse them.[39]

In general, it seems that women must be harmed before change is made. But haven't generations of women endured harm enough to warrant radical change now? Countless women died because of unwanted, unplanned, or dangerous pregnancies prior to *Roe* and since *Dobbs*. Famous women's lives are upended because their every (perceived) weakness is flaunted, ad nauseam, by unforgiving media outlets in an unforgiving social media fishbowl. Non-famous women are forced into fame when they behave (for good or for ill) in ways that violate deep-rooted cultural norms regarding gender and sexuality. Young girls are boxed into expected roles and suffer when they do not fit those roles, but cannot identify any meaningful alternatives. Non-White, non-hetero, non-cis, non-able-bodied girls and women are doubly, triply, quadruply harmed in a society that expects girls and women to live uniform lives that adhere to rigid, exclusive, and sexist narratives. Girls and women who grow up in this environment (that is, all girls and women) learn that these harmful actions are an acceptable way to treat *other* girls and women (even if it feels crappy when *they* are treated this way).

Towards the end of her memoir, Sinéad O'Connor introduces her four children, all of whom have different fathers. She tells a story of preparing for a performance in Germany, where her children and their male nanny were visiting her. Border Patrol officers were reluctant to let the group across the border because they all had different last names, and the adult male accompanying them was not related to any of them. O'Connor recalls, "It took about twenty minutes to explain to the customs agent what the story was. Nothing made sense to him until I said, 'Look, I was a bit of a slut.' And then he said, 'Oh, okay.'"[40] To the reader, she shares, "But I was joking," and goes on to explain that she did not consider herself a slut, never felt the need to marry just because she was having a child with a person, and that in many ways, she lived her life with male privilege. "In short, while it's okay in society for men to have children with different women, sometimes women get looked down upon for having four children with four different men or, really, any amount of children with different men."[41] Her celebrity, notoriety, and willingness to make it easy for border guards to find a path to understanding her motherhood made an otherwise dicey situation easier to navigate.

When women occupy positions that are easily understood or assimilated, they are granted a certain freedom. To counter the centering and silencing of women and girls in pop culture and lived experience, these problematic narratives need to be called out, interrogated, re-imagined, and shifted. Let us spend more time with these stories and more time examining them closely through the lens of gender equity, inclusivity, and empathy. Let us do the work to imagine a different relationship to and with gender, for ourselves and each other. The future of patriarchy—and a better world beyond it—is up to all of us.

NOTES

1. Jan Hoffman, "Alabama Says Embryos in a Lab Are Children. What Are the Implications?" *New York Times*, February 21, 2024; Rebecca Kluchin, "If Courts Recognize Fetal Personhood, Women's Rights Are Curtailed," *Washington Post*, May 12, 2022.
2. Hoffman, "Alabama Says Embryos."
3. Rebecca Solnit, *Men Explain Things To Me* (Haymarket Books, 2014), 32.
4. Linda Greenhouse, "A Forgotten Chapter of Abortion History Repeats Itself," *New York Times*, December 22, 2023.
5. Soon after *Dobbs* was made public, "camping trips" became coded language for travel support for people willing to help those living in highly restrictive states secure abortion. See Morgan Sung and Ben Goggin, "Post-*Roe*, 'Camping' Has Become Code for Abortions. Activists Say it May Put People at Risk," NBC News, June 30, 2025; Republican-dominant Florida led a strong, but ultimately unsuccessful, campaign to protect abortion rights. See Mara Gay, "In Florida, Democrats Hope Abortion Will Revive Their Fortunes," *New York Times*, May 29, 2024. Regan McCarthy, "Florida's Amendment to Protect Abortion Rights Fell Short of Passing by Just 3% Votes," NPR, November 9. 2024. Medical providers take risks to support women in states where abortion is banned. See Pam Belluck, "A Day With One Abortion Pill Prescriber," *New York Times*, June 9, 2025.
6. Claire Cain Miller and Margot Sanger-Katz, "Despite State Bans, Legal Abortions Didn't Fall Nationwide in Year After Dobbs," *New York Times*, October 24, 2023; Associated Press, "Study Finds More People Are Obtaining Abortions but Fewer Are Traveling to Other States for It," *Cleveland.com*, April 15, 2025.
7. Molly Cook Escobar, Amy Schoenfeld Walker, Allison McCann, Scott Reinhard, and Helmuth Rosales, "171,000 Traveled For Abortions Last Year. See Where They Went," *New York Times*, June 13, 2024.
8. Cain Miller and Sanger-Katz, "Despite State Bans."
9. Lisa Lerer and Nicholas Nehamas, "Kamala Harris Visits Abortion Clinic, in Historic First," *New York Times*, March 13, 2024.
10. Kamala Harris, "Kamala Harris Says Abortion Ruling Calls Into Question Other Rights," posted June 24, 2022, by USA Today, YouTube, June 24, 2022.
11. "Did Biden Say Abortion Yet?" accessed August 4, 2025.
12. David D. Kirkpatrick, "The Next Targets for the Group That Overturned Roe," *New Yorker*, October 2, 2023.
13. Kirkpatrick, "The Next Targets for the Group That Overturned Roe."
14. Kirkpatrick, "The Next Targets for the Group That Overturned Roe."
15. *Mrs. America*, showrun by Davhi Waller, television series (FX on Hulu, 2020).
16. Libby Torres and Rebecca Cohen, "Anna Sorokin Acknowledges That Defrauding Banks Was Wrong but Doesn't Think She Owes Them an Apology," *Business Insider*, June 16, 2022; Jessica Pressler, "Maybe She Has So Much Money She Just Lost Track of It," *The Cut*, May 28, 2018.
17. Sarah Marshall, host, *You're Wrong About*, "Rosie Ruiz and the Marathon Women, with Maggie Mertens," August 5, 2024, 60 minutes; Richard Sandomir, "Rosie Ruiz, Who Faked Victory in Boston Marathon, Dies at 66,"

	New York Times. August 8, 2019.
18	Marshall, "Rosie Ruiz and the Marathon Women, with Maggie Mertens."
19	Christine Blasey Ford, *One Way Back: A Memoir* (St. Martin's Press, 2024), 139.
20	Blasey Ford, *One Way Back*, 139.
21	Fiona Sturges, "Riot Grrrl Pioneer Kathleen Hanna: 'A Lot of Men Really Get off on Watching a Woman Get Angry,'" *The Guardian*, May 13, 2024.
22	Jia Tolentino, "Gloria Allred's Crusade," *New Yorker*, September 25, 2017.
23	Mona Gable, *Searching for Savanna: The Murder of One Native American Woman and the Violence Against Many* (Atria Books, 2023); see also Jeramy Dominguez, Katrina Tend, and James Byers, "Missing And Murdered Indigenous Women And Girls," *Project Censored*, December 1, 2020.
24	Francine Prose, "New York Supergals Love That Naughty Prez," *New York Observer*, February 9, 1998.
25	Monica Lewinsky, host, *Reclaiming*, Wondery, 2025–present, 60+ minutes.
26	Eron Gjoni, "Why Does This Exist?" *The ZoePost*, accessed August 4, 2025.
27	John Koblin, "Ellen Degeneres Is Ending Her Show After Years of Dancing and 'Be Kind,'" *New York Times*, May 12, 2021.
28	Jason Zinoman, "Ellen DeGeneres is in Her Boss Era on Her New Netflix Special," *New York Times*, September 24, 2024.
29	bell hooks, *Feminist Theory: From Margin to Center* (Routledge, 1984).
30	hooks, *Feminist Theory*, 1.
31	hooks, *Feminist Theory*.
32	David Buckingham, *Media Education: Literacy, Learning and Contemporary Culture* (Polity Press, 2003). Douglas Kellner and Jeff Share, *The Critical Media Literacy Guide: Engaging Media and Transforming Education* (Brill-Sense Publishers, 2019).
33	Buckingham, *Media Education*.
34	Buckingham, *Media Education*; David Buckingham, *The Media Education Manifesto* (Polity Press, 2019); Allison Butler, *Educating Media Literacy: The Need For Critical Media Literacy in Teacher Education* (Brill-Sense Publishers, 2020).
35	Rachel Louise Snyder, "We Underestimate the Manosphere at Our Peril," *New York Times*, March 28, 2025; Joseph Bernstein, "The 'Manosphere'? It's Planet Earth," *New York Times*, February 1, 2025; Avishay Artsy, "How Andrew Tate Sells Men on Toxic Masculinity," *Vox*, January 10, 2023.
36	Kate Manne, *Down Girl: The Logic of Misogyny* (Oxford University Press, 2018), 14.
37	June Eric-Udorie, "Introduction," in *Can We All be Feminists?* edited by June Eric-Udorie (Penguin Books, 2018), xxiv.
38	Naiymah Sanchez, "Trans Women are Women: Avoiding the Mistakes of our Predecessors," *ACLU*, March 17, 2021.
39	Jia Tolentino, "Gloria Allred's Crusade," *New Yorker*, September 25, 2017.
40	Sinéad O'Connor, *Rememberings* (Houghton-Mifflin-Harcourt Publishers, 2021), 265.
41	O'Connor, *Rememberings*, 266.
42	Rachel Louise Snyder, "We Underestimate the Manosphere at Our Peril," *New York Times*, March 28, 2025; Joseph Bernstein, "The 'Manosphere'? It's Planet Earth," *New York Times*, February 1, 2025; Avishay Artsy, "How Andrew Tate Sells Men on Toxic Masculinity," *Vox*, January 10, 2023.

273 *THE JUDGMENT OF GENDER*

BIBLIOGRAPHY

Academic and Popular Works

Agtuca, Jacqueline. "Beloved Women: Life Givers, Caretakers, Teachers of Future Generations." In *Sharing Our Stories of Survival: Native Women Surviving Violence*, edited by Sarah Deer, Bonnie Clairmont, Carrie A. Martell, and Maureen L. White Eagle. AltaMira Press, 2007.

Anderson Brower, Kate. *First Women: The Grace and Power of America's Modern First Ladies.* Harper, 2016.

Aufderheide, Patricia. *Media Literacy–A Report of the National Leadership Conference on Media Literacy.* The Aspen Institute, 1993.

Bohannon, Cat. *Eve: How the Female Body Drove 200 Million Years of Human Evolution.* Knopf, 2023.

Buckingham, David. *Media Education: Literacy, Learning and Contemporary Culture.* Polity Press, 2003.

Buckingham, David. *The Media Education Manifesto.* Polity Press, 2019.

Butler, Allison. *Educating Media Literacy: The Need for Critical Media Literacy in Teacher Education.* Brill-Sense Publishers, 2020.

Butler, Judith. *Gender Trouble: Feminism and the Subversion of Identity.* Routledge, 1999.

Chang, Emily. *Brotopia: Breaking up the Boys' Club of Silicon Valley.* Portfolio, 2018.

Chesler, Phyllis. *Patriarchy: Notes of an Expert Witness.* Common Courage Press, 1994.

Chesler, Phyllis. *Woman's Inhumanity to Woman.* Chicago Review Press, 2009.

Child, Brenda J. *Boarding School Seasons: American Indian Families, 1900–1940.* University of Nebraska Press, 2000.

Crenshaw, Kimberlé. "Demarginalizing the Intersection of Race and Sex: A Black Feminist Critique of Antidiscrimination Doctrine, Feminist Theory, and Antiracist Politics." University of Chicago Legal Forum 1989, no. 2 (1989): 138–67.

Criado-Perez, Caroline. *Invisible Women: Data Bias in a World Designed for Men.* Abrams Press, 2019.

Crowley Jack, Dana. *Silencing the Self: Women and Depression.* William Morrow, 1991.

D'Ignazio, Catherine, and Lauren Klein. Data Feminism. MIT Press, 2020.

Dans, Paul, and Steven Groves, eds. Mandate for Leadership: The Conservative Promise. The Heritage Foundation, 2023.

Davis, Angela. *Women, Race and Class.* Vintage Press, 1981.

Eric-Udorie, June. "Introduction." In *Can We All Be Feminists?*, edited by June Eric-Udorie. Penguin Books, 2018

Fessler, Ann. *The Girls Who Went Away: The Hidden History of Women Who Surrendered Children for Adoption in the Decades Before Roe v. Wade*. Penguin Books, 2006.

Flock, Elizabeth. *The Furies: Women, Vengeance, and Justice.* Harper Collins, 2023.

Friedan, Betty. *The Feminine Mystique*. WW Norton, 1963.

Gable, Mona. *Searching for Savanna: The Murder of One Native American Woman and the Violence Against Many.* Atria Books, 2023.

Gilbert, Sophie. *Girl on Girl: How Pop Culture Turned a Generation of Women Against Themselves.* Penguin Press, 2025.

Godfrey, Rebecca. *Under the Bridge: The True Story of the Murder of Reena Virk.* Gallery Books, 2025.

Gordon, Timothy. *The Case for Patriarchy*. Sophia Institute Press, 2021.

Haver, Mary Claire. *The New Menopause: Navigating Your Path Through Hormonal Change with Purpose, Power, and Facts.* Rodale, 2024.

Hirsch, Afua. "Imperial Feminism." In *Can We All Be Feminists?*, edited by June Eric-Udorie. Penguin Books, 2018.

hooks, bell. "Madonna: Plantation Mistress or Soul Sister?" In *Gender, Race and Class in Media*, edited by Gail Dines and Jean M. Humez. Sage Publications, 1995.

hooks, bell. *Feminist Theory: From Margin to Center.* Routledge, 1984.

Kantor, Jodi, and Megan Twohey. *She Said: Breaking the Sexual Harassment Story That Helped Ignite a Movement.* Penguin Books, 2019.

Karakatsanis, Alec. *Copaganda: How Police and the Media Manipulate Our News.* The New Press, 2025.

Kellner, Douglas, and Jeff Share. "Critical Media Literacy, Democracy, and the Reconstruction of Education." In *Media Literacy: A Reader*, edited by Donaldo Macedo and Shirley Steinberg. Peter Lang, 2007.

Kellner, Douglas, and Jeff Share. *The Critical Media Literacy Guide: Engaging Media and Transforming Education.* Brill-Sense Publishers, 2019.

LaPointe, Charlene Ann. "Sexual Violence: An Introduction to the Social and Legal Issues for Native Women." In *Sharing Our Stories of Survival: Native Women Surviving Violence*, edited by Sarah Deer, Bonnie Clairmont, Carrie A. Martell, and Maureen L. White Eagle. AltaMira Press, 2008.

Lorenz, Taylor. *Extremely Online: The Untold Story of Fame, Influence and Power on the Internet.* Simon and Schuster, 2023.

Manne, Kate. *Down Girl: The Logic of Misogyny.* Oxford University Press, 2018.

McDiarmid, Jessica. *Highway of Tears.* Atria, 2019.

McKinney, Kelsey. *You Didn't Hear This from Me: (Mostly) True Notes on Gossip.* Grand Central Publishing, 2025.

Mikel Brown, Lyn, and Carol Gilligan. *Meeting at the Crossroads: Women's Psychology and Girls' Development.* Harvard University Press, 1992.

Motz, Anna. *If Love Could Kill: Myths and Truths of Women Who Commit Violence.* Knopf, 2024.

Noble, Safiya Umoja. *Algorithms of Oppression: How Search Engines Reinforce Racism*. NYU Press, 2024.

Owens, Deirdre Cooper. "Listening to Black Women Saves Lives." *The Lancet* 397, no 10276 (2021): 788–89.

Petersen, Anne Helen. *Too Fat, Too Slutty, Too Loud: The Rise and Reign of the Unruly Woman*. Plume, 2017.

Pipher, Mary. *Reviving Ophelia: Saving the Selves of Adolescent Girls*. Penguin, 1994.

Rogers, Katie. *American Woman: The Transformation of the Modern First Lady from Hillary Clinton to Jill Biden*. Crown Books, 2024.

Rosenthal, Lisa, and Marci Lobel. "Stereotypes of Black American Women Related to Sexuality and Motherhood." *Psychology of Women Quarterly* 40, no. 3 (2016): 414–27.

Shane, Charlotte. "No Wave Feminism." In *Can We All Be Feminists?* Edited by June Eric-Udorie. Penguin Books, 2018.

Solnit, Rebecca. *Men Explain Things to Me*. Haymarket Books, 2014.

Tapper, Jake, and Alex Thompson. *Original Sin: President Biden's Decline, Its Cover-Up, and His Disastrous Choice to Run Again*. Penguin Press, 2025.

Teegee, Mary (White Wolf). "Foreword." In *Highway of Tears*, author Jessica McDiarmid. Atria, 2019.

Thompson, Selina. "Fat Demands." In *Can We All Be Feminists?*, edited by June Eric-Udorie. Penguin Books, 2018.

Turk, Katherine. *The Women of NOW: How Feminists Built an Organization That Transformed America.* Farrar, Straus & Giroux, 2023.

Walsh, Matt. *What Is a Woman: One Man's Journey to Answer the Question of a Generation.* DW Books, 2022.

Weiss, Theresa R., and Sandra M. Bulmer. "Young Women's Experiences Living with Polycystic Ovary Syndrome." *Journal of Obstetric, Gynecologic & Neonatal Nursing* 40, no. 6 (2011): 709–18.

Winddance Twine, France. *Geek Girls: Inequality and Opportunity in Silicon Valley.* NYU Press, 2022.

Yarrow, Allison. *90s Bitch: Media, Culture, and the Failed Promise of Gender Equality.* Harper Perennial, 2018.

Ybanez, Victoria. "Domestic Violence: An Introduction to the Social and Legal Issues for Native Women." In *Sharing Our Stories of Survival: Native Women Surviving Violence,* edited by Sarah Deer, Bonnie Clairmont, Carrie A. Martell, and Maureen L. White Eagle. AltaMira Press, 2008.

Zeisler, Andi. *We Were Feminists Once: From Riot Grrrl to Covergirl®, the Buying and Selling of a Political Movement.* Public Affairs, 2016.

Memoirs, Biographies & Documentaries

Blasey Ford, Christine. *One Way Back: A Memoir.* St. Martin's Press, 2024.

Brock, David. *Blinded by the Right: The Conscience of an Ex-Conservative.* Crown Books, 2023.

Brock, David. *Stench: The Making of the Thomas Court and the Unmaking of America.* Penguin-Random House, 2024.

Brock, David. *The Real Anita Hill: The Untold Story.* Free Press, 1993.

Burke, Tarana. *Unbound: My Story of Liberation and the Birth of the MeToo Movement.* Flatiron Books, 2021.

Carey, Ashley B. et al., producers. *Harry and Meghan.* Television series. Netflix, 2022.

Clinton, William. *My Life.* Alfred A. Knopf, 2004.

Cutler, R.J., director. *Martha.* Netflix, 2024.

Desborough, James. *Inside Gamergate: A Social History Of The Gamer Revolt.* Postmortem Studios, 2017.

Doneen, Derek, director. *Dancing for the Devil: The 7M Tik-Tok Cult.* Television series. Netflix, 2024.

Folk, Justin, director. *What Is A Woman?* The Daily Wire, 2022.

Gabriel, Mary. *Madonna: A Rebel Life.* Hatchette Books, 2023.

Hanna, Kathleen. *Rebel Girl: My Life as a Feminist Punk.* Ecco, 2024.

Hill, Anita. *Speaking Truth to Power.* Anchor Books, 1997.

Isaac, Mike. *Super Pumped: The Battle for Uber.* WW Norton, 2019.

Keshishian, Alek, and Mark Aldo Miceli, directors. *Madonna: Truth Or Dare.* Miramax Films, 1991.

Lee Karr, Erin, director. *At the Heart of Gold: Inside the US Gymnastics Scandal.* SJ Gibson Films, 2019.

Marcus, Sara. *Girls to the Front: The True Story of the Riot Grrrl Revolution.* Harper Perennial, 2010.

McCabe, Allyson. *Why Sinéad O'Connor Matters*. University of Texas Press, 2023.

Morton, Andrew. *Diana, Her True Story–In Her Own Words*. Michael O'Mara Books, 1992.

Morton, Andrew. *Monica's Story*. St. Martin's Press, 1999.

NoiseCat, Julian Brave, and Emily Kassie, directors. *Sugarcane*. Impact Partners, 2024.

O'Connor, Sinéad. *Rememberings*. Houghton-Mifflin-Harcourt Publishers, 2021.

Perkins, Ed, director. *The Princess*. Lightbox Productions, 2022.

Prince Harry, The Duke of Sussex. *Spare*. Random House, 2023.

Quinn, Zoë. *Crash Override: How Gamergate [Nearly] Destroyed My Life and How We Can Win the Fight Against Online Hate*. PublicAffairs, 2017.

Rofé, Joshua, director. *Lorena*. Amazon Prime Video, 2019.

Sandberg, Sheryl. *Lean In: Women, Work, and the Will to Lead*. Alfred A. Knopf, 2013.

Semenya, Caster. *The Race to be Myself: A Memoir*. WW Norton, 2023.

Shetterly, Margot Lee. *Hidden Figures: The American Dream and the Untold Story of the Black Women Who Helped Win the Space Race*. William Morrow, 2016.

Siney, Kate, director. *Taylor Swift vs Scooter Braun: Bad Blood*. Optomen Productions, 2014.

Spears, Britney. *The Woman In Me*. Gallery Books, 2023.

Spears, Lynne. *Through the Storm: A Real Story of Fame and Family in a Tabloid World.* Thomas Nelson, 2008.

Stark, Samantha, director. *Controlling Britney Spears.* The New York Times, 2021.

Stark, Samantha, director. *Framing Britney Spears.* The New York Times, 2021.

Tripp, Linda, with Dennis Carstens. *A Basket of Deplorables: What I Saw Inside the Clinton White House.* Post Hill Press, 2020.

Van Tassel, Sabrina, director. *Missing from Fire Trail Road.* Canal+, 2024.

Walsh, Katie, director. *Simone Biles Rising.* Netflix, 2024.

Warren, Elizabeth. *Persist.* Metropolitan Books, 2021.

Films, Television Shows, and Novels

Aglok MacDonald, Stacey, and Alethea Arnaquq-Baril, creators. *North of North.* Television series. Northwood Entertainment and Red Marrow Media, 2025–present.

Armstrong, Valerie, Rashida Jones, Will McCormack, and Craig DiGregorio, executive producers. *Kevin Can F**k Himself.* Television series. AMC, 2021–2022.

Baldoni, Justin, director. *It Ends With Us.* Sony Pictures Releasing, 2024.

Beck, Max, composer. *The Secret Lives of Mormon Wives.* Hulu, 2024.

Bergman, Andrew, director. *Striptease*. Columbia Pictures, 1996.

Brancato, Chris, Carlo Bernard, and Doug Miro, creators. *Narcos*. Netflix, 2015–2018.

Calderón Kellett, Gloria, and Mike Royce, developers. *One Day at a Time*. Television series. Act III Productions, 2017–2020.

Cronin, Mark, Courtland Cox, Nadine Rajabi, Lauren Simms, Rebecca Henning, James Bruce, and Elise Duran, producers. *Below Deck, Season 2: Ohana*. Television series. Bravo, 2014.

Gerwig, Greta, director. *Barbie*. Warner Bros. Pictures, 2023.

Green, Kitty, director. *The Assistant*. Bleecker Street, 2019.

Harjo, Sterling, Taika Waititi, and Garrett Basch, executive producers. *Reservation Dogs*. Television series. Waititi Productions, 2021–2023.

Hoover, Colleen. *It Ends With Us*. Atria Books, 2016.

Johnston, Greg, Lois Curran, and Rod Aissa, executive producers. *The Newlyweds: Nick and Jessica*. Television series. MTV, 2003–2005.

Lloyd, Christopher, and Steven Levitan, creators. *Modern Family*. ABC, 2009–2020.

López, Issa, showrunner *True Detective: Night Country*. HBO, 2024.

Melfi, Theodore, director. *Hidden Figures*. 20th Century Studios, 2017.

Pesci, Joe. "Opening Monologue." Saturday Night Live, aired October 10, 1992, posted October 2, 2013 by NBC, YouTube, 03:20.

Sheridan, Taylor, creator. *1883: A Yellowstone Origin Story*. 101 Studios, 2021.

Tevis, Walter. *The Queen's Gambit*. Random House, 1983.

Podcasts

Baker, Elna, special host. *Reclaiming*. Episode 1, "Monica Lewinsky." Wondery, February 18, 2025. Podcast, 60 minutes.

Barker, Tess, and Babs Gray, hosts. *Toxic: The Britney Spears Story*. Season 1, episode 3, "Boys." Stitcher Studios, July 13, 2021. Podcast, 40 minutes.

Barker, Tess, and Babs Gray, hosts. *Toxic: The Britney Spears Story*. Season 1, episode 4, "Lonely." Stitcher Studios, July 20, 2021. Podcast, 40 minutes.

Estes, Nick, and Jen Marley, hosts. *The Red Nation Podcast*. 2019–2024. Podcast, 20–90 minutes.

Gladstone, Brooke, host. *On the Media*, "Maligned Women." WNYC Studios, August 20, 2021. Podcast, 60 minutes.

Hamam, Rhiannon, Michael Liroff, and Peter Shamshiri, hosts. *5-4*. "Garland v Cargill." Prologue Projects, June 25, 2024. Podcast, 45–60 minutes.

Hobbes, Michael, and Sarah Marshall, hosts. *You're Wrong About*. "Anita Hill." May 26, 2018. Podcast, 60 minutes.

Hobbes, Michael, and Sarah Marshall, hosts. *You're Wrong About*. "Monica Lewinsky." June 2, 2018. Podcast, 60 minutes.

Hobbes, Michael, and Sarah Marshall, hosts. *You're Wrong*

About. "Quarantine Deep Dive: Jessica Simpson's *Open Book*." May 7, 14, 28, 2020; and June 8, 2020. Podcast, 60 minutes.

Hobbes, Michael, and Sarah Marshall, hosts. *You're Wrong About*. "Marcia Clark." November 14, 2020, and September 30, 2020. Podcast, 60 minutes.

Hobbes, Michael, and Sarah Marshall, hosts. *You're Wrong About*. "Princess Diana." September 28, 2020; October 5, 12, 2020; and November 2, 9, 2020. Podcast, 60 minutes.

Hobbes, Michael, and Sarah Marshall, hosts. *You're Wrong About*. "Tonya Harding." July 18, 26, 2019. Podcast, 74 minutes.

Jarvis, Rebecca, host. *The Dropout*. Season 1, ABC News, 2019. Podcast, 37–45 minutes.

Korte, Cara, and Bo Erickson, hosts. *Missing Justice*. CBS News, 2022. Podcast, 34 minutes.

Lewinsky, Monica, host. *Reclaiming*. "Tarana Burke." Wondery, March 18, 2025. Podcast, 60 minutes.

Lewinsky, Monica, host. *Reclaiming*. Wondery, 2025–present. Podcast, 60+ minutes.

Luse, Brittany, host. "Olympic Hurdles for Women Athletes; Plus, Big Trucks and Big Questions." *It's Been a Minute*, July 26, 2024. Podcast, 32 minutes.

Marshall, Sarah, host. *You're Wrong About*. "Has the Supreme Court Always Been This Terrible? With Mackenzie Joy Brennan." June 22, 2024. Podcast, 60 minutes.

Marshall, Sarah, host. *You're Wrong About*. "Phones Are Good, Actually, with Taylor Lorenz." June 25, 2024. Podcast, 60 minutes.

Marshall, Sarah, host. *You're Wrong About*. "Revolutions and Resistance with Kellie Carter Jackson." October 12, 2024. Podcast, 65 minutes.

Marshall, Sarah, host. *You're Wrong About*. "Rosie Ruiz and the Marathon Women, with Maggie Mertens." August 5, 2024. Podcast, 60 minutes.

Marshall, Sarah, host. *You're Wrong About*. "The Jane Collective with Moira Donega." September 4, 2024. Podcast, 69 minutes.

Marshall, Sarah, host. *You're Wrong About*. 2018–present. Podcast, 60+ minutes.

Neyfakh, Leon, host. *Slow Burn: The Clinton Impeachment*. Season 2, episode 4, "Alone, Together." *Slate*, August 29, 2018. Podcast, 50–60 minutes.

Walker, Connie, host. *Missing & Murdered*. CBC, 2016–2018. Podcast, 30–60 minutes.

Walker, Connie, host. *Stolen*. Spotify, 2021–present. Podcast, 50–60 minutes.

Social Media & Websites

"2003 Pulitzer Prizes." *Boston Globe*, accessed September 11, 2025.

"2025 Anti-Trans Bill Tracker." The Legislation Tracker, accessed August 4, 2025.

"About." *The Real Mrs. America*, accessed August 4, 2025.

Ballerina Farm (@ballerinafarm). Instagram.

Biles, Simone (@simonebiles). Instagram.

Blake Brown Beauty, accessed August 4, 2025.

Brut (@brutamerica). TikTok.

Center for Reproductive Rights. "Roe v. Wade." Center for Reproductive Rights, accessed August 4, 2025.

"*Declaration of Sentiments*." National Parks Service, accessed August 4, 2025.

"Did Biden Say Abortion Yet?", accessed August 4, 2025.

"Elizabeth Holmes' Emotional Testimony at Theranos Trial." Posted November 29, 2021, by ABC News. YouTube, 04:24.

"The Fake Socialite Who Scammed New York's Elite." Posted in June 12, 2019, by Cheddar. YouTube, 10:50.

"Feminism." Merriam-Webster Dictionary, accessed August 4, 2025.

"Feminist Frequency." Tumblr, accessed August 4, 2025.

"Griselda | Official Trailer | Netflix." Posted November 30, 2024, by Netflix. YouTube, 02:32.

Griswold *v* Connecticut (1965). Oyez, accessed August 4, 2025.

Gjoni, Eron. "Why Does This Exist?" The ZoePost, accessed August 4, 2025.

Haley, Nikki (@nikkihaley). Instagram.

"Jessica Simpson (Tuna? Chicken?)." Posted April 29, 2010, by Meza Jandro. YouTube, 01:16.

julieta.la.chulita (@julieta.la.chulita). TikTok.

"Justin Baldoni Made 'It Ends with Us' for the Lily Blooms." Posted August 9, 2024, by Entertainment Tonight. TikTok, 0:41.

luffyfathom (@luffyfathom). TikTok.

"Madonna Woman Of The Year Full Speech." Posted on December 14, 2016, by Billboard. YouTube, 10:29.

Maher, Ilona (ilonamaher). TikTok.

"Maureen Dowd of the New York Times." The Pulitzer Prizes, accessed September 11, 2025.

Media Matters for America. Media Matters for America, accessed August 4, 2025.

"Miley Cyrus Wiki." Fandom, accessed August 4, 2025.

Planned Parenthood of Southeastern Pennsylvania v Casey. Oyez, accessed August 4, 2025.

Project 2025: Presidential Transition Project. Project 2025, accessed August 4, 2025.

Rubin, Dave (@daveclips). X.

"The Scandal That Changed How the Media Covers Politics." Posted in February 26, 2019, by CNN. YouTube, 17:50.

"Sex Discrimination." US Department of Justice, Civil Rights Division, accessed August 4, 2025.

Soule, Jay. Built on Genocide, accessed August 4, 2025.

Spears, Britney (@britneyspears). Instagram.

Starr, Kenneth W. Communication from Kenneth W. Starr, Independent Counsel. September 11, 1998.

"Title IX and Sex Discrimination." US Department of Education, accessed August 4, 2025.

Townhall.com (@townhallcom). "Don Lemon: "Nikki Haley isn't in her prime." X, February 16, 2023.

unfabled.co (@unfabled.co). TikTok.

"User Clip: Clarence Thomas Lynching." C-SPAN, October 11, 1991. Video, 03:27.

viki_g23 (@viki_g23). TikTok.

"Violence Against Women Act." National Network to End Domestic Violence (NNEDV), accessed August 4, 2025.

Walsh, Matt. "What Is a Woman? One Man's Journey to Answer the Question of a Generation by Matt Walsh." Book synopsis. Posted by Goodreads, 2022.

We R Native. "Lateral Violence." We R Native, accessed September 5, 2025, via Wayback Machine.

Whitehouse, Sheldon. "Unworthy Of Reliance: The Flawed Supplemental Background Investigation into Sexual-Assault Allegations Against Justice Brett Kavanaugh." U.S. Senator Sheldon Whitehouse, October 2024.

Williams, Estee (@esteecwilliams). TikTok.

"Women and the Military." The Feminist Majority Foundation, accessed September 8, 2025.

"Women's Airforce Service Pilots (WASP)." Air Force Historical Support Division, accessed August 4, 2025.

"The Worst TikTok Husband? Matt & Abby." Posted November 14, 2023, by Dani Green. YouTube, 21:06.

Biopics

Brownell, Jess, Holden Chang, and Jessica Pressler, producers. *Inventing Anna*. Television series. Netflix, 2022.

Frank, Scott, writer/director. *The Queen's Gambit*. Netflix, 2020.

Frears, Stephen, director. *The Queen*. Pathé Renn Production, 2006.

Gillespie, Craig, director. *I, Tonya*. 30West, 2018.

Jenkins, Patty, director. *Monster*. Denver and Delilah Productions, 2003.

Newman, Eric, Sofía Vergara, Andrés Baiz, Luis Balaguer, Carlo Bernard, Ingrid Escajeda, and Doug Miro, producers. *Griselda*. Television series. Latin World Entertainment, 2024.

Stebbing, Andy, Martin Harrison, Michael Casey, Andrew Eaton, Oona O'Beirn, and Faye Ward, producers. *The Crown*. Television series. Left Bank Pictures, 2016–2023.

Vucelich, Chip, Eric Kovtun, Lou Eyrich, Eryn Mekash Krueger, Beanie Feldstein, and Monica Lewinsky, producers. *Impeachment: American Crime Story*. Television series. FX Productions, 2021.

Waller, Davhi, showrunner. *Mrs. America*. FX on Hulu, 2020.

Popular Press

Agnew, Megan. "Meet the Queen of the 'Trad Wives' (And Her Eight Children)." *The Times*, July 20, 2024.

Agnew, Megan. "My Day with the Tradwife Queen and What It Taught Me." *The Times*, July 29, 2024.

Aguiar, Annie. "What *'It Ends With Us'* Gets Wrong (and Right) About Domestic Abuse." *New York Times*, August 21, 2024.

Albright, Madeleine. "My Undiplomatic Moment." *New York Times*, February 12, 2016.

American Medical Association. "AMA to States: Stop Interfering in Health Care of Transgender Children." *American Medical Association*, April 26, 2021.

Artsy, Avishay. "How Andrew Tate Sells Men on Toxic Masculinity." *Vox*, January 10, 2023.

Associated Press. "Study Finds More People Are Obtaining Abortions but Fewer Are Traveling to Other States for It." *Cleveland.com*, April 15, 2025.

Astor, Maggie. "Taylor Swift's Call to Vote Sent Hundreds of Thousands to Registration Tools." *New York Times*, September 12, 2024.

Ball, Aaratrika. "Diddy Conspiracy Theory Suggests Jay-Z and Beyoncé Are Involved in Aaliyah's Death." *SportsSkeeda*, October 4, 2024.

Barnes, Brooks. "What 'Pocahontas' Tells Us About Disney, for Better and Worse." *New York Times*, December 16, 2023.

Bauer, Lauren, and Noadia Steinmetz-Silber. 2024. "Prime-Age Women Are Still Driving the Labor Market Recovery." *Brookings Institution*, July 26, 2024.

Beckwith, Sean. "Why Would Anyone Date Taylor Swift?" *DeadSpin*, September 20, 2023.

Beggin, Riley, and Jeff Stein. "White House Has No Plan to Mandate IVF Care, Despite Campaign Pledge." *Washington Post*, August 3, 2025.

Belluck, Pam. "A Day With One Abortion Pill Prescriber." *New York Times*, June 9, 2025.

Bennet, James. "The President Under Fire: The Overview; Clinton Emphatically Denies an Affair with Ex-Intern: Lawyers Say He Is Distracted by Events." *New York Times*, January 27, 1998.

Bennett, Jessica. "The Joy of Communal Girlhood, the Anguish of Teen Girls." *New York Times*, December 22, 2023.

Bernstein, Joseph. "The 'Manosphere'? It's Planet Earth." *New York Times*, February 1, 2025.

Berwick, Louise. "Harry to Marry Into Gangster Royalty? New Love 'From Crime-Ridden Neighbourhood'." *Daily Star*, November 3, 2016.

Bezzant, Niki. "'She Will Not Become Dull and Unattractive': The Charming History of Menopause and HRT." *The Guardian*, January 17, 2022.

Biggs, Joanna. "At 23, She Had a Termination. 55 Years Later, She's Ready to Write About It." *New York Times*, August 7, 2024.

Blickley, Leigh. "TikTok Couple Matt and Abby Howard's Most Controversial Parenting Moments." *US Weekly*, June 9, 2024.

Bluestone, Gabrielle. "Dancing in The Name of the Lord." *The Cut*, June 3, 2024.

Boguhn, Alexandrea. "Maureen Dowd's Advice for Hillary Clinton Is Full of Sexist Tropes." *Media Matters*, April 19, 2015.

Box Office Mojo. "Taylor Swift: The *Eras* Tour." BoxOfficeMojo, accessed July 25, 2025.

Boykin-Patterson, Eboni. "SNL Boss Lorne Michaels Changes Tune on Sinéad O'Connor's Infamous Stunt." *The Daily Beast*, January 24, 2025.

Branch, John. "They Called It 'Improper' to Have Women in the Olympics. But She Persisted." *New York Times*, July 10, 2024.

Bray, Rosemary L. "Taking Sides Against Ourselves." *New York Times*, November 17, 1991.

Breedon, Aurelien. "Over 200,000 Minors Abused by Clergy in France Since 1950, Report Estimates." *New York Times*, October 5, 2021.

Briggs, Zakeycia, and Melissa Harden. "#7. Underreporting of Missing and Victimized Black Women and Girls." *Project Censored*, December 1, 2020.

Brown, Emma. "California Professor, Writer of Confidential Brett Kavanaugh Letter, Speaks Out About Her Allegation of Sexual Assault." *Washington Post*, September 16, 2018.

Burns, Katelyn. "The Rise of Anti-Trans 'Radical' Feminists, Explained." *Vox*, September 5, 2019.

Burton, Nylah. "Black 'Tradwives' Say Marriage Is the Key to Escaping Burnout." *Refinery29*, December 21, 2022.

Butler, Allison. "CNN's Don Lemon Still Gets It Wrong. His Non-Apology for Sexist Comments Is What Not to Do." *USA Today*, February 22, 2023.

Cain Miller, Claire, and Margot Sanger-Katz. "Despite State Bans, Legal Abortions Didn't Fall Nationwide in Year After Dobbs." *New York Times*, October 24, 2023.

CBS/AP. "Fox News Calls Michelle Obama 'Baby Mama'." CBS News, June 13, 2008.

CBS/AP. "Judge Rules Breonna Taylor's Boyfriend Caused Her Death, Throws Out Major Charges Against Ex-Louisville Officers." CBS News, August 26, 2024.

Cep, Casey. "On Native Grounds." *New Yorker*, May 6, 2024, 28–39.

Cherelus, Gina. "Bumble to Users: You Need Sex. Users to Bumble: Get Lost." New York Times, May 14, 2024.

Christie, Grazie Sophia. "The Case for Marrying an Older Man." The Cut, March 27, 2024.

Clarity, James F. "Ireland's Catholic Hierarchy Confronts Sex Abuse of Children." New York Times, October 19, 1995.

Cleghorn, Elinor. "Medical Myths About Gender Roles go Back to Ancient Greece. Women Are Still Paying the Price Today." Time, June 17, 2021.

Coaston, Jane. "The Intersectionality Wars." Vox, May 28, 2019.

Cohen, Luc. "Ghislaine Maxwell Convicted of Recruiting Teenage Girls for Epstein Sex Abuse." Reuters, December 30, 2021.

Cohen, Rebecca, and Libby Torres. "Anna Sorokin Acknowledges That Defrauding Banks Was Wrong but Doesn't Think She Owes Them an Apology." Business Insider, June 16, 2022.

Colino, Stacey. "Women Are Still Under-Represented in Medical Research. Here's Where the Gender Gap Is Most Pronounced." Time, November 1, 2024.

Collins, Gail, and Brett Stephens. "Harris vs. Trump Is Taking Shape. And Then There's Vance." *New York Times*, July 29, 2024.

Cook Escobar, Molly, Amy Schoenfeld Walker, Allison McCann, Scott Reinhard, and Helmuth Rosales. "171,000 Traveled For Abortions Last Year. See Where They Went." *New York Times*, June 13, 2024.

Cook, Jesselynn. "A Powerful New Deepfake Tool Has Digitally Undressed Thousands of Women." *Huffington Post*, August 10, 2021.

Cooper, Michael. "Comments Bring Wives Into Fray in Wisconsin." *New York Times*, February 20, 2008.

Coscarelli, Joe. "Britney Spears Announces 'Indefinite Work Hiatus,' Cancels Las Vegas Residency." *New York Times*, January 4, 2019.

Coscarelli, Joe. "Cassie's Trip From Star to Star Witness May Spell Trouble for Sean Combs." *New York Times*, May 13, 2025.

Cottin Pogrebin, Letty. "A Thank You Note to Anita Hill." *The Nation*, October 5, 2011.

Cramer, Maria. "Harvey Weinstein's New York Conviction Is Overturned." *New York Times*, April 25, 2024.

Crenshaw, Kimberlé. "Black Women Still in Defense of Ourselves." *The Nation*, October 5, 2011.

Dargis, Manohla. "Demi Moore and the Subversive Politics of the Naked Body." *New York Times*, September 9, 2024.

Davidson, Kavitha A. "What Olympics Star Ilona Maher Doesn't Have to Explain to You About Her Body." *MSNBC*, July 31, 2024.

Davis O'Brien, Rebecca, and Reid J. Epstein. "Take My Wife, Please: For Political Damage Control, Just Blame Your Spouse." *New York Times*, May 17, 2024.

Deer, Ka'Nhehsí:io. "National Billboard Campaign Honours Missing and Murdered Indigenous Women." *CBC*, June 19, 2019.

Del Rosario, Alexandra. "Madonna Blames 'Ageism,' 'Misogyny' for Remarks About Her Face; Some Fans Don't Agree." *LA Times*, February 8, 2023.

Diamond, Anna. "Overlooked no More: Mabel Addis, Who Pioneered Storytelling in Video Gaming." *New York Times*, August 27, 2024.

Diaz, Jaclyn. "Negligence, Staff Failures Led to Jeffrey Epstein's Suicide, a DOJ Report Says." *NPR*, June 27, 2023.

Dibdin, Emma. "What to Know About Linda Tripp, a Key Player in the Clinton-Lewinsky Scandal." *Elle*, September 7, 2021.

Dienst, Jonathan, and Erica Byfield. "Sen. Menendez Found Guilty on All Counts in Federal Corruption Trial." *NBC News, New York*, July 16, 2024.

Ditum, Sarah. "For Most Women, Trad Wives Are a Freak Show." *The Times*, July 22, 2024.

Dodd, Sophie, and Zoey Lyttle. "A Comprehensive Guide to All of the Kardashian-Jenner Siblings' Business Ventures." *People*, September 28, 2023.

Dominguez, Jeramy, Katrina Tend, and James Byers. "#1. Missing and Murdered Indigenous Women and Girls." *Project Censored*, December 1, 2020.

Dowd, Maureen. "Granny Get Your Gun." *New York Times*, April 18, 2015.

Dowd, Maureen. "Monica's Frowny Face." *New York Times*, May 31, 1998.

Dowd, Maureen. "President Irresistible." *New York Times*, February 18, 1998.

Dowd, Maureen. "Roadkill on Capitol Hill." *New York Times*, December 9, 2017.

Dowd, Maureen. "The Slander Strategy." *New York Times*, January 28, 1998.

Elmhirst, Sophie. "The Rise and Fall of the Trad Wife." *New Yorker*, March 29, 2024.

Epstein, Joseph. "Is There a Doctor in the White House? Not If You Need an M.D." *Wall Street Journal*, December 11, 2020.

Erbland, Kate. "'It Ends with Us' Is a Movie About Domestic Violence, so Why Are Blake Lively and Colleen Hoover Acting like It Isn't?" IndieWire, August 16, 2024.

Eulogy for: Beat up Anita Sarkeesian. Newgrounds, July 5, 2012.

Eyal, Maytal. "Self-Silencing is Making Women Sick." *Time*, October 3, 2023.

Farrow, Ronan, and Jia Tolentino. "Britney Spears's Conservatorship Nightmare." *The New Yorker*, July 3, 2021.

Farrow, Ronan. "From Aggressive Overtures to Sexual Assault: Harvey Weinstein's Accusers Tell Their Stories." *New Yorker*, October 10, 2017.

Ferrier, Lindsay. "And the Award for the Worst Celebrity Mom Goes To …" Suburban Turmoil, September 22, 2008.

Freedman, Bryan. "Statement to the *New York Times* from

Bryan Freedman, Attorney for Justin Baldoni, Wayfarer Studios and all its Representatives." *New York Times*, December 21, 2024.

Friedman, Vanessa. "The Ugly Effect of Physical Insults." *New York Times*, May 17, 2024.

Frommer, Frederic J. "Justice Ginsburg Thought Roe Was the Wrong Case to Settle the Abortion Issue." *Washington Post*, May 6, 2022.

Gabler, Ellen, Jim Rutenberg, Michael M. Grynbaum, and Rachel Abrams. "NBC Fires Matt Lauer, the Face Of 'Today'." *New York Times*, November 29, 2017.

Gabriel, Mary, and Kristin J. Lieb. "The Nerve of Madonna to Pull it Off, Again." *New York Times*, May 16, 2024.

Gachman, Dina. "Sympathy for the Diva: Why We Love 'Difficult' Stars." *New York Times*, July 24, 2024.

Gajanan, Mahita. "Sen. Orrin Hatch Calls Christine Blasey Ford an 'Attractive' Witness." *Time*, September 27, 2018.

Galbraith, Alex. "'I Admired the Bravery': Lorne Michaels Has Come Around on Sinead O'Connor's 'SNL' Pope Photo Stunt." *Salon*, January 24, 2025.

Gay, Mara. "In Florida, Democrats Hope Abortion Will Revive Their Fortunes." *New York Times*, May 29, 2024.

George, Robin. "What is Red Dress Day? How Missing and Murdered Indigenous women, Girls, and Two-Spirit People are Honoured on May 5." *Globe and Mail*, May 5, 2025.

Georgetown Law. "Myths and Facts About Sexual Violence." Georgetown Law, accessed August 4, 2025.

Gibb, Bobbi. "A Run of One's Own." Running Past, accessed August 4, 2025.

Gilbert, Sophie. "What Meghan Markle Means for the Royal Family." The Atlantic, November 27, 2017.

Gissen, Lillian. "Disturbing It Ends with Us Detail Sparks Fury Among Fans as Blake Lively and Justin Baldoni Drama Continues." Daily Mail UK, August 16, 2024.

Gleiberman, Owen. "'Martha' Review: R.J. Cutler's Splendid Documentary Taps Into Everything We Love, and Don't, About Martha Stewart." Variety, October 30, 2024.

Glenza, Jessica, and Alana Casanova-Burgess. "The US Air Force Gave Her a Choice: Your Baby or Your Job." The Guardian, December 13, 2019.

Goldberg, Michelle. "Funny Business." Tablet Magazine, November 29, 2011.

Goldfield, Hannah. "The Portland Bar That Screens Only Women's Sports." New Yorker, June 16, 2025.

Goldmacher, Shane. "Harris Raises More Than $50 Million As Biden's Exit Unleashes Cash Wave." New York Times, July 22, 2024.

Gonzalez, Shivani. "'*It Ends With Us*': The Press Tour Drama, Explained." New York Times, August 16, 2024.

Goodman, J. David, and Edgar Sandoval. "After Nonbinary Students' Death, Schools Chief Defends Restrictive Gender Policies." New York Times, February 23, 2024.

Grabenstein, Hannah. "Are the 2024 Paris Olympics Gender Equal? That Depends How You Measure It." PBS, July 26, 2024.

Grady, Constance. "The Taylor Swift/Scooter Braun Controversy, Explained." *Vox*, July 1, 2019.

Grayson, Nathan. "The Indie Game Reality TV Show That Went to Hell." *Kotaku*, March 31, 2014.

Greenblatt, Leah. "In Britney Spears's Memoir, She's Stronger than Ever." *New York Times*, October 19, 2023.

Greenhouse, Linda. "A Forgotten Chapter of Abortion History Repeats Itself." *New York Times*, December 22, 2023.

Grose, Jessica. "'Tradwife' Content Isn't Really for Women. It's for Men Who Want Submissive Wives." *New York Times*, May 15, 2024.

Grynbaum, Michael M., and John Koblin. "Uproar Hits CNN as Don Lemon Is Rebuked for Comments About Women." *New York Times*, February 17, 2023.

Guccione Jr., Bob. "Lorne Michaels Talks SNL, Sinead O'Connor, Wayne's World, and More in Our 1993 Interview." *Spin*, February 27, 2018.

Haberman, Maggie, and Peter Baker. "Trump Taunts Christine Blasey Ford at Rally." *New York Times*, October 2, 2018.

Harris, Kamala. "Kamala Harris Says Abortion Ruling Calls Into Question Other Rights." Posted June 24, 2022. by *USA Today*. YouTube, 01:37.

Hays, Constance L. "Monica Lewinsky Meets Jenny Craig, and a Spokeswoman Is Born." *New York Times*, December 28, 1999.

Henley, Jon. "How the Boston Globe Exposed the Abuse Scandal That Rocked the Catholic Church." *The Guardian*, April 21, 2010.

Hess, Amanda. "'Ditsy, Predatory White House Intern'" *Slate*, May 7, 2014.

Hess, Amanda. "Watching Britney Spears, as a Girl and a Woman." *New York Times*, October 30, 2023.

Hesse, Monica. "Tradwives, Stay-at-Home Girlfriends and the Dream of Feminine Leisure." *Washington Post*, April 10, 2024.

Hoffman, Jan. "Alabama Says Embryos in a Lab Are Children. What Are the Implications?" *New York Times*, February 21, 2024.

Hoffman, Jan. "Pregnant, Addicted and Fighting the Pull of Drugs." *New York Times*, June 16, 2024.

Holpuch, Amanda. "In a 911 Call, Sonya Massey's Mother Asked That Police Not Hurt Her." *New York Times*, August 1, 2024.

Hsu, Tiffany. "Kate Middleton, Britney Spears and the Online Trolls Doubting Their Existence." *New York Times*, March 20, 2024.

Hymes, Clare. "Jury Finds Ghislaine Maxwell Guilty on Charges Tied to Jeffrey Epstein's Sex Trafficking Ring." CBS News, December 30, 2021.

Isikoff, Michael, and Evan Thomas. "Clinton and the Intern." *Newsweek*, February 2, 1998.

Jacobs, Julia, and Ben Sisario. "Sean Combs's New Home: A Troubled Brooklyn Jail." *New York Times*, September 18, 2024.

Jacobs, Julia, and Ben Sisario. "Sean Combs's Winning Defense: He's Abusive, but He's Not a Racketeer." *New York Times*, July 3, 2025.

Jacobs, Julia, and Sarah Bahr. "The Britney Spears Transcript, Annotated: 'Hear What I Have to Say,'" *New York Times*, June 24, 2021.

Jacobs, Julia, Ben Sisario, Benjamin Weiser, and Thomas Fuller. "Sean Combs Trial Begins with Explicit Accounts of Sex and Violence." *New York Times*, May 12, 2025.

Janetsky, Megan. "Vitriol About Female Boxer Imane Khelif Fuels Concern of Backlash Against LGBTQ+ and Women Athletes." *Associated Press*, August 2, 2024.

Jenkins, Craig. "The Diddy Discourse Has Lost the Plot." *Vulture*, October 7, 2024.

Jezer-Morton, Kathryn. "Did Moms Exist Before Social Media?" *New York Times*, April 16, 2020.

Jimenez, Jesus. "Britney Spears Announces Engagement to Longtime Boyfriend, Sam Asghari." *New York Times*, September 12, 2021.

Jocelyn, Hannah. "Motherhood in the Age of Reproductive Surveillance." *New Yorker*, April 25, 2025.

Kahn, Mattie. "Gisele Bündchen on Healthy Eating and Unhealthy Relationships." *New York Times*, March 23, 2024.

Kantor, Jodi, and Megan Twohey. "Harvey Weinstein Paid off Sexual Harassment Accusers for Decades." *New York Times*, October 5, 2017.

Kaszovitz, Shara. "5 Reasons Why Victims Wait to Disclose That They Were Sexually Assaulted." *Jackson Women's Health System*, accessed September 11, 2025.

Kaufman, Sarah L. "Why Was Trump Lurking Behind Clinton? How Body Language Dominated the Debate." *Washington Post*, October 10, 2016.

Keller, Erin. "Trump's Transgender Ad About 'Misplaced Priorities,' Campaign Director Says." *Newsweek*, November 11, 2024.

Khalili, Isabel. "This Former Sitcom Star Made History for Her Recent Dramatic Turn." *CBR*. August 3, 2024.

King, Michelle Penelope. "Alyssa Milano on What Is Next for #MeToo." *Forbes*, February 27, 2018.

Kirkpatrick, David. "The Next Targets for the Group That Overturned Roe." *New Yorker*, October 2, 2023.

Kitchener, Caroline. "White House Assesses Ways to Persuade Women to Have More Children." *New York Times*, April 23, 2025.

Kluchin, Rebecca. "If Courts Recognize Fetal Personhood, Women's Rights Are Curtailed." *Washington Post*, May 12, 2022.

Koblin, John. "Ellen DeGeneres Is Ending Her Show After Years of Dancing and 'Be Kind'." *New York Times*, May 12, 2021.

Kohler, Meagan. "Unfair Media Portrayals — Not a Rich Family Life — Are Erasing Hannah Neeleman's True Identity." *Deseret News*, August 2, 2024.

Kraft, Coralie. "Trolls Used Her Face to Make Fake Porn. There Was Nothing She Could Do." *New York Times*, July 31, 2024.

Krauthammer, Charles. "Revenge Disguised as Self-Defense." *Washington Post*, January 13, 1994.

Kristof, Nicholas. "The Online Degradation of Women and Girls That We Meet with a Shrug." *New York Times*, March 23, 2024.

Kuczynski, Alex, and William Glaberson. "Book Author Says He Lied in His Attacks on Anita Hill in Bid to Aid Justice Thomas." *New York Times*, June 27, 2001.

Kurhayez, Arden. "#16. Femicide Census Connects UK Killings with Global Wave of Violence Against Women." *Project Censored*, November 9, 2021.

Kurtz, Howard. "Sex & the Single Stiletto." *Washington Post*, November 5, 2005.

Kurtzleben, Danielle. "Trump Signs Order That Seeks to Ban Transgender Athletes from Women's Sports." *NPR*, February 5, 2025.

Leishman, Rachel. "Fine, We Can Talk About the Fever Dream That Is Brett Cooper's 'Daily Wire' Show." *The Mary Sue*, October 23, 2023.

Lerer, Lisa, and Nicholas Nehamas. "Kamala Harris Will Visit Abortion Clinic, in Historic First." *New York Times*, March 13, 2024.

Lewinsky, Monica. "Shame and Survival." *Vanity Fair*, May 28, 2014.

Lewis, Helen. "Dear the Internet, This Is Why You Can't Have Anything Nice." *New Statesman*, June 12, 2012.

Lewis, Helen. "Harry and Meghan Won't Play the Game." *The Atlantic*, January 9, 2020.

Light, Alan. "Sinead O'Connor Speaks." *Rolling Stone*, October 29, 1992.

Little, Olivia. "Study: Tradwife Influencers Are Quietly Spreading Far-Right Conspiracy Theories." Media Matters, May 1, 2024.

Longman, Jere. "How the Women Won." New York Times, June 23, 1996.

Lucchesi, Annita (Southern Cheyenne), and Abigail Echo-Hawk (Pawnee). "Missing and Murdered Indigenous Women and Girls." Urban Health Institute, accessed September 11, 2025.

Macur, Juliet. "Simone Biles Is Done Being Judged." New York Times, July 28, 2024.

Macur, Juliet. "Stalkers, Disease and Doubt: A Gymnast's Hard Road Back to the Games." New York Times, July 29, 2024.

Magee, Zoe, and Kevin Shalvey. "Kate Middleton Apologizes for 'Confusion' Caused by Edited Photo." GMA, March 11, 2024.

Manatt, Phelps, and Phillips. 2024. Complaint for Damages.

Margolick, David. "Lorena Bobbitt Acquitted in Mutilation of Husband." New York Times, January 22, 1994.

Marshall, Sarah. "Making an Ice Queen." The Baffler, December 11, 2017.

Marshall, Sarah. "Remote Control: Tonya Harding, Nancy Kerrigan, and the Spectacles of Female Power and Pain." The Believer, January 1, 2014.

Massie, Victoria M. "How Racism and Sexism Shaped the Clarence Thomas/Anita Hill Hearing." Vox, April 16, 2016.

Masters, Kim. "Lorena Bobbitt: Sex, Lies, and an 8-Inch Carving Knife." Vanity Fair, November 1, 1993.

Masterson, Victoria. "How Paris 2024 Aims to Become the First-Ever Gender-Equal Olympics." World Economic Forum, April 5, 2024.

Mazzei, Patricia. "Judge Strikes Down Florida's Ban on Transgender Care for Minors." New York Times, June 11, 2024.

McCarthy, Regan. "Florida's Amendment to Protect Abortion Rights Fell Short of Passing by Just 3% Votes." NPR, November 9, 2024.

McDermott, Maeve. "BBC Host Danny Baker Fired After Tweet Depicting Royal Baby as a Monkey." USA Today, May 9, 2019.

McDermott, Peter. "Echo Profile: A Necessary Woman." Irish Times, February 22–28, 2006.

McGann, Laura. "Maureen Dowd Smeared Monica Lewinsky. Now She's Undermining #MeToo." Vox, March 25, 2018.

Medina, Mekahlo. "First Women's Sports Bar in California Officially Opens." NBC Los Angeles, July 27, 2024.

Metz, Nina. "Latinas on TV, from 'Modern Family' to 'Superstore.'" Detroit News, November 6, 2018.

Millar, Will. "Sinéad O'Connor: The Devastating and Dark Story Behind the Irish Singer's Shaved Head." Edinburgh News, July 27, 2023.

Miller, Maya C. "Democrats Seek Criminal Investigation of Justice Thomas Over Travel and Gifts." New York Times, July 9, 2024.

Moore, Kate. "Declared Insane for Speaking Up: The Dark American History of Silencing Women Through Psychiatry." Time, June 22, 2021.

Musgrave, Shawn. "Trump White House Got in the Way of Brett Kavanaugh Sexual Assault Investigation." *The Intercept*, October 8, 2024.

National Organization of Women (NOW). n.d. "Women and the Military." *The Feminist Majority Foundation*, 1980.

Nayyar, Rhea. "What Are Those Giant Painted Heads Floating in the Seine?" *HyperAllergic*, July 30, 2024.

Nehamas, Nicholas, Theodore Schleifer, and Nick Corasaniti. "Taylor Swift Endorses Kamala Harris." *New York Times*, September 10, 2024.

Newsweek staff. "Revolution, Girl Style." *Newsweek*, November 22, 1992.

Nichols, Morgan. "#10. Activists Call Out Legacy of Racism and Sexism in Forced Sterilization." *Project Censored*, November 9, 2021.

Nittle, Nadra Kareem. "How MTV Handled Accusations of Racism and Became More Inclusive." *LiveAbout*, January 14, 2020.

Nittle, Nadra. "'We Are Not Believed': For Black Women, the 'Diddy' Verdict Is a Reminder of Justice Denied." *The 19th*, July 3, 2025.

Nolan, Emma. "Fact Check: Did Ray J, Kim Kardashian, Kris Jenner Make Sex Tape 'Deal'?" *Newsweek*, May 5, 2022.

O'Meara, Sarah. "Internet Trolls up Their Harassment Game with 'Beat up Anita Sarkeesian'." *The Huffington Post*, June 7, 2012.

Oppel Jr., Richard A., Derrick Bryson Taylor, and Nicholas Bogel-Burroughs. "What to Know About Breonna Taylor's Death." *New York Times*, December 13, 2023.

Orlean, Susan. "The Tonya Harding Fan Club." *New Yorker*, February 14. 1994.

Paglia, Camille. "Madonna—Finally, a Real Feminist." *New York Times*, December 14, 1990.

Paglia, Camille. "My Op-Ed Moment." *New York Times*, September 24, 2010. Video, 02:32.

Parker, Kim. "What's Behind the Growing Gap Between Men and Women in College Completion?" *Pew Research Center*, November 8, 2021.

Parkin, Simon. "Gamergate: A Scandal Erupts in the Video-Game Community." *New Yorker*, October 17, 2014.

Pate, Caroline. "Proof That Slut-Shaming Seriously Hurts." *Bustle*, May 6, 2014.

Pauly, Madison, and Henry Carnell. "'Dystopian': Trump Issues New Order to Stamp Out Trans Youth Healthcare." *Mother Jones*, January 28, 2025.

Petri, Alexandra E. "Deputy Fatally Shot Woman over Pot of Hot Water, Records Show." *New York Times*, July 17, 2024.

Philipps, Dave. "'This is Unacceptable.' Military Reports a Surge of Sexual Assaults in the Ranks." *New York Times*, May 2, 2019.

Porter, Catherine, and Ségolène Le Stradic. "A 'Love Activist' D.J. Opened the Olympics. Then Came a Wave of Hate." *New York Times*, August 2, 2024.

Potgieter, Heili. "Swift Justice – The Tale of Copyright Cat-and-Mouse in Taylor's Version." *Spoor-Fisher*, April 11, 2024.

Pressler, Jessica. "Maybe She Has So Much Money She Just Lost Track of It." *The Cut*. May 28, 2018.

Prose, Francine. "New York Supergals Love That Naughty Prez." *New York Observer*, February 9, 1998.

Ramage, Jack. "Who Is Estee Williams? Meet the Gen Z Tradwife Taking TikTok by Storm." *Screenshot*, April 2, 2024.

Reilly, William M. "Steamroller Crushes Sinéad O'Connor Recordings." *UPI*, October 21, 1992.

Renfro, Kim, and Charise Frazier. "An Essential Timeline of the Fallout from Janet Jackson and Justin Timberlake's Super Bowl Halftime Show." *Business Insider*, January 30, 2022.

Rice, Kylie. "A Brief History on the Forced Sterilization of Indigenous Peoples in the US." The Indigenous Foundation, accessed August 4, 2025.

Richardson, Kalia. "The True Story of Griselda Blanco, Deadly 'Cocaine Godmother' of Miami." *Rolling Stone*, February 10, 2024.

Robinson, Lori, and Michael E. O'Hanlon. "Women Warriors: The Ongoing Story of Integrating and Diversifying the American Armed Forces." Brookings Institution, May, 2020.

Rolling Stone. "All the Artists Who Have Shown up in Support of Kamala Harris." November 4, 2024.

Roy, Reena. "Teen Convicted, Sentenced to Life in Prison for Killing Mother, Attempted Murder of Stepdad." ABC News, September 23, 2024.

Rubin, Rebecca. "'It Ends with Us' Crosses $100 Million at Domestic Box Office After 11 Days." *Variety*, August 20, 2024.

Ryan, Erika, Courtney Dorning, and Ari Shapiro. "Powerful Women Tend to Be Called by Their First Name. It's Not an Accident." NPR, July 24, 2024.

Sanchez, Naiymah. "Trans Women Are Women: Avoiding the Mistakes of Our Predecessors." *ACLU*, March 17, 2021.

Sanchez, Ray. "Who Was Sandra Bland?" *CNN*, July 23, 2015.

Sandomir, Richard. "Rosie Ruiz, Who Faked Victory in Boston Marathon, Dies at 66." *New York Times*. August 8, 2019.

Sandoval, Edgar. "Autopsy Shows Nex Benedict Died by Suicide." *New York Times*, March 13, 2024.

Schreckinger, Ben, and Daniel Lippman. "Meet the Woman Who Ties Jeffrey Epstein to Trump and the Clintons." *Politico*, July 21, 2019.

Schwartz, Alexandra. "When Women Commit Violence." *New Yorker*, February 5, 2024.

Schwiegershausen, Erica. "Do Women Really Need 10 Hours of Sleep?" *The Cut*, May 3, 2024.

Shear, Michael D. "Biden Drops Out of Presidential Race and Endorses Harris." *New York Times*, July 21, updated July 23, 2024.

Shear, Michael D. and Peter Baker. "Election Live Updates: Harris Moves To Clear Path To Democratic Nomination." *New York Times,* July 22, 2024.

Sherman, Gabriel. "Megyn Kelly Told Murdoch Investigators That Roger Ailes Sexually Assaulted Her." *New York Magazine*, July 19, 2016.

Shorey, Eric. "6 of the Most Insane Things Howard Stern Said About Lorena Bobbitt." *Oxygen True Crime*, February 19, 2019.

Singer, Natasha. "Spurred by Teen Girls, States Move to Ban Deepfake Nudes." *New York Times*, April 22, 2024.

Sisario, Ben, and Julia Jacobs. "Drugs, Sex, Baby Oil: The 'Freak-Offs' at the Core of Sean Combs's Troubles." *New York Times*, September 22, 2024.

Sisario, Ben, and Julia Jacobs. "Sean Combs's Trial: What to Know." *New York Times*, May 21, 2025.

Sisario, Ben. "Sean Combs's Arrest Has the Music World Asking: Is Our #MeToo Here?" *New York Times*, September 23, 2024.

Smith, Danyel. "I Knew Diddy for Years. What I Now Remember Haunts Me." *New York Times*, July 12, 2024.

Snyder, Rachel Louise. "Chrystul Kizer Got 11 Years in Prison for Killing Her Abuser. This Is Justice?" *New York Times*, August 22, 2024.

Snyder, Rachel Louise. "We Underestimate the Manosphere at Our Peril." *New York Times*, March 28, 2025.

Snyder, Rachel Louise. "Who Gets to Kill in Self-Defense?" *New York Times*, September 4, 2024.

Solnit, Rebecca. "Trans Women Pose No Threat to Cis Women, but We Pose a Threat to Them If We Make Them Outcasts." *The Guardian*, August 10, 2020.

Spangler, Todd. "Candace Owens is Out at *Daily Wire*, CEO Says." *Variety*, March 22, 2024.

Specter, Emma. "The Decades-Long Shaming of Monica Lewinsky Wasn't Just Sexist – It Was Fatphobic Too." *Vogue*, September 8, 2021.

Spence, Amanda. "Why Princess Diana Was Seen as 'a Problem' to the Royal Family." *Royals*, October 10, 2019.

Sperling, Nicole. "'Barbie' Was Supposed to Change Hollywood for Women. Why Didn't It?" *New York Times*, July 22, 2024.

Stancy, Diana. "Jill Biden Should Have to Answer for 'Cover Up' of Former President's Decline, White House Says." Fox News, May 29, 2025.

Stanley, W.A. "Gamergate Doesn't Pay: The Cautionary Tale of Adam Baldwin." Medium, May 21, 2017.

Steel, Emily, and Michael S. Schmidt. "Bill O'Reilly Settled New Harassment Claim, Then Fox Renewed His Contract." *New York Times*, October 12, 2017.

Stewart, Laura. "Missing and Murdered Indigenous Women and Girls: A Crisis Hiding in Plain Sight." *Cultural Survival*, June 1, 2023.

Sturges, Fiona. "Riot Grrrl Pioneer Kathleen Hanna: 'A Lot of Men Really Get off on Watching a Woman Get Angry'." *The Guardian*, May 13, 2024.

Sung, Morgan, and Ben Goggin. "Post-Roe, 'Camping' Has Become Code for Abortions. Activists Say It May Put People at Risk." NBC News, June 30, 2025.

Switzer, Kathrine. "The Girl Who Started it All." *Runner's World*, March 26, 2007.

Szalai, Jennifer. "First He Went After Anita Hill. Now He's Coming for Clarence Thomas." *New York Times*, September 16, 2024.

Taibbi, Matt. "Sandra Bland Was Murdered." *Rolling Stone*, July 24, 2015.

Tamblyn, Amber. "Britney Spears's Raw Anger, and Mine." *New York Times*, June 26, 2021.

Tani, Maxwell. "Maureen Dowd: The Only Thing I Wish I Could Take Back Is a Negative Column I Wrote About Seinfeld." *Insider*, September 14, 2016.

Taylor-Coleman, Jasmine. "The Dark Depths of Hatred for Hillary Clinton." *BBC News*, October 12, 2016.

Taylor, Andrene. "Our Patriarchal Society Doesn't Always Tell the Stories of Black Women." *Andscape*, July 22, 2020.

Tenbarge, Kat. "Blake Lively vs. The 'Misogyny Slop Ecosystem'." *New York Times*, July 7, 2025.

Thomas, Louisa. "Hou Yifan and the Wait for Chess's First Woman World Champion." *New Yorker*, July 26, 2021.

Tognotti, Chris. "Zoë Quinn Talks About Being Harassed Online." *Bustle*, September 29, 2014.

Tolentino, Jia. "Gloria Allred's Crusade." *New Yorker*, September 25, 2017.

Totenberg, Nina, host. "David Brock Interview Transcript." NPR, July 7, 2001.

Totilo, Stephen. "Another Woman in Gaming Flees Home Following Death Threats." *Kotaku*, October 12, 2014.

Tron, Gina. "The Unbelievable Sexism Prosecutor Marcia Clark Faced During the O.J. Simpson Trial." *Oxygen*, December 29, 2017.

Truth Sojourner. "Ain't I a Woman?" Speech, Akron, Ohio, December 1851. Fordham University, accessed August 4, 2025.

Tufekci, Zeynep. "Kate Middleton's Story is About so Much More Than Kate Middleton." *New York Times*, March 13, 2024.

Turnbull, Tiffanie. "Olympics Commentator Axed over Sexist Remark." *BBC*, July 29, 2024.

Twersky, Carolyn, and Leah Campano. "What You Should Know Before Sending Nudes." *Seventeen*, April 6, 2023.

Twohey, Megan, and Jacob Bernstein. "'The 'Lady of the House' Who Was Long Entangled with Jeffrey Epstein." *New York Times*, July 15, 2019.

Twohey, Megan, Mike McIntire, and Julie Tate. "'We Can Bury Anyone:' Inside a Hollywood Smear Machine." *New York Times*, December 21, 2024.

Vadukul, Alex. "Mattel Unveils Blind Barbie." *New York Times*, July 23, 2024.

Valentino-DeVries, Jennifer, and Michael H. Keller. "A Marketplace of Girl Influencers Managed by Moms and Stalked by Men." *New York Times*, February 22, 2024.

Valentino-DeVries, Jennifer, and Michael K. Heller. "The Men Who Use Instagram to Groom Child Influencers." *New York Times*, December 30, 2024.

VanSickle, Abbie. "Justice Thomas Failed to Reveal More Private Flights, Senator Says." *New York Times*, August 5, 2024.

Vlessing, Etan. "Martha Stewart Dishes on 'Cookie-Cutter Life,' Insider Trading Scandal in 'Martha' Netflix Documentary Trailer." *Hollywood Reporter*, October 10, 2024.

Voitl, Shealeigh. "From #MeToo to Misdirection." *Project Censored*, January 23, 2025.

315 *THE JUDGMENT OF GENDER*

INDEX

A Basket of Deplorables (book), 230, 233, 245
Abortion, 15–18, 44, 130, 132, 242, 248–50, 271. *See also* reproductive autonomy
Abzug, Bella, 253
Addis, Mabel, 165, 179
Alliance Defending Freedom (ADF), 200, 250
Allred, Gloria, 239, 240, 246, 254, 255, 269, 272
The Assistant (film), 138, 148

Baldoni, Justin, 209–11, 216
Baldwin, Adam, 160, 161, 165, 178
Barbie, 21, 28, 29, 44, 46, 102
Beyoncé, 28, 29, 46, 215
Biden, Jill, 81, 167, 172, 173 179, 180
Biden, Joe, 14, 44, 93, 95, 165, 167, 170, 172, 182, 250, 271
Bikini Kill, 18, 37, 153–57, 254
Biles, Simone, 69, 70, 76, 81, 82, 144, 145, 149
Blanco, Griselda, 174, 175, 180. *See also Griselda* (TV series)
Bland, Sandra, 201, 202, 215, 216
Blasey Ford, Christine, 33, 47, 86, 87, 97–99, 117, 140, 141, 254, 272
Bloomberg, Michael, 139, 140
Book, Lauren, 196
Boston Globe, 125, 147
Brock, David, 35, 36, 47, 92–94, 116
Burke, Tarana, 142, 143, 149, 206, 215
Burnett, Carol, 37, 47
Bush, Laura, 167, 168

Carlson, Gretchen, 142, 149
Carpenter, Sabrina, 103
Catherine, Princess of Wales. *See* Princess Kate
Clark, Caitlin, 76, 82
Clark, Marcia, 173, 174, 180
Clinton, Bill, 33, 169–71, 182, 220–37, 244, 245, 251, 255, 267
Clinton, Hillary, 61, 81, 169–172, 179, 180, 219, 221, 228–33, 235, 243–45 267
Cobain, Kurt, 155
Combs, Sean "Diddy", 46, 81, 205–7, 215, 216
COVID-19, 28, 82, 167
Crenshaw, Kimberlé, 67, 68, 81, 86
Cyrus, Miley, 103, 117

Data feminism, 60, 80
Davis, Angela, 69, 80, 108, 110, 118, 183, 212
Deepfake, 36, 195–97, 214
DeGeneres, Ellen, 256, 272
Desborough, James, 164, 165, 179
Destiny's Child, 154
Diana, Princess of Wales. *See* Princess Diana
Dobbs v Jackson Women's Health Organization, 56, 248, 249, 251, 269, 271
Dowd, Maureen, 220, 221, 227, 228, 233–37, 244, 245

1883 (TV series), 194, 213
Ellen (series), 254. *See also* DeGeneres, Ellen
Emily's List, 100
Equal Rights Amendment (ERA), 17, 18, 32

The Feminine Mystique (book), 20, 44, 64, 257
Feminism, 18–21, 44, 60, 67, 68, 77, 80, 81, 103, 108, 109, 118, 154, 156, 157, 238, 240, 246, 256, 257, 269
    and women of color, 20, 67–70 257
    in history, 18–20, 108, 109, 256, 257
Feminist Frequency, 162, 164, 179

First Lady/ies, 61, 81, 152, 166–70, 172, 179
First Nations women, 189
Forced sterilization, 131, 148, 187, 193, 212
Fox News, 138, 169, 180
Friedan, Betty, 20, 44, 64, 257

Gallo, Lorena (FKA Bobbitt), 32, 46, 144, 149
Gamergate, 152, 160, 164, 165, 178, 179, 184, 256
Garcia, Ileana, 196
Gibb, Bobbi, 150, 151
Gjoni, Eron, 160, 161, 178, 179, 272
Goldberg, Lucianne, 230
Griselda (TV series), 174, 175, 180
Griswold v. Connecticut, 199, 214

Haley, Nikki, 36, 47, 267
Hanna, Kathleen, 25, 37, 45–47, 152–59, 178, 184, 198, 212, 214, 254, 272
Harding, Tonya, 71–75, 81, 82, 144, 149
Harris, Kamala, 14, 15, 44, 46, 104, 166, 172, 249, 250, 267, 271
Hatch, Orrin, 89, 98, 117, 268
Hill, Anita, 35, 36, 41, 86, 87, 89–96 98–100, 102, 115–17, 140, 141, 174, 206
Holmes, Elizabeth, 120–22, 146
hooks, bell, 81, 105, 106, 118, 257, 272
Hoover, Colleen, 207, 209, 210, 216
Hormone replacement therapy (HRT), 54, 55, 78
"Human computers", 60, 165

I, Tonya (film), 144, 149
Impeachment: American Crime Story (TV series), 237, 246
Indian Civil Rights Act of 1968, 185
Indigenous women, 24, 34, 35, 47, 70, 182, 184–89, 191–95, 198, 201, 212, 213, 255, 272. *See also* Native American women or First Nations women

Inventing Anna (TV series), 120, 146
Isikoff, Michael, 230, 231, 244, 245
It Ends With Us (film), 207, 209, 210, 216

Jackson, Janet, 68, 69, 81
Javellana, Sabrina, 195, 196
Jenner, Kris, 238, 246
Joneswork PR, 210
Judd, Ashley, 142

Kardashian, Kim, 238, 246
Kavanaugh, Brett, 33, 97–100, 116, 117, 248, 254
Kelly, Megyn, 142, 149
Kerrigan, Nancy, 73–75, 81, 144, 149
*Kevin Can F*** Himself* (TV series), 38, 47
Kantor, Jodi, 31, 46, 138, 139, 148, 246
Kizer, Chrystul, 34, 47

Lane, Harriet, 166
Lateral violence, 58, 79
Lauer, Matt, 127, 147
Lee, Sunisa (Suni), 76
Lemon, Don, 36, 47
Lewinsky, Monica, 33, 41, 47, 142, 149, 215, 220–37, 244–46, 251, 255, 272
Lively, Blake, 209–11, 216

Madonna, 63, 80, 86, 101–7, 117, 118, 124, 153, 155
Major Crimes Act of 1885, 185
Markle, Meghan, 33, 85, 86, 115
Marshall, Sarah, 44, 46, 72, 81, 82, 115, 117, 118, 143, 149, 178–80, 244, 271, 272
Massey, Sonya, 203, 215
McGowan, Rose, 141, 142
Menopause, 53–55, 78, 107
MeToo, 97, 141–43, 147, 149, 206, 207, 215, 235–37
Michaels, Lorne, 37, 123, 125, 146, 147
Milano, Alyssa, 142, 143, 149
Missing and murdered Indigenous

women and girls (MMIWG), 34, 47, 184, 187, 192–94, 201, 212, 213, 255, 272
Missing from Fire Trail Road (film), 194, 212, 213
Missing Justice (podcast), 193, 213
Mommy blogs, 63, 64, 66, 111
Monica's Story (book), 222, 223, 244, 245
Moore, Demi, 31, 46
Morton, Andrew, 84, 115, 222–24, 229, 244, 245
Mrs. America (TV series), 32, 46, 118, 253, 271
MTV, 101, 104, 105, 117, 118, 123, 127, 128
My Life (book), 222, 244, 245

National Organization for Women (NOW), 17, 44, 45
Native American women, 45, 81, 186, 212, 272. *See also* Indigenous women
Native American residential schools, 186, 188, 193–95
Neeleman, Hannah, 112, 113, 119
The Newlyweds (TV series), 104, 105, 117
No More Foundation, 208
Non-disclosure agreements (NDAs), 138–40, 240
North of North (TV series), 194, 214
"Nudify" apps, 36, 196, 197

Obama, Michelle, 34, 167–69, 176, 180
O'Connor, Sinéad, 34, 41, 47, 122–26, 137, 144, 146, 147, 204, 205, 215, 252, 270. 272
Oliphant v. *Suquamish Indian Tribe*, 185
Olympics, 30, 36, 46, 47, 70, 74–77, 82, 144, 145, 150, 178
One Day At A Time (TV series), 176, 181
O'Reilly, Bill, 138, 148

Paglia, Camille, 102, 103, 105, 117,118 155
Patriarchy, 18, 21, 23–29, 39, 42, 45, 46, 56, 57, 68, 69, 72, 77, 79, 92, 93, 100, 106, 113, 116, 117, 141, 149, 166, 177, 205, 211, 219, 220, 221, 235, 237–39, 242, 243, 267, 270
Prince, 124, 203–5, 215
Princess Diana, 84–86, 102, 115, 127
Princess Kate, 85, 86

Quinn, Zoë, 152, 160–62, 164, 165, 178, 179, 197, 255, 256

Reagan, Nancy, 168, 173
Reproductive autonomy, 15, 221, 250
Reservation Dogs, 195, 214
Riot Grrrl movement, 44, 117, 118, 152–56, 158, 178, 184, 198, 254, 272
Roe v *Wade*, 15, 16, 32, 44, 46, 214
Roosevelt, Eleanor, 168
Royal Canadian Mounted Police (RCMP), 188–90, 192
Ruiz, Rosie, 253, 254, 271, 272

Sandberg, Sheryl, 71, 81, 240, 241, 246
Sarkeesian, Anita, 152, 160–64, 179
Saturday Night Live (SNL) (TV series), 37, 47, 123, 125, 126, 146, 147
Sawyer, Diane, 127, 133, 134
Schlafly, Phyllis, 18, 32, 108, 253
The Secret Lives of Mormon Wives (TV series), 111, 112, 119
Semenya, Caster, 34, 47, 75, 82, 151, 178
Seneca Falls, 19, 66
Sex and gender distinctions, 22–26, 75–77, 151, 152
Sexual assault, 15, 27, 33, 35, 76, 91, 95, 97, 99, 100, 116, 117, 122, 138, 140, 149, 158, 176, 177, 181–83, 211, 222, 227, 239, 250, 252, 266
Sexual harassment, 27, 28, 35, 46, 59, 67, 86, 87, 90, 91, 93–99, 142,

147, 148, 210, 211, 239, 240, 246
Simpson, Jessica, 90, 104, 105, 117, 118
Solnit, Rebecca, 24, 25, 28, 41, 45, 48, 77, 82, 90, 96, 111, 115, 116, 118, 183, 212, 271
Sorokin, Anna (AKA Anna Delvey), 120, 121, 146, 253, 271
Spears, Britney, 41, 47, 104, 122, 126–37, 144, 146–48, 252
Spears, Jamie Lynn, 129, 130
Spears, Lynne, 129, 130, 135, 147
Spice Girls, 154
Starr, Kenneth, 41, 221, 222, 227, 229, 233, 244
Stay-at-home girlfriends (SAHGs), 107, 118
Stewart, Martha, 121, 122, 146, 212
Striptease (film), 31, 46
Sugarcane (film), 194, 213
The Sumerian Game (video game), 165
Swift, Taylor, 14, 28, 29, 44, 46, 103, 104, 106, 117
Switzer, Kathrine, 151, 178

Taylor, Breonna, 202, 203, 215
Taylor, Elizabeth, 62, 80
Technology and gender, 29, 59, 60, 160–65, 197
TikTok, 42, 65, 66, 80, 82, 107, 109, 112, 117, 118, 121, 144, 146, 149, 216
Timberlake, Justin, 68, 69, 81, 132–34
Tradwives, 87, 107–13, 118, 119, 253
Trans exclusive radical feminists (TERFs), 24
Trans girls & women, 24, 28, 45, 67, 199–201, 214, 250, 251, 268, 272
Tripp, Linda, 220, 227–33, 237, 245
Trump, Ivanka, 166
Trump, Melania, 166, 167, 179
True Detective (TV series), 194, 213
Truth or Dare (film), 105, 106, 118
Truth, Sojourner, 66, 81
Twohey, Megan, 31, 46, 138, 139, 148, 149, 216, 246

The US Military, 17, 61, 173, 175–77, 180, 181
and abortion, 17
and sexual assault, 176, 177
and women's roles, 173, 175–77

Vail, Tobi, 18
Vergara, Sofía, 175
Violence Against Women Act (VAWA), 182, 183, 212, 221, 249

Waggoner, Kristen, 200, 248, 249
Walsh, Matt, 22, 23, 44, 45
Warren, Elizabeth, 139, 140, 148
Weinstein, Harvey, 31, 46, 138, 140–42, 149, 206
Williams, Estee, 108, 118
Williams, Juan, 87, 115
Wilson, Edith Bolling Galt, 168
Wuornos, Aileen, 32
Wu, Brianna, 152, 160, 161, 163, 179

You're Wrong About, 12, 44, 46, 81, 82, 115, 117, 143, 144, 149, 178, 180, 244, 271
YouTube, 42, 65, 66, 80, 106, 118, 121, 146, 175, 180, 246, 271

Zines, 152–56, 158
The Zoe Post (blog), 161

www.ingramcontent.com/pod-product-compliance
Lightning Source LLC
LaVergne TN
LVHW091712070526
838199LV00050B/2362